Close-up

STUDENT'S BOOK

B1

Angela Healan
Katrina Gormley
with Karen Ludlow

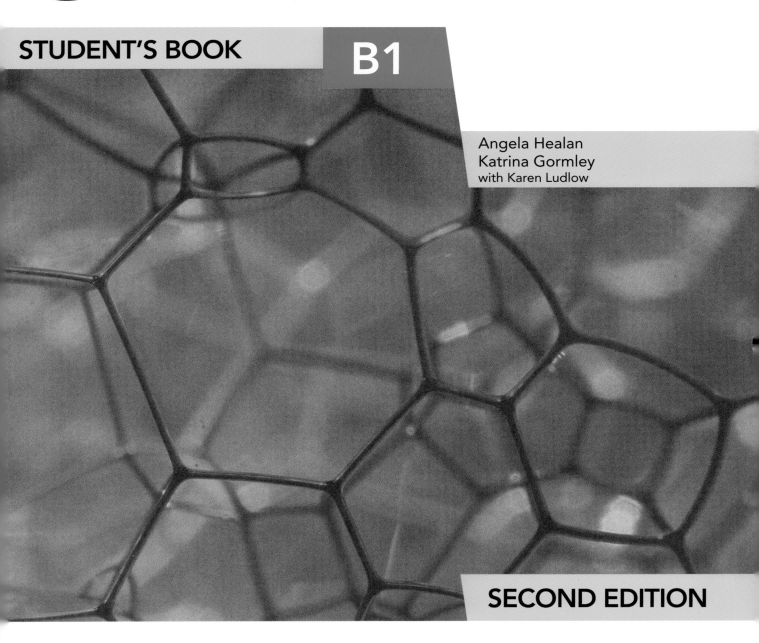

SECOND EDITION

NATIONAL
GEOGRAPHIC
L E A R N I N G

Australia · Brazil · Mexico · Singapore · United Kingdom · United States

Contents

Speaking	Vocabulary	Grammar	Writing	Video
talking about family, describing photos, describing in detail	collocations & expressions	countable & uncountable nouns, quantifiers	email, using abbreviations, including all the information, inviting, asking for a reply, writing about special events	One Woman's Choice
talking about food & restaurants, describing photos, using different adjectives, using adjectives	word formation	used to & would, be used to & get used to	review, ordering adjectives, making your writing interesting, recommending, adjectives for food & restaurants	Greek Olives
talking about the environment, listening to instructions, opening discussions	prepositions, reading a multiple choice text first	articles	informal email, planning your work, friendly openings & endings, useful phrases	Swimming with Sharks
relationships, problem solving, considering advantages & disadvantages, giving advice	phrasal verbs	temporals	story (1), thinking of ideas, organising a story / ideas, describing people	Man's Best Friend
talking about homes, general conversations, expanding on the topic, talking about a topic	collocations & expressions	future plans & events, future predictions	informal letter, replying to a letter, using informal language, accepting/ rejecting invitations, responding to news, making suggestions	Living in Venice
talking about sport, decision making, giving opinions, agreeing & disagreeing asking if someone agrees, giving your opinions	word formation	second conditional, if	sentence transformation (1), clauses of purpose, transforming sentences	Water Sports Adventure
describing photos, talking about extreme situations, paraphrasing	prepositions, collocations & expressions	question tags, subject & object questions, negative questions	story (2), using narrative tenses, creating suspense, reviewing your writing	Coast Guard School
talking about free-time activities, decision making, talking about all the options, talking about possibility	phrasal verbs	modals & semi-modals (2)	postcard, linking words & phrases, writing the correct amount, writing a postcard	Young Adventurers
talking about technology, decision making, making a decision, deciding	prepositions	the passive voice: gerunds, infinitives & modal verbs	sentence transformation (2), using collocations, checking the meaning	Mars Rovers
talking about entertainment, describing photos, talking about a photo, describing people, places & things	phrasal verbs	reported speech: questions, commands & requests	letter or story, ordering ideas, choosing the right question, free-time activities	Steel Drums
talking about school and education, decision making, changing opinions, changing your mind	collocations & expressions, prepositions	gerunds, infinitives	report, remembering common errors, checking for common errors, introducing & closing reports, school facilities and equipment, after-school activities	The Maasai Teacher
talking about your body, general conversations, interacting with your partner, talking about health and fitness	phrasal verbs	comparison of adjectives & adverbs	dramatic stories, making stories more interesting, leaving enough time, relationships	The Memory Man

Collocations & Expressions: p 184   Phrasal Verbs: p 186
Prepositions: p 185

1 Family Ties

Reading:	true/false, reading the exam question first
Vocabulary:	family-related words, collocations & expressions
Grammar:	present simple, present continuous, stative verbs, countable & uncountable nouns, quantifiers
Listening:	multiple-choice questions (pictures), identifying differences
Speaking:	talking about family, describing photos, describing in detail
Writing:	email, using abbreviations, including all the information, inviting, asking for a reply, writing about special events

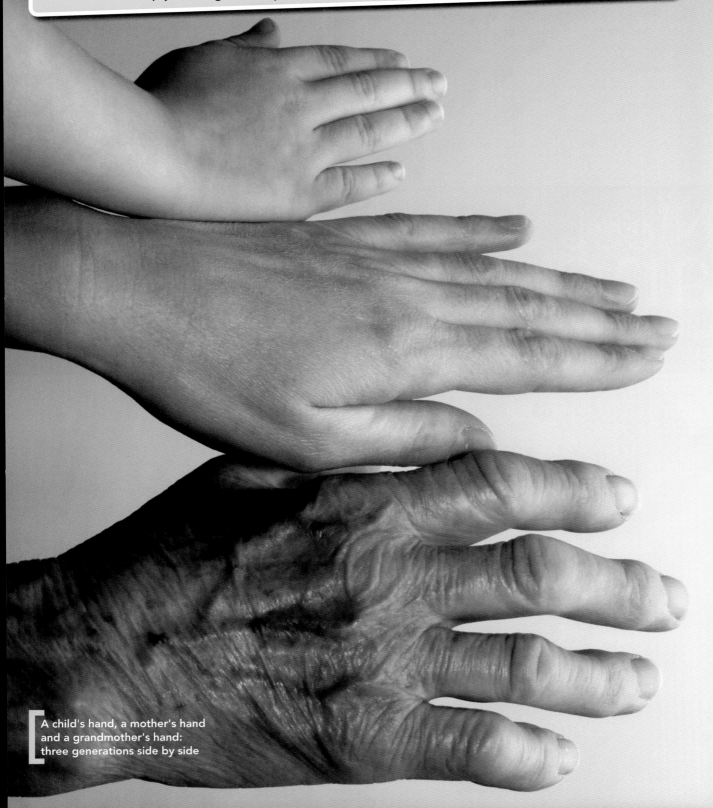

A child's hand, a mother's hand and a grandmother's hand: three generations side by side

Reading

A Work in pairs. How many words for family members can you think of? Write as many as you can in one minute.

B How can you learn about your family's past? Write down the different ways in your notebook. Then, quickly read the text. Are your answers the same?

C Read the text about family history and match the headings below with the correct sections in the text.

   A Your turn ☐
   B What is genealogy? ☐
   C Research and records ☐

Meet the ancestors

What makes you who you are? Part of the answer is in your family's past. Become a detective and find clues to your family history.

Word Focus

gene: part of a cell passed from parents to children that determines how they look
generation: the people of about the same age in a particular family
ancestor: person related to you who lived a long time ago
genealogy: the study of family history

1. When you look in the mirror, do you see your father's smile? Maybe you take after your mother or look like a grandparent? That's because of DNA. Our DNA contains genes that make each person in the world different - no two people look, think or act the same. We pass down our genes through generations. Scientists can test your DNA to find out which part of the world your ancestors were from.

2. Your family's history may be a mystery to you, but there's a way to find out about it. It's called genealogy, and it's the study of the people you are related to. Genealogy helps you put together your family history. It starts with the relatives you know, such as parents and grandparents, and then you can learn about ancestors who lived and died before you were born.

D Read the *Exam Close-up*. Then read the *Exam Task* below and underline the key words in the text.

Exam Task

Look at the sentences below about studying your family history. Read the text to decide if each sentence is correct or incorrect. Write T (True) or F (False).

1 We look the way we do because of the genes in our DNA. ☐

2 A DNA test can show where in the world our ancestors lived. ☐

3 You can find out the number of relatives you have in a DNA test. ☐

4 Genealogy is the history of our past and present family members. ☐

5 Relatives who are alive could have information about ancestors. ☐

6 A family tree shows how you are related to other people in your family. ☐

7 A detective can help you to find information about your family. ☐

8 It is possible to buy old newspapers at some libraries. ☐

9 Public records tell you when people were born. ☐

10 The text says that websites can help you find information about your ancestors. ☐

Exam Close-up

Reading the exam question first

- It's a good idea to read the exam sentences very carefully before you read the text.
- Underline the key words in each statement so you know what information you need to look for.
- Then read the text quickly so you know what it is about.
- Read the text again and look for words and phrases in the text that are similar to the word you underlined in each exam sentence.
- The statements are in the same order as the information in the text.

E Now complete the *Exam Task*. Use the words you underlined to help you.

F Find the underlined words in the text and think about what they mean.
Then circle the correct meanings below.

1 **take after:** to follow somebody / to be like somebody

2 **look like:** to have a similar appearance / to see things you enjoy

3 **pass down:** transfer to / respect the next generation

4 **relative:** family member / close friend

5 **find out:** to take outside / to discover or learn

6 **look for:** to be similar to / to try to find

3. It isn't difficult to learn about your past. You can begin by asking your relatives questions about your ancestors. While you are talking with family members, take notes. This helps you organise any information you get. Make sure you write down any names, dates or places people mention. Then you can draw a family tree with your name at the top. Then you would add all the relatives from you to your great grandparents so you can see how everyone is related.

4. If there any blank boxes in your tree it's time for some detective work! Many people begin at a library where they can <u>look for</u> family names in old newspapers. Public records are usually a very good thing to look at too. They have information about births, marriages and death certificates too. Some records show when people moved to a country. Sometimes, records tell you where people went to school and what their job was. You can also search the Internet. With every bit of research you do, you are discovering your family's history.

- If you could choose someone famous to be in your family, who would you choose and why?
- If you could go back in time, which one of your ancestors would you like to meet? Why? / Why not?

Ideas Focus

Vocabulary

A Match the definitions with the members of the family.

1 Your mum's mother.
2 Your brother's or sister's daughter.
3 Your uncle's and aunt's children.
4 Your brother or sister's son.
5 Your mother's sister.
6 Your father's wife if he marries again.

a aunt
b niece
c step-mother
d grandmother
e nephew
f cousins

B Complete the sentences using two of the words in each group.

1 | height slim tall |

Peter has always been very _____ ;
he was 1.98m when he was 14 years-old! He's also
quite _____ even though he eats a lot.

2 | weigh overweight build |

Annabel and Claire have got the same
_____. They aren't very tall and
they're both a bit _____.

3 | beard blonde straight |

I love your son's curly _____ hair. Mine
is very _____ and dark.

4 | elderly middle-aged young |

Sunday was boring! We spent it with our
_____ grandparents and our
_____ parents.

5 | hard-working jealous generous |

My aunt is a very _____ person. She
gives money to people in need. She's also very
_____ and spends lots of time helping at
the care centre.

6 | relax honest nervous |

My cousin Jack is very _____. He needs
to do more exercise to help him _____.

7 | unkind easy-going scruffy |

Granddad is very _____ and fun-loving,
and he always dresses in _____ clothes.

8 | lazy clever reliable |

Jack isn't very _____. If you ask him to do
something he forgets. He's very _____
though and does very well at school.

C Complete the text with these words.

| young kind easy-going height elderly hard-working nervous weigh |

Elephants: animals of higher intelligence

Elephants are interesting animals because they are very sociable and
family is important to them. They can grow to a (1) _____
of over 3 metres and usually (2) _____ about 3,800 kilos.
Normally they are quite relaxed and (3) _____ animals,
but sometimes they can get (4) _____ when they are
looking after (5) _____ elephants. They are also quite
clever and (6) _____, and slow down and help feed
(7) _____ or ill members of the family group.
These qualities and the fact that they are so strong and
(8) _____ is why people want to protect them and the
land they live on for the future.

African elephant mother and baby

Ideas Focus

• Is family important to you? Why / Why not?
• Do you think young people can learn things from elderly
members of their family? Why? / Why not?

Grammar

Present Simple & Present Continuous

A **Read the sentences below. Match each sentence with one use of the Present Simple.**

1 Water **boils** at 100°C.
2 His parents **work** at a bank.
3 We **have** a dance class next week.
4 The English **drink** a lot of tea.

a habits and repeated actions ☐
b permanent situations ☐
c scientific facts ☐
d future actions based on timetables and schedules ☐

> **Be careful**
> We often use adverbs of frequency with the Present Simple. They go after the verb *be* but before all other main verbs.

B **Read the sentences below. Match each sentence with one use of the Present Continuous.**

1 You **are** always **interrupting** me!
2 What **are** you **doing** at the weekend?
3 I **am saving** up for a car.
4 The baby **is crying**! It must be hungry.
5 Families **are becoming** smaller and smaller these days.

a actions happening now ☐
b temporary situations ☐
c future plans ☐
d annoying habits ☐
e changing and developing situations in the present ☐

Stative Verbs

C **Read the sentences below and underline the verbs.**

1 Peter hates his new school.
2 He understands the problem now.
3 These flowers smell wonderful.
4 Who owns the blue car outside?

D **Complete the rule with the Present Simple or Present Continuous.**

We don't use some verbs in continuous tenses. They are called stative because they describe states and not actions. To talk about the present, we use these verbs in the _____ tense.

E **Some verbs can be both stative and action verbs, but with a different meaning. How does the meaning of *think* change in the sentences below?**

1 They **think** that having a lot of children is fantastic.
2 They **are thinking** of moving house this year.

▶ Grammar Focus pp.161 & 162 (1.1 to 1.4)

F **Choose the correct answers.**

1 Quiet William! Why _____ so noisy this morning?
   a are you be   b are you being
2 Who's that? I _____ her name.
   a 'm not remembering b don't remember
3 Irene _____ with her cousin for a few weeks.
   a lives   b is living
4 Granddad isn't feeling well. He _____ the doctor later today.
   a 's seeing   b sees
5 Tony _____ his grandfather.
   a is looking like   b looks like
6 Mum and Dad always _____ us with them on holidays.
   a take   b are taking
7 Bob and Sue _____ to their aunt Maisie's house every weekend.
   a are going   b go
8 Why _____ children are jealous of each other?
   a do you think   b are you thinking

G **Complete the text with the correct Present Simple or Present Continuous form of the verbs in brackets.**

Identical twins

I (**1**) _____ (think) that identical twins are fascinating. They (**2**) _____ (have) the same DNA, but they've got different fingerprints and they often have different personalities too. My sisters Katy and Sandy (**3**) _____ (be) identical twins, and my parents and I (**4**) _____ (not / know) which twin is which most of the time. In fact, they (**5**) _____ (always / play) tricks on us, which is not funny! They (**6**) _____ (wear) different clothes every morning, so we know who is who but then they (**7**) _____ (sometimes / change) clothes later just to confuse us. There is only one thing that helps us tell who is who: Katy (**8**) _____ (spend) a lot of her free time reading books, but Sandy (**9**) _____ (hate) reading. She often complains about it, saying 'Katy (**10**) _____ (read) again!'.

Listening

A Look carefully at the pictures below. What can you see in each one?

1
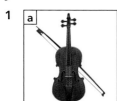 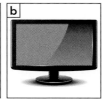 

2
 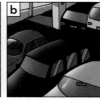 

3

B Look at the pictures in A again and match them to these questions.

1 Where did the woman meet her cousin? ☐

2 Who does the man's niece take after? ☐

3 How does the man's daughter spend her free time? ☐

C 1.1 ▶❚❚ Now listen to the three conversations and circle the correct answers (a, b or c) in Task B.

D Read the *Exam Close-up*. Then read the *Exam Task* below and study the pictures carefully. Write notes about the differences, similarities or connections between them.

E 1.2 ▶❚❚ Now complete the *Exam Task*.

F 1.2 ▶❚❚ Now listen again.

Exam Close-up

Identifying differences

- Before you listen, read the question for each set of pictures first and underline any key words.
- Then look at the pictures carefully and make sure you understand them.
- It's important to identify the differences between them before you listen.

Exam Task

There are six questions in this part. For each question, there are three pictures and a short recording. Circle the correct picture **a**, **b** or **c**.

1 Which girl is her sister?

 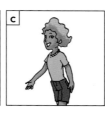

2 Who are the neighbours' children?

  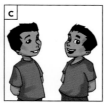

3 What time will the boy leave?

4 Where do Sophie and her family live now?

5 When will they have their picnic?

6 What did the boy think of his friend's father?

Speaking

A Work with a partner and answer these questions.

- Do you come from a big or small family?
- What do you enjoy doing with your family in your free time?

B Look at the photos in the *Exam Task*. Then write 1 (photo 1), 2 (photo 2) or B (both photos) next to the words below.

a pets ☐   f jeans ☐
b board game ☐   g garden ☐
c parents ☐   h outdoors ☐
d children ☐   i indoors ☐
e friendly ☐   j relaxed ☐

Useful Expressions

Describing photos

… lying on the floor.
I can see a … in the foreground / background.
There's a white …
There are four …
She's got long …
He's behind / in front of / next to / on the right
He's wearing …
She's … tall, slim good-looking
He / She's got… long, dark hair
They look … relaxed / happy / easy-going

C Complete the sentences about the two photos in the *Exam Task*. Use the words in the box.

> right background next to behind left foreground on

1 In the _____ I can see some trees.
2 The father and son are sitting _____ the sofa.
3 The girl with long, blonde hair is _____ her mum.
4 In the _____ there is a mother and daughter.
5 The teenage boy is _____ the white dog.
6 The boy in the striped T-shirt is on the _____.
7 The father with the dogs is on the _____.

D Read the *Exam Close-up* and then work in pairs to complete the *Exam Task*. Use the *Useful Expressions* to help you.

Exam Close-up

Describing in detail

- In the exam, look at the photo for a moment before you start speaking.
- Try and describe the photo in as much detail as possible – think about what you can see in the background and foreground.
- Use adjectives to describe people and things, e.g. what they are wearing, their personality, etc.
- Use prepositions to say where things are in the photograph.

Exam Task

Student A looks at photograph 1 and describes what he or she can see. Student B listens. Then student B describes photograph 2 and student A listens.

- Would you prefer to live in a big family / small family? Why / Why not?
- Do parents nowadays spend enough time with their children? Why? / Why not?

Ideas Focus

Vocabulary
Collocations & Expressions

A Complete the phrases with *keep*, *fall*, *pay*, *get* and *have*.

1 _____ a compliment / a visit
2 _____ a diary / a secret
3 _____ a family / sympathy
4 _____ married / divorced
5 _____ in love / to pieces

B Complete sentences 1–10 with collocations and expressions from A.

1 I'm not ready for children now, but I'd love to **have** _____ in a few years.
2 Shhh! You mustn't tell anyone about it! Can you **keep** _____?
3 I don't think I'll ever **fall** _____ again. My divorce was very upsetting.
4 My husband **paid** me _____ yesterday. He said I looked lovely.
5 Tom and I want to **get** _____ as soon as possible. We love each other.
6 I'd never **keep** _____. My sister might read it!
7 **Have** some _____ Pete; your brother has just lost his job.
8 If they can't sort out their problems soon, they may **get** _____.
9 Why not **pay** Grandma _____, Tom? She'll be pleased to see you.
10 It is difficult not to **fall** _____ when someone close to you passes away.

C Complete the sentences with the correct form of the expressions from A.

1 After 20 years, Susie's parents are _____.
   Naturally she's very upset.
2 Sam's father left his mother. Sam's worried that she'll
   _____.
3 I _____ a lot of _____ for
   children of separated or divorced parents.
4 My grandmother's house is near here; let's
   _____ her _____.
5 Mum, do you remember what it was that made you
   _____ with Dad?
6 Pam, can you _____? Good, come here and I'll
   whisper it in your ear.
7 A lot of my friends _____; they write in it every
   day.
8 My sister is _____ at the end of the month
   – she's having a very unusual wedding.
9 'Do you plan to _____ when you grow up?'
   'I want a big one with five children!'
10 My boyfriend _____ me _____
   today; he said I was very clever!

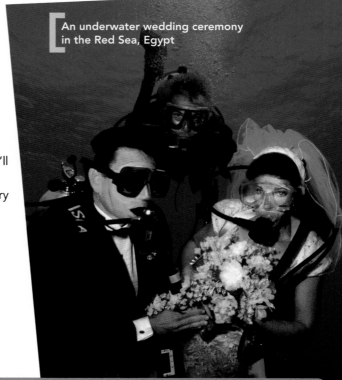

An underwater wedding ceremony in the Red Sea, Egypt

Ideas Focus

- Do you think it is better to have a family when you are young? Why? / Why not?
- Do you think people can only really fall in love once in their lives? Why? / Why not?
- Do you think it is a good idea to keep a diary so you can look at it when you are old? Why? / Why not?

Grammar

Countable / Uncountable Nouns & Quantifiers

A Look at the nouns in bold. Which are countable and which are uncountable? Write C (countable) and U (uncountable).

1 Granddad told us a **story** about our ancestors. ☐
2 Each country has its own **traditions**. ☐
3 **Information** about our genes comes from our DNA. ☐
4 A mother feels great **love** for her children. ☐
5 An **aunt** of mine gave me this picture. ☐

B Circle the correct words to complete the rules.

1 Countable / Uncountable nouns refer to separate items. They can be singular and plural. We use an article *(a/an/the)* before singular countable nouns.
2 Countable / Uncountable nouns refer to things that cannot be counted or abstract ideas. These nouns do not have a plural form.

C Some nouns can be both countable and uncountable depending on their meaning. How is the meaning of *hair* different in these sentences?

1 My sister washes her **hair** every day.
2 Oh no! There are dog **hairs** all over the sofa.

D Complete the table with the words below.

| a lot of | a kilo of | a number of | any | a few | a little | lots of | many | much | some |

Only Countable	Only Uncountable	Both
	✗	
✗	✗	
✗	✗	

> **Be careful**
> Remember that some plural countable nouns don't end in –s, and that some uncountable nouns do end in –s.
> *Children are* usually friendly.
> *The news is* very good!

● Grammar Focus p.162 (1.5 to 1.7)

E Write the words in the correct column.

| advice | food | generation | information | mirror |
| people | maths | family | research | tradition |

Countable	Uncountable

F *Chocolate* and *time* can also be countable and uncountable depending on their meaning. Write a sentence for each meaning.

_____
_____
_____
_____
_____

G Complete the dialogues with *a*, *an* or *some*.

1 **A:** Can I have _____ orange, please?
  B: Of course!
2 **A:** What's that, Dad?
  B: It's _____ old watch that Granddad gave me.
3 **A:** I saw _____ cool audio equipment in a shop this morning.
  B: Oh, did you buy anything?
4 **A:** Mum wants to make _____ apple pie, but there are only two apples.
  B: Oh, well, I'll go and buy _____.
5 **A:** What did you get for your birthday?
  B: I got _____ delicious chocolate and _____ great book!
6 **A:** Could I have _____ milk?
  B: Oh, there isn't any left.
7 **A:** Did you buy _____ present for your grandmother?
  B: Yes, I bought her _____ Italian bag.
8 **A:** Do you want _____ sugar in your tea?
  B: No, thanks.

Writing: an email

Learning Focus

Using abbreviations

We often use abbreviations in notes and postcards. These are the most common:

- morning and afternoon – am and pm
- people's titles – Mrs, Mr, Miss, Ms, Dr
- ordinal numbers – 10th (tenth), 40th (fortieth)
- parts of the language – e.g. (for example), etc. (etcetera), i.e. (that's to say)
- some countries – USA, UK, UAE
- in addresses – Rd (road), Ave (avenue), St (street)

A Rewrite the sentences below with abbreviations in your notebooks

1 I look like my mother's side of the family; that's to say, my grandmother, my aunt and my cousins.
2 It's mum's thirty-fifth birthday next week.
3 Carol lives in the United Arab Emirates.
4 Please bring food. For example, fruit, sandwiches or hotdogs.
5 I'm seeing Doctor Andrews at four o'clock in the afternoon.
6 Mister Jones says lessons start at eight forty-five in the morning.
7 Sixty-two Greendale Street, London, United Kingdom.
8 Buses leave at ten in the morning, eleven in the morning, twelve in the morning, etcetera.

B Read the writing task below and answer the questions.

> *You are preparing for a special family occasion. Write an email inviting one of your relatives to the party.*
>
> In your invitation, you should:
> - say what the invitation is for
> - say when the party is
> - say who is coming (35–45 words)

1 What do you have to write?
2 Who will read it?
3 Why are you writing?

C Read the example email and underline the abbreviations.

Hi Uncle Sam,

How are you?

We're having a surprise party on Saturday 11th April at 6pm because it's Dad's 50th birthday. Can you come?

All the family are coming, as well as Dad's friends.

I hope you can come too. Let me know.

Love,

Rashida

D Read the example email again and tick (☒) the things Rashida has included.

1 a greeting ☐
2 the reason for the party ☐
3 the time the party starts ☐
4 the date of the party ☐
5 details about the food ☐
6 told the reader to keep a secret ☐
7 asked the reader to reply to the invitation ☐
8 informal expressions ☐

E Match the items to make a plan.

1 Greeting
2 Paragraph 1
3 Paragraph 2
4 Paragraph 3
5 Paragraph 4
6 Signing off

a Give the reason why you are writing.
b Love, Rashida
c Ask the reader to reply to your invitation.
d Ask about the reader.
e Hi Uncle Sam,
f Give more details about the party.

F Read the *Exam Close-up* and the *Exam Task*. Then make a plan.

G Now complete the *Exam Task*. Remember to include all the important information.

Exam Close-up

Including all the information
- Make sure you read the exam question carefully.
- Underline the information you need to include in your writing.
- When you have finished, read the exam question again and check you have included all the points in your note.

Exam Task

You have done very well at school this year and your parents want to have a party to celebrate.

Write an **email** to a friend to invite them to the party. In your email you should:

- tell your friend why you are emailing
- give information about the party (time, place, date)
- ask your friend to reply (35–45 words)

Useful Expressions

Inviting
You're invited to …
Can you come?
I want to invite you to …

Asking for a reply
Let me know if you can come.
Tell me if you can come or not.

Writing about special events
celebration
guests
invitation
special occasion
surprise party
celebrate
invite
organise
plan
have a party

1 One Woman's Choice

Tanzania, Africa

Before you watch

A Work with a partner and answer these questions.

- What do you think 'family ties' are?
- Are family ties important to you? Why? / Why not?
- What reasons would a person cut family ties for?

While you watch

B Watch the video and decide if these statements are T (True) or F (False).

1 Flora Salonik has a university degree but nowadays she lives on a farm. ☐
2 Flora's life changed because she fell in love with a man from the Dorobo people. ☐
3 The remote village of Kijunga is a forty-minute walk from Arusha. ☐
4 Flora's family didn't know she was leaving the comforts of the city and moving to a faraway village. ☐
5 Flora and her husband Loshero raise cattle and grow crops to feed their family. ☐
6 Since Flora has been away for so long, the busy streets of her hometown are familiar to Flora. ☐

After you watch

C Complete the summary of the video below using these words.

belonged	city	decision	farm	grew	happy	married	stayed

Flora Salonik (**1**) _____ up in Arusha, which is one of Tanzania's busiest cities. She went to university and learnt to speak four languages. However, Flora's life changed dramatically after she got (**2**) _____. Her husband brought her home to the small village of Kijungu, very far away from Arusha. Besides looking after their three children, Flora also took care of the family's (**3**) _____ as her husband was away for most of the time. It was difficult for her to stop thinking about her past and she wondered how her life would be if she lived in the (**4**) _____. Flora had to make a (**5**) _____ about her family's future. She decided to go back to Arusha to figure things out. Flora was very (**6**) _____ to see her mother and (**7**) _____ with her for a while. She also visited all the places she used to know. Finally, Flora made her decision; she (**8**) _____ in Kijungu.

A family packages recently harvested plants, Tanzania

Ideas Focus

- Do you think it's better to raise a family in a village or in a city? Why / Why not?
- Would you like to live close to your childhood home when you grow up? Why? / Why not?

2 Food, Food, Food!

Take 136 kg of meat, 23 kg of cheese, 9 kg of onions, 5.5 kg of pickles and 13.5 kg of lettuce and slide them onto a massive bun and you have the biggest hamburger in the world! The burger was grilled on a colossal custom charcoal grill made by Napoleon Gourmet Grills. Toronto, Canada

17

Reading

A How much do you know about olives? Do the quiz and find out!

1 People have been growing olive trees for
   a 2,000 years.
   b 4,000 years.
   c 6,000 years.

2 Which country produces the most olive oil in the world?
   a Spain
   b Italy
   c Tunisia

3 People used to use olive oil to
   a attack people.
   b make cleaning products.
   c fight religion.

4 We now know exactly why olive oil is good because of
   a olive growers.
   b ancient traditions.
   c modern science.

B Quickly read the text and check your answers to the quiz.

C Read the incomplete sentence below. Then look at each gap carefully. What type of word do you need for each gap?

Butter and olive oil are both fats but olive oil is a (**1**) _____ fat and is better (**2**) _____ you because it (**3**) _____ your body from (**4**) _____.

An Oil for Life

Word Focus

crush: to press something very hard and break it
harvest: to pick and collect crops
fresh: not preserved or old
improve: to make something better

Maria Alcalá of Madrid speaks for many Mediterranean people when she says that "a meal without olive oil is boring". (**1**) _____ knows when the Mediterraneans first fell in love with olives because it was before people wrote and kept records. However, there is some evidence that people began growing olive trees around the Mediterranean Sea approximately 6,000 years ago. The Mediterranean countries still (**2**) _____ 99% of the world's olive oil with Spain being the world's biggest producer.

From ancient times (**3**) _____ today, the basic process of producing the oil is the same. First, farmers crush the olives. Then, they take the liquid and separate the oil from the water.

Many olive growers keep their ancient traditions and still harvest the olives (**4**) _____ hand. "We harvest in the traditional way", says Don Celso, an olive farmer from Tuscany, Italy. "It is less expensive to do it with machines but it's more a social thing. Twenty people come to help with the harvest and we pay them in oil".

Ancient civilisations used olive oil (**5**) _____ money and medicine. They even used it during war – they would heat it up and drop it down on the enemy! (**6**) _____ days, it is still used in religious ceremonies as it was in ancient times. It is also great for making fish and cheese stay fresh. There are even olive oil lamps and olive oil soaps.

D Find the words 1–5 in the text and match them to their definitions a–e.

1 evidence ☐   a something like water that you can pour easily
2 process ☐   b a series of things that you do to make something
3 liquid ☐   c reasons for believing that something is or isn't true
4 civilisation ☐   d an illness; something that makes you very sick
5 disease ☐   e a large group of people with its own culture

E Choose the correct words to complete the sentence in Exercise C.

1 lunch / good / unhealthy / old
2 eat / on / from / for
3 makes / likes / protects / healthy
4 fat / thin / infection / sleep

Exam Task

Read the text and choose the correct word for each space. For each question, mark the correct letter, **a, b, c** or **d**.

1   a Anyone   b Everyone   c No one   d Someone
2   a better   b want   c buy   d produce
3   a since   b for   c through   d until
4   a by   b in   c on   d with
5   a as   b at   c on   d of
6   a There   b These   c This   d Those
7   a lightest   b lowest   c healthiest   d smallest
8   a amounts   b groups   c lots   d numbers
9   a food   b dish   c diet   d plate
10   a give   b offer   c share   d show

Exam Close-up

Choosing the correct option

- First, read all the text to find out the topic and to get the general meaning.
- Then go back and read each sentence with a gap carefully. Make sure you read the complete sentence. Think about the type of word that could fit in each gap.
- Read the options. Then read the sentence again with each option in the gap. Which word fits the best?
- Be careful and write the correct option on the exam paper. Go back and check again!

F Read the *Exam Close-up* and the *Exam Task*. Then carefully read each sentence in the text with a gap.

G Now complete the *Exam Task*. Remember to check your answers.

One important study showed that Mediterranean people have the (**7**) _____ hearts in the western world. This is partly to do with frequently using olive oil. Other studies have shown that using olive oil can help to protect people from some types of <u>diseases</u>. The world is beginning to understand the advantages of using olive oil and it isn't an unusual thing to see on dinner tables outside the Mediterranean region anymore. The olive oil producing countries now sell large (**8**) _____ of olive oil to countries in Europe, Asia, Africa, and North and South America.

Olive oil <u>improves</u> the lives of people everywhere when it is part of a well-balanced (**9**) _____. Ancient people knew about its benefits and modern science has confirmed them. Luckily, the Mediterranean people are happy to (**10**) _____ their secret with the world.

Ideas Focus

- Is your country famous for a particular type of food? Do you enjoy it? Why? / Why not?
- Do you prefer to eat at a restaurant or at home? Why?
- Would you rather eat a salad or vegetables with your main meal of the day? Why? / Why not?

Vocabulary

A **Number the foods in the picture.**

1	pizza	**6**	sweetcorn
2	aubergine	**7**	rice
3	eggs	**8**	cupcake
4	wheat	**9**	chicken
5	broccoli	**10**	croissant

B **Copy and complete the table with the words from Exercise A.**

Grains and cereals	Fruit and vegetables	Protein and dairy	Sugar and fat

C **Circle the odd ones out.**

1 thirsty   hungry   bread   **5** bite   breakfast   chew

2 dessert   starter   lunch   **6** horrible   delicious   mix

3 kitchen   chop   peel   **7** fridge   jug   bowl

4 grill   boil   meat   **8** fry   stir   knife

A monk at Shaolin temple in China carries a takeaway burger meal

D **Complete the sentences with some of the words from Exercise C.**

1 Don't _____ the egg in this oil.

2 Have we got a _____ for the chicken and rice to go in?

3 It was a great restaurant. The strawberry and ice-cream _____ was delicious!

4 The _____ isn't working. All the food is warm.

5 Please _____ the apple for the baby – he can't eat the skin.

6 I'll need a sharp knife to _____ the brocolli.

7 You have to _____ the sauce, so it doesn't stick.

8 Don't _____ with your mouth open! It's horrible!

E **Read the text and choose the correct answers.**

The story of the hamburger

The (**1**) _____ hamburger is one of the most popular foods in the world, but where did it come from? Nobody really knows.

One theory is that about 800 years ago Mongolian soldiers, who didn't have (**2**) _____ or cookers, put meat under their saddles while they rode their horses to make it soft. In the evening they ate the meat without cooking it.

Another story is that immigrants to America from the city of Hamburg in Germany brought their 'Hamburg steak' with them – a type of (**3**) _____ meat in (**4**) _____.

Or perhaps Otta Kuasw from Hamburg made the first hamburger. Otto (**5**) _____ meat with (**6**) _____, fried it and put it between bread and sold it to young, hard-working and (**7**) _____ sailors for their (**8**) _____. When the sailors went back to America they asked their families to make the same thing and so the hamburger was born.

1	**a** horrible	**b** delicious	**c** breakfast		**5**	**a** chewed	**b** bit	**c** mixed
2	**a** meat	**b** food	**c** fridges		**6**	**a** breakfast	**b** eggs	**c** starter
3	**a** fried	**b** peeled	**c** stirred		**7**	**a** starter	**b** kitchen	**c** hungry
4	**a** bowl	**b** bread	**c** kitchen		**8**	**a** dessert	**b** lunch	**c** meat

Grammar

Past Simple

A Read the sentences below. Which sentence has a regular verb in the Past Simple?

1 Natalie went to the shops, bought a pizza and took it home.
2 I cooked fish last week.
3 James had croissants for breakfast every day when he was in France.

B Match each sentence in A with one use of the Past Simple below.

a past routines and habits ☐
b actions which happened one after the other in the past ☐
c actions or situations which started and finished in the past ☐

Past Continuous

C Read the sentences below. How do we form the Past continuous?

1 Jennifer **was watching** TV while her mum **was cooking** dinner.
2 It **was raining**, the wind **was blowing** and we **were shaking** from the cold.
3 I **was making** coffee at seven o'clock this morning.
4 Dad **was chopping** carrots when the phone **rang**.

D Match each sentence in C with one use of the Past Continuous below.

a an action that was in progress at a specific time in the past. ☐
b two or more actions that were in progress at the same time in the past. ☐
c an action that was in progress in the past but was interrupted by another action. ☐
d to give background information in a story. ☐

> **Be careful**
> Remember that we don't use stative verbs in continuous tenses.

▶ Grammar Focus p.163 (2.1 & 2.2)

F Write sentences with the Past Continuous in your notebooks.

1 the students / not eat / breakfast / in the classroom / this morning
2 we / not have / lunch / at one o'clock today
3 ? / you / make / cupcakes / all morning
4 this time last week / we / sample / French cheese
5 my sister / peel / potatoes / for hours this morning
6 ? / Cathy / prepare / dinner / on her own / last night

G Complete the sentences with the correct form of the Past Simple or the Past Continuous of the verbs in brackets.

1 We _____ (eat) some ice cream after we _____ (finish) cleaning the kitchen.
2 _____ (Joey / call) you while you _____ (watch) Jamie Oliver's cookery programme?
3 My dad _____ (cook) dinner on Saturday because Mum _____ (be) ill.
4 The children _____ (order) pizza when I _____ (walk) into their bedroom.
5 I _____ (not / fry) the hamburgers, I _____ (grill) them. They're healthier that way.
6 Karen _____ (make) lunch while Peter _____ (set) the table.
7 _____ (they / have) a barbeque when it _____ (start) to rain?
8 _____ (you / order) a dessert after you _____ (have) your main course?

E Complete the text with the Past Simple of the verbs in brackets.

Pizza, pizza, pizza!

Most people, love pizza and it's been around for a very long time. (**1**) _____ (you / know) that something similar to pizza was prepared in Ancient Greece? The Ancient Greeks (**2**) _____ (cover) their bread with oil, herbs and cheese. The Romans later (**3**) _____ (develop) *placenta*, which was a type of bread with cheese, honey and bay leaves. However, pizza as we know it (**4**) _____ (originate) in Italy as a Neapolitan pie with tomato.

A lot of people enjoy making their own pizza, and there's even a World Pizza Championship which is held every year in Italy. People also try to break the record for the largest pizza. The current record was set in Johannesburg, South Africa. The pizza (**5**) _____ (be) 37.4 metres in diameter. Many people (**6**) _____ (work) together for many hours to get this record. Some (**7**) _____ (make) the base and others (**8**) _____ (grate) the cheese. They used 500 kg of flour, 800 kg of cheese and 900 kg of tomato puree. The result was one enormous magnificent pizza!

Listening

A 2.1 ▶❙❙ **Read the numbers below. Then listen and choose the correct option a, b or c.**

1   **a** 2010   **b** 2011   **c** 2025

2   **a** 35   **b** 25   **c** 29

3   **a** 550   **b** 150   **c** 950

4   **a** 25th   **b** 21st   **c** 26th

5   **a** 250   **b** 260   **c** 160

B **Imagine that you are listening to a chef talking about the restaurant where he used to work. Look at the possible answers below and write down what the questions could be.**

The Gourmet Odyssey bus, London

1 _____

   a 6 months   **b** 1 year   **c** 2 years

2 _____

   a pasta dishes   **b** pizzas   **c** seafood risottos

3 _____

   a he didn't like the restaurant owner

   b to start his own restaurant

   c to work in a different type of restaurant

C **Read the *Exam Close-up*. Then read the *Exam Task* below and underline the important words and numbers.**

D 2.2 ▶❙❙ **Listen and complete the *Exam Task*.**

Exam Close-up

Listening for numbers

- Before you listen, read the questions carefully and check you understand the topic.
- Underline the important words, numbers or dates in the main question and a–c options.
- Be careful with numbers and dates! Sometimes they sound very similar. When you listen the second time, check your answers carefully.

Exam Task

You will hear a radio interview about a restaurant festival. For each question, circle the correct option a, b or c.

1   How many restaurants took part in the festival in 2009?
   a over 415
   b over 800
   c over 450

2   What does each restaurant do at the festival?
   a offer classes to the public with their favourite chef
   b prepare a special menu
   c offer four different dishes in a menu

3   How does the festival help charities?
   a It provides meals for people living on the streets.
   b It donates money to a charity for people living on the streets.
   c It has set up a website for people living on the streets.

4   What does the Gourmet Odyssey offer people?
   a four courses in four different restaurants
   b travel between the restaurants in a bus
   c the chance to meet the chefs

5   How much does the walking version of the Gourmet Odyssey cost?
   a £35
   b £95
   c £135

6   Faye Wallis says …
   a Gordon Ramsey will cook every night.
   b all the London Eye capsules will become dining rooms.
   c Gordon Ramsey's meal will raise money for charity.

E 2.2 ▶❙❙ **Now listen again.**

Speaking

A Work with a partner and answer these questions.

- Can you cook? What can you cook?
- Who normally does the cooking at home?
- What's your favourite food and what food do you never eat? Why?

B Choose the correct adjective to complete the sentences.

1 The chocolate cake with strawberries was delicious / horrible. I ate three pieces!
2 This chicken is undercooked / overcooked. It's black!
3 My dad really loves bland / spicy food, like a hot, Indian curry.
4 This salad looks really tasty / tasteless! It's bright and colourful / grey.
5 Some people don't like the bitter / sweet taste of lemons.
6 Too much healthy / processed food isn't good for you.
7 They usually eat grilled / fried fish because it is healthier.
8 I waited a long time for these eggs and now they're cold / hot!

C Read the *Exam Close-up*. Then work with a partner and make a list of all the food and drink you can see in each photo in the *Exam Task* below. Choose adjectives from B to describe them.

D Now complete the *Exam Task*. Use the *Useful Expressions* to help you.

Useful Expressions

Using adjectives

It looks / seems to be + adjective

I think they / he / she are + adjective

That is / isn't good for you because it's + adjective

I often eat / don't usually eat that because it's + adjective

I like / don't like that because it's + adjective

Exam Close-up

Using different adjectives

- When you describe people or things try to use lots of different adjectives.
- Try not to use adjectives like *nice*, *good* or *bad* all the time.
- Look carefully at the photo first and think about positive or negative ways to describe the things you can see.
- You can also give your opinion and say if you like or dislike what you see.

Exam Task

Student A looks at photograph 1 and describes what he or she can see. Student B listens. Then student B describes photograph 2 and student A listens.

- Do you enjoy eating fast food? Why? / Why not?
- Do young people still eat lots of traditional types of food? Why / Why not?

Ideas Focus

Vocabulary
Word formation

A Copy and complete the table.

noun	verb	adjective
(1) _____	colour	coloured/colourful
taste	(2) _____	tasty/tasteless
tradition	✗	(3) _____
decision	(4) _____	decisive
choice	(5) _____	choosy
custom/ (6) _____	✗	customary
mixture	(7) _____	mixed/mixing
(8) _____	✗	trendy
(9) _____	brighten	bright
variety	vary	(10) _____

C Complete the text with the correct form of the words.

B Complete the sentences with the words from the table in A.

1 What a nice old restaurant! Reds, yellows, dark blues – it's so _____!

2 There were a lot of _____ waiting to get into *The Hummingbird Bakery*.

3 Look at all those different types of cake! I can't _____ which one to get for mum. Which one do you think I should _____?

4 They left the dark street and went into the _____ restaurant with lots of colourful lights.

5 Hot dogs are a(n) _____ snack served at American baseball games.

6 Can I have another biscuit, please? They're very _____.

7 That new café might be modern and _____, but they make terrible coffee!

8 The quality of vegetables you can buy can _____ from market stall to market stall.

9 I had a _____ of vanilla, chocolate and strawberry ice-cream for dessert.

The Hummingbird Bakery

Do you like sweet things? Love sugar? Dream about chocolate? If you do then 'The Hummingbird Bakery' in London is the place for you.

These shops are full of the most delicious and (1) _____ cupcakes you can imagine. These (2) _____ treats are so popular that there are now three branches of the bakery in London with a fourth planned for next year. The first bakery opened in 2004 after a group of Americans couldn't find (3) _____ American-style cupcakes anywhere in London. They decided to make their own and sell them. It certainly proved to be a great (4) _____!

Those who visit the bakery will definitely be spoilt for (5) _____! But the favourite with the (6) _____ is the 'Red Velvet Cupcake'. This is a delicious (7) _____ of bright red vanilla cake with cream cheese and chocolate on top.

The newest shop to open in London is in (8) _____ Soho. It is decorated with (9) _____ -coloured cupcake art and a large TV screen showing the bakery's 50 different (10) _____ of cakes.

So if you're in London and you didn't have a dessert at lunchtime, why not drop by and try the delicious delights the Hummingbird Bakery has to offer.

COLOUR
TASTE

TRADITION

DECIDE
CHOOSE
CUSTOM
MIX

TREND
BRIGHT
VARY

Ideas Focus

• It is difficult for you to decide what to have when you are in a restaurant? Why? / Why not?
• Do you like to taste new things? Why? / Why not?

Grammar

used to & would

A Tick (✓) the sentence where *used to* can be replaced with *would*.

1 Lisa used to like olives when she was young. ☐

2 My grandmother used to make her own pasta when she lived in the countryside. ☐

B Complete the rule with *used to* and *would*.

- _____ can be used to talk about states or repeated actions in the past, but _____ can only be used to talk about repeated actions in the past. It cannot be used to talk about past states.

be used to & get used to

C Look at the sentences and answer the questions.

1 I am getting used to eating healthy food.

2 I am used to eating healthy food.

a Which sentence refers to something that is already usual or familiar? ☐

b Which sentence refers to something that is becoming familiar now? ☐

D Complete the rules with *be used to* and *get used to*.

- We use _____ + verb + -*ing* or a noun to talk about actions or states that are usual or familiar. We use _____ + verb + -*ing* or a noun to talk about actions or states that are becoming familiar to us.

▶ Grammar Focus p.163 (2.3 & 2.4)

E Tick (✓) the sentences where the words in bold can be replaced with *would*.

1 My mum **used to** give us croissants every Sunday morning. ☐

2 These chocolates **used to** cost much less. ☐

3 **Did** you **use to** like vegetables when you were younger? ☐

4 We **used to** have picnics at the beach every weekend. ☐

5 I **didn't use to** own a fridge, but now I do. ☐

6 David **used to** eat a lot of rice when he lived in China. ☐

7 Our cat Max **used to** hide its food in the garden. ☐

8 **Did** Susan **use to** be slim when she was at university? ☐

F Choose the correct answers.

1 I ___ having bread and cheese for breakfast.
   a am used to   b used to   c am getting used

2 My cookery teacher ___ be a chef.
   a is getting used to   b is used to   c used to

3 ___ preparing food when you lived at home?
   a Did you use to   b Are you getting used to   c Were you used to

4 Jessica loved India, but she ___ the spicy food.
   a didn't use to   b couldn't get used to   c used to

5 Maria and Natalie ___ the lunches at their new school's canteen.
   a are getting used to   b used to   c get used to

6 ___ watching his weight?
   a Did Ted use to   b Is Ted used to   c Is Ted getting used

7 I ___ eating anything I wanted before I went on a diet.
   a was used to   b am getting used to   c used to

8 ___ help your mum set the table?
   a Did you get used to   b Did you use to   c Were you used to

writing: a review

Learning Focus

Ordering adjectives

- When you have two or more adjectives before a noun, remember to put them in this order: **opinion** (*delicious*), **size** (*tiny*), **age** (*old*), **shape** (*square*), **colour** (*purple*), **origin** (*German*) and **material** (*silk*).
- When you have two adjectives of the same kind before a noun, put *and* between them and put them in alphabetical order (*black and white*).

A Tick (✓) the correct sentences and then correct the order of adjectives in the wrong ones.

1 The waiters were wearing blue nice uniforms. _____
2 We sat at a big round table by the window. _____
3 Have you been to the Chinese fantastic new restaurant? _____
4 Please change this dirty old tablecloth! _____
5 The walls are decorated with modern interesting pictures. _____
6 There were lovely fresh flowers on the table. _____
7 I recommend our tasty little pizzas. _____
8 It's worth a try if you're thirsty and hungry. _____

B Read the writing task below and then decide if the statements are T (True) or F (False).

> *You recently had a meal in a new restaurant. Write a review of the restaurant for your school magazine giving your opinion and saying why you would / wouldn't recommend it. (100 words)*

1 You should write about some food you enjoyed. ☐
2 The review is for people the same age as you. ☐
3 The review can be either positive or negative. ☐
4 You should say why you liked or didn't like the food. ☐
5 You need to say if you think other people should go to the restaurant. ☐

C Read the example review and complete it with the adjectives in brackets in the correct order.

Gino's: a good choice for hungry shoppers

Are you bored with (**1**) (grey / tasteless) _____ fast-food? Next time you are hungry, why not pay a visit to the (**2**) (Italian / new) _____ restaurant, Gino's?

I was shopping last weekend when I saw the (**3**) (colourful / modern) _____ restaurant in the city centre, so I decided to try it. I had a (**4**) (healthy / small) _____ starter of grilled aubergine and chicken pasta for my main. The aubergine was (**5**) (tasty / sweet) _____ and the pasta was delicious.

Gino's is a(n) (**6**) (easy-going / small) _____ restaurant with (**7**) (red / lovely / cotton) _____ tablecloths, trendy pictures, and (**8**) (young / friendly) _____ waiters. It's the perfect place for lunch for everyone!

D Read the example review again and answer these questions.

1 Is the title a good one for this review? Why? / Why not?
2 How does the writer attract the reader's attention in Paragraph 1?
3 What adjectives does the writer use to describe the food?
4 What other descriptions does the writer give?
5 Who does the writer think the restaurant is good for?

E Complete the plan for the example review with these descriptions.

a Describe the meal you ate. ☐ Paragraph 1
b Give your opinion of the restaurant and make a recommendation. ☐ Paragraph 2
c Give details about the restaurant. ☐ Paragraph 3
d Introduce what you are reviewing. ☐ Paragraph 4

F Read the *Exam Close-up* and the *Exam Task*. Do you need to write a positive or negative review?

G Read the *Useful Expressions* and write P (positive) or N (negative) for each one.

H Complete the *Exam Task*. Remember to make a plan before you start and to think about different adjectives you can use in each paragraph.

Useful Expressions

Recommending

I highly recommend …	☐
I wouldn't / don't recommend …	☐
It's the perfect place / cafe / restaurant for …	☐
It's the worst …	☐

Adjectives for food

bitter	☐
undercooked	☐
overcooked	☐
colourful	☐
delicious	☐
healthy	☐
unhealthy	☐
bland	☐
processed	☐
tasty	☐
tasteless	☐

Adjectives for restaurants

scruffy	☐
dirty	☐
trendy	☐
bright	☐
old-fashioned	☐
expensive	☐
slow	☐
unfriendly	☐
rude	☐

Exam Task

You recently ate at a new restaurant but you were very unhappy with your meal.

Write a **review** of the restaurant for your school magazine. Give your opinion and say why you wouldn't recommend it to others. (100 words)

Exam Close-up

Making your writing interesting

• It is a good idea to use lots of different vocabulary in your writing to make it more interesting.
• When you are planning in the exam, think about the words you can use to describe people, places or things.
• Try to use lots of different adjectives and not the same ones all the time.

2 Greek Olives

Naxos, Greece

Before you watch

A How much do you know about olives? Look at the statements below and write T (True) or F (False).

1 Green, black and brown olives each come from a different type of tree. ☐
2 The olive branch is a symbol of peace. ☐
3 Olive trees are easy to recognise. ☐

While you watch

B Watch the video and see if your answers for A are correct.

C Watch the video again and circle the words you hear.

1 In fact, most people wouldn't know / recognise an olive tree.
2 Some trees have been alive / lived for thousands of years.
3 If people want to end a war, they are said to 'offer an olive tree / branch'.
4 You can make a kind / type of tea from the leaves.
5 To produce the best liquid / oil, olives are collected and processed once they have become black.
6 They're very important / valuable for vitamins and their oils are very healthy.

After you watch

D Complete the summary of the video below using these words.

account associated assume carries evidence incorrect live produce

On the Greek island of Naxos, olives grow in many sizes and colours. Many people (**1**) _____ that they come from different kinds of trees, but this is (**2**) _____. Green olives are young and black ones are older. It is usually the black olives that are processed in order to (**3**) _____ oil. Greek olives (**4**) _____ for a lot of the world's olive production.

Olives have been an important part of life in Greece for many thousands of years. For example, in ancient stories of gods and goddesses, Eirene, the goddess of peace, (**5**) _____ an olive branch. Today, around the world, the olive branch is still (**6**) _____ with peace and the end of wars.

Olive oil is also said to have remarkable health benefits. There is even (**7**) _____ that those who use it (**8**) _____ longer.

Ideas Focus

- Do you and your family eat a lot of olives, or use a lot of olive oil? Why? / Why not?
- What other foods do you know that have health benefits?

Review 1

Vocabulary

A Circle the correct words.

1 Do you want to have / get a large family when you are older?
2 My sister pay / keeps a diary, but she won't let me read it.
3 We should pay / get a visit to the new Italian restaurant in town.
4 My cousin is getting / keeping married in the summer.
5 Suzie was so upset when she dropped her father's birthday cake. She fell / had to pieces.
6 Can you have / keep a secret? I'm in love.
7 The meal was so delicious that my mother paid / got the chef a compliment.
8 David's met a wonderful girl and they've got / fallen in love.

B Complete the word groups with these words.

fry   look like   main course   middle-aged   plate   reliable   sweet   unkind

1 young	elderly	_____
2 jug	bowl	_____
3 dessert	starter	_____
4 generous	honest	_____
5 boil	grill	_____
6 similar	take after	_____
7 tasty	delicious	_____
8 lazy	nervous	_____

C Complete the sentences with both words.

1   decide   decision
   a Vicky can never make a _____ about what to order in a restaurant.
   b Can we _____ what to eat for lunch today?

2   choice   choosy
   a My mother is very _____ about what meat she buys.
   b 'There's not much _____ on the menu, is there?' she said.

3   mixture   mix
   a His hamburger was a _____ of fried meat and eggs put between bread.
   b Would you like to _____ the chicken with the rice?

4   custom   customary
   a It's _____ to offer a visitor a cup of tea or coffee when they arrive.
   b There is a _____ here of cooking special vegetables on Christmas Day.

5   bright   brighten
   a Light colours _____ the restaurant and make it very relaxing
   b There is a very _____ light in the kitchen.

6   variety   vary
   a There are a _____ of pizzas to choose from.
   b The restaurant tries to _____ the menu every day.

D Complete the sentences with these prepositions.

after   down   for   like   out

1 My father is looking _____ a cousin in Australia.
2 I take _____ my mother; I have her sense of humour.
3 Do you think she looks _____ her older sister or her grandmother?
4 We're trying to find _____ more about our family tree.
5 Traditional stories are passed _____ from generation to generation.

Review 1   Units 1 & 2

Grammar

A Complete the sentences with the Present Simple, the Present Continuous, the Past Simple or the Past Continuous of the verbs in brackets.

1 You _____ (be) disgusting! You _____ (always / eat) with your mouth open!

2 I _____ (miss) my favourite cookery programme on TV last night. What time _____ (it / start)?

3 Shelly _____ (not / see) her parents very often, but she _____ (often / visit) her grandparents.

4 A three-course meal at *Mama Mia* _____ (cost) about £45 per person.

5 We all _____ (know) that fruit and vegetables _____ (be) very good for us, but _____ (we / eat) enough each day?

6 Mum _____ (make) pizza for lunch when she _____ (realise) that she _____ (not / have) any cheese. We _____ (have) sandwiches instead!

7 I _____ (think) of cooking chicken on Sunday. What _____ (you / think)?

8 Bill _____ (not / be) a chef, but he _____ (work) at a restaurant in town at the moment.

9 Pete and Lucy _____ (spend) last weekend with us.

10 _____ (the children / enjoy) the party on Saturday?

11 Sam _____ (have) eight sisters! I _____ (have) only got one.

12 Carrie _____ (go) to the doctor's yesterday and he _____ (tell) her about the importance of a well-balanced diet.

B Circle the correct words.

1 I found an / the information about olives on the Internet.

2 Physics is / are my brother's favourite subject at school.

3 Please buy some cheese and any / some bread when you're at the supermarket.

4 There are a number of / a lot good restaurants down by the sea.

5 Put a little / few olive oil on your salad and it will taste delicious.

6 I'd like a sandwich and a can / cup of coffee for lunch, please.

7 How much / many spaghetti do you want?

8 Men enjoy / enjoys cooking – lots of chefs are men.

C Complete the second sentences so that they have a similar meaning to the first sentences. Use the words in bold.

1 We don't eat out during the week any more. **used**
   We _____ during the week.

2 Sooner or later your new school won't feel so strange. **get**
   Sooner or later, you _____ your new school.

3 Cooking for lots of people is nothing new for Geoff. **is**
   Geoff _____ for lots of people.

4 Tammy didn't eat meat when she was younger. **use**
   Tammy _____ meat when she was younger.

5 Looking after a small baby is something new for my sister and her husband. **not**
   My sister and her husband _____ after a small baby.

6 Mum used to read me stories when I was young. **would**
   Mum _____ me stories when I was young.

30

3 The Wonders of Nature

The sleeping Mud Maid is a sculpture that
changes with every change of the season.
The base is made of wood, mud and cement.
The Mud Maid can be admired in the Lost
Gardens of Heligan, Cornwall, England.

Reading

A Work with a partner. What do you usually read? Look at the ideas below. Which ones do you read the most?

- books
- ebooks
- magazines
- text messages
- newspapers
- notices and posters
- websites
- blogs
- adverts
- postcards

B Look at the ideas in A again. With a partner, decide if the information you read in each …

- gives facts
- entertains the reader
- is educational
- gives personal opinions

C Read the text quickly. Where could you read this type of text? What type of information does it have in it?

D Read the *Exam Close-up*. Then read the *Exam Task* and underline the key words.

E Now complete the *Exam Task*.

A diver uses cyanide to collect fish from a coral reef in the Philippines. Traders can receive a high price for reef fish in aquarium markets

Cities Beneath the Sea

Coral polyps are truly the animals that helped make the world. For millions of years, tiny coral polyps have been building underwater cities. The polyps create something called limestone which they then live on top of. There are huge amounts of limestone under the ocean in islands and mountains. These limestone islands and mountains are called coral reefs. Some reefs are bigger than anything people have ever made. The Egyptians used it to build the Great Pyramids. We have used limestone to build many buildings, and crushed limestone is used to make cement.

A Variety of Life

Living coral reefs are amazing 'cities beneath the sea' that are full of life. The reefs develop well in the warm oceans near the Equator. Among the world's most colourful places, coral reefs are full of brightly-coloured fish. Reef fish are an important food source for humans and many are caught for food around the world.

The Biggest of Them All

The Great Barrier Reef, in Australia, is the largest reef in the world. It is 2,000 kilometres long. Over 400 types of coral, 1,500 species of fish and approximately 4,000 types of mollusc live in, on and around the reef.

Each year, thousands of visitors come to see this remarkable world beneath the waves. However, there are rules – visitors can only visit 5% of the reef. In this way, they can still enjoy the reef while it remains protected for future generations.

Threats to Coral Reefs

In recent years, a number of dangers have threatened coral reefs and the life that depends on them. One of the biggest threats is an illegal way of fishing

Exam Task

Read the text and questions below. For each question, choose the correct letter **a**, **b**, **c** or **d**.

1 What does the writer want to do with this text?
   a entertain the reader
   b give information about reefs
   c give advice on conservation
   d advertise a place to go on holiday
2 What are coral reefs made of?
   a molluscs
   b mountains
   c cement
   d a kind of rock
3 Which statement about coral reefs is NOT true?
   a They are an important source of fish.
   b They are very colourful places.
   c They are usually found in deep ocean waters.
   d They can be larger than man-made things.
4 How is the Great Barrier Reef protected?
   a Only a small part of the reef can be seen by visitors.
   b Just 5% of visitors are allowed to see it.
   c Visitors must be very strict.
   d The reef is not open every year.

Exam Close-up

Understanding text types

- Identifying the type of texts in an exam can help you understand the information in it.
- Read the text quickly to find out what kind of text it is, e.g. a review, a notice, a letter, etc. and the type of information it has in it.
- Then read each paragraph carefully, one at a time. What is each paragraph about? What information does the writer want you to know? Try to answer these questions before you read the next paragraph.
- Use the title and any headings in the text to help you.

5 Which is the best summary of the text?
   a Polyps are very important because they create the rock known as limestone, which is used to build things.
   b The coral reefs are natural wonders that are in danger and we should do everything we can to save them.
   c The fish from coral reefs are very beautiful and you can see them in aquariums around the world.
   d There are many different ways to catch fish but some of them are not safe for the environment.

Word Focus

coral polyp: a small animal that lives in the sea
limestone: a rock that is made of calcium carbonate
cement: a grey powder that is mixed with sand and water to make concrete
Equator: an imaginary line drawn around the middle of the earth
mollusc: an animal that has a soft body and is often covered with a shell
stun: make unconscious and unable to move for a short time

F Work in pairs. One of these statements about the Great Barrier Reef is not true. Which one do you think it is? Discuss your answers.

1 It is a World Heritage Site.
2 It is the world's largest coral reef system.
3 It is one of the Seven Ancient Wonders of the World.
4 It can be seen from outer space.

The Great Barrier Reef, Australia

that explodes bombs in the water to kill as many fish as possible. It kills most living things and causes great damage to the reef's structure.

Fishing with an extremely dangerous chemical called cyanide is another threat to reefs, particularly in the Philippines. Fishermen put this poisonous chemical into the reef water because it stuns the fish and they can't move. They catch the fish easily and then sell them for big money to aquariums or restaurants. The chemical they use kills coral polyps, and causes large areas of the reef to die.

Water pollution also damages reefs. In addition, warmer water in the oceans has been causing many areas of reefs to turn white. Biologists are worried that further warming may damage coral reefs even more.

Reasons for Hope

Threats to coral reefs are serious, but there is reason to hope that they will survive. Coral reef conservation can help these tiny coral polyps, which have survived natural threats for millions of years, to rebuild the damaged reefs that so many ocean creatures and plants depend on.

Ideas Focus

- Do you agree with protecting coral reefs from tourists? Why? / Why not?
- Which structures on earth do you think can be seen from outer space?

Vocabulary

A Label the pictures with these words.

cave   cliff   coast   glacier   pond   rainforest   stream   valley

_____   _____   _____   _____

_____   _____   _____   _____

B Read the text in the box and find the words to help you match 1–8 to a–h below.

1 fossil ☐
2 conservation ☐
3 climate ☐
4 natural ☐
5 solar ☐
6 power ☐
7 endangered ☐
8 renewable ☐

a habitats
b energy
c change
d fuels
e areas
f stations
g power
h species

What's new?

Every day we read or hear how humans are creating climate change by burning fossil fuels in huge power stations instead of using renewable energy, such as solar power. The news is full of stories of how people are destroying natural habitats and putting animals and insects in danger of extinction.

However, there is some good news – scientists are still making new discoveries in the darkest parts of our rainforests, caves and coasts. We know of about two million species in the world, but there are probably another eight million kinds of animals and insects that we don't know about yet.

However, as scientists discover these new animals and insects, they already know there are endangered species. Many countries have set up conservation areas to create safe places for them to live and be protected from humans.

C Match each sentence 1–8 with the sentence a–h that logically follows it.

1 Renewable energy is very important. ☐
2 Humans are using all the planet's fossil fuels quickly. ☐
3 Many people think climate change is a big problem. ☐
4 Conservation areas are very important. ☐
5 An animal's natural habitat is the place where it lives. ☐
6 Many animals are on the list of endangered species. ☐
7 Solar power is available everywhere. ☐
8 Power stations are often huge. ☐

a They help to give animals and insects in danger of extinction a safe place to live.
b The temperature of the earth and sea has gone up by about 1°C in the last 100 years.
c If we don't protect them, they will become extinct.
d Most of our electricity is still produced in them.
e It is the power we get from the sun, wind and sea.
f It's important that we don't destroy the land they live on.
g We get it from the sun and it is very easy to use.
h It took millions of years for oil, coal and gas to form and we are using them up too fast.

Ideas Focus

• Glaciers are melting and rainforests are being destroyed. Do you agree that it's all our fault but we can't do anything to change the situation? Why? / Why not?

Grammar

Present Perfect Simple

A **Read the sentences. How do we form the affirmative and negative in the Present Perfect Simple?**

1 The scientist **has won** many prizes.
2 The students **have** just **completed** a project on the environment.
3 I can't show you how to use the camera because I **haven't read** the instructions.
4 I**'ve lost** my map of the rainforest.

B **Match each sentence with one use of the Present Perfect Simple.**

a actions that have just finished ☐
b experiences and achievements ☐
c actions that happened in the past but have results that affect the present ☐
d actions that happened at an indefinite time in the past ☐

| **Be careful**
Remember that we use the Past Simple to describe
● actions that began and ended in the past, but
we use the Present Perfect Simple to describe
completed actions when we don't know or don't
mention when they happened.

Present Perfect Continuous

C **Read the sentences. How do you think we form the negative of the Present Perfect Continuous?**

1 He is sunburnt because he **has been walking** on the beach.
2 We **have been recycling** for many years.
3 The explorers **have been travelling** through the jungle for ten months.

D **Match each sentence with one use of the Present Perfect Continuous.**

a for actions that began in the past and are still in progress or have happened repeatedly until now ☐
b for actions that happened for a period of time and have finished, but that have results that affect the present ☐
c to emphasise how long actions have been in progress for ☐

| **Be careful**
We don't use the Present Perfect Continuous when
● we mention the number of times an action occurred
or when we mention specific quantities. We use the
Present Perfect Simple.

➦ **Grammar Focus p.163 & 164 (3.1 to 3.6)**

E **Choose the correct answers.**

1 Many explorers have ___ to the North Pole.
   a go   **b** been   **c** going
2 Nobody is here. They have ___ to find new species in the rainforest.
   a gone   **b** been   **c** going
3 Edmund Hillary and Tenzing Norgay got to the top of Mount Everest ___.
   a since 1953   **b** almost 60 years ago   **c** for almost 60 years
4 Kate has been studying endangered species ___.
   a for ten years   **b** since ten years   **c** ten years
5 He has been collecting fossils ___ he was a student.
   a for   **b** ago   **c** since

F **Circle the correct words.**

1 Animal conservation became / has become more important in the last 100 years.
2 Climate change caused / has caused many glaciers to melt.
3 The Giant Panda has been / was an endangered species for years.
4 The puppy has been drinking / drank milk from a bottle for two months.
5 The fisherman has been catching / has caught 50 kilos of fish since yesterday.
6 The scientists haven't finished / haven't been finishing their research yet.

G **Complete the text with the correct form of the Present Perfect Simple, the Present Perfect Continuous or the Past Simple of the verbs in brackets.**

Icebergs

The word 'iceberg' probably comes from the Norwegian word 'isberg', which means 'ice mountain'. Every year about 10,000–15,000 icebergs form around the world. Although modern ships know where icebergs are now, in the past icebergs (**1**) _____ (be) one of the biggest dangers in the sea. The famous Titanic (**2**) _____ (sink) when it hit an iceberg in 1912 and many people (**3**) _____ (die). Because of this accident, thirteen countries (**4**) _____ (form) the International Ice Patrol in 1914. This organisation (**5**) _____ (give) information to ships about icebergs ever since.

Biologists (**6**) _____ (study) icebergs for a long time to find out how they change sea life. When an iceberg melts, nutrients go into the sea. Recently, scientist (**7**) _____ (show) that the water near icebergs is full of plankton, fish and other sea life.

Scientists (**8**) _____ (notice) the way icebergs fall to pieces when they are in warmer waters. One of the biggest icebergs (**9**) _____ (break) off from the Ross Ice Shelf in Antarctica in 2000. It was 295km long and 37km wide!

Listening

A Look at the notes below before you listen. Which of the missing words will NOT be numbers? Say what you think those words might be.

1 The average length of a Great White Shark is _____ metres.
2 The biggest shark ever found was _____ kg.
3 Great Whites are in fact not all white, but mostly _____.
4 A Great White Shark has got approximately _____ teeth.
5 Its fastest speed is _____ kilometres per hour.
6 _____ is the Great White Shark's most important sense.

B 3.1 ▶❚❚ Now listen and complete the notes in A.

C Read the *Exam Close-up*. Then think about the words which could go in each gap in the *Exam Task*.

A great white shark in its natural habitat

D 3.2 ▶❚❚ Now listen and complete the *Exam Task*.

Exam Task

You will hear an interview with a scientist who studies sharks. For each question, fill in the missing information in the numbered space.

Wildlife Watch shark investigation

Number of people who died from shark attacks in 2008. (**1**) _____
Number of different (**2**) _____ of shark.
Reason why sharks bite: to find out (**3**) _____ about objects.
Sharks probably don't usually eat humans because humans have too many (**4**) _____.
Approximately (**5**) _____ sharks are killed by humans each year.
Many sharks are now (**6**) _____ extinction.

E 3.2 ▶❚❚ Now listen again.

Exam Close-up

Thinking about the answers first
- It's a good idea to understand what type of information you need to complete the gaps before you listen.
- Read the words before and after each gap and try to think of the type of words or numbers which could complete the gap.
- Then listen and write the exact same words or information you hear.
- In each gap you will normally need to write between one and three words.

Speaking

A Work with a partner and answer these questions.

- Why is our planet in danger?
- How do people damage the environment?
- How many endangered species do you know of? Make a list in your notebook.

B 3.3 ▶❚❚ Read the *Exam Close-up*. Listen and complete the instructions for the *Exam Task* below.

I'm going to describe a situation to you.
A (1) _____ committee is trying to decide what (2) _____ its students could do to help (3) _____ the environment. Talk together about the (4) _____ things the students could do and then (5) _____ which project would be (6) _____.

Exam Close-up

Listening to instructions

- In the exam, listen to the instructions carefully and make sure you understand what you have to talk about.
- If you aren't sure or you are nervous, you can politely ask the examiner to repeat the instructions.
- Start by talking about the first picture then discuss each one before making a decision.

C Match the verbs 1–5 with words a–e. Then find them in the *Exam Task*.

1	start ☐	a	rubbish and litter on the beach
2	recycle ☐	b	posters for a campaign
3	plant ☐	c	trees
4	clear up ☐	d	a school blog
5	put up ☐	e	plastic, paper and cans

Useful Expressions

Opening discussions

Shall we start with this …?   To begin with, …
Let's begin / start by looking at …   Let's move on to …
First of all, …   Shall we talk about … now?

D Now work in pairs to complete the *Exam Task*. Use the *Useful Expressions* to help you.

Exam Task

recycling

cleaning up the beach

a campaign

Ways to protect the environment

planting trees

writing a school blog

Ideas Focus

- Are zoos a good or bad idea? Why? / Why not?
- Should you help to protect the environment? Why / Why not?
- If we don't protect the environment, what do you think will happen in the future?

Vocabulary
Prepositions

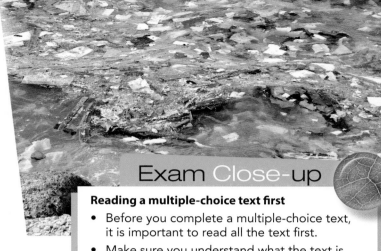

A Complete the phrases with the correct preposition.

1 (after / across) _____ years of something
2 take action (on / onto) _____ something
3 for (between / over) _____ 20 years
4 go from here (to / in) _____ there
5 get (for / from) _____ this to this
6 appear (in / into) _____ something
7 get (during / onto) _____ something
8 (on / at) _____ the moment
9 turn (at / into) _____ something
10 (before / on) _____ something happens

Exam Close-up

Reading a multiple-choice text first
- Before you complete a multiple-choice text, it is important to read all the text first.
- Make sure you understand what the text is about before you start to choose the correct answers.
- When you have chosen the answers, go back and read the text again and check that it makes sense.

B Complete the sentences with the correct prepositions.

in into to over at onto before from

1 We need to protect the rainforest _____ it disappears.
2 I have been using solar power for _____ a decade now. Twelve years in fact.
3 In Iceland, you can explore anything _____ caves to glaciers.
4 They are turning this land _____ a conservation area.

5 The stream goes from the top of the mountain _____ the bottom of the valley.
6 Species from the rainforest have appeared _____ people's garden ponds.
7 Bacteria on animals can get _____ our hands.
8 I can't talk right now; I'm very busy _____ the moment.

C Read the *Exam Close-up* and then read the *Exam Task* text. How could the 'Great Garbage Patch' be dangerous?

D Now complete the *Exam Task*. Remember to read the text again when you have finished.

Exam Task

What a load of rubbish!!
It's difficult to believe that (**1**) ___ years of people working hard to fight pollution and take action (**2**) ___ the environment, we still have a long way to go before we succeed.

Oceanographers have discovered a huge 'plastic soup' made from rubbish floating in the Pacific Ocean. This island of rubbish has been growing slowly for (**3**) ___ 60 years and is now so big it goes from California (**4**) ___ Hawaii and nearly to Japan. It contains everything you could imagine, (**5**) ___ plastic bags to children's toys and even plastic swimming pools!

The 'Great Garbage Patch' as it's sometimes called, causes lots of problems. One of these is the chemicals it produces in the sea. These chemicals and small pieces of plastic are now appearing (**6**) ___ fish, and obviously, this means the plastic-filled fish could get (**7**) ___ our dinner plates!

It's not all bad news though. (**8**) ___ the moment, a conservation group are investigating if the 100 million tons of waste can be turned (**9**) ___ fuel and used in a positive way.

Let's hope they take action (**10**) ___ the 'plastic soup' now before it gets any bigger!

	a		b		c		d	
1	a	after	b	about	c	across	d	over
2	a	around	b	above	c	about	d	on
3	a	between	b	over	c	below	d	on
4	a	in	b	outside	c	to	d	for
5	a	for	b	to	c	from	d	before
6	a	after	b	in	c	at	d	from
7	a	over	b	behind	c	onto	d	into
8	a	At	b	On	c	In	d	Over
9	a	instead of	b	into	c	inside	d	between
10	a	behind	b	during	c	before	d	on

Ideas Focus
- Do you think we should recycle 100% of our household waste? Why? / Why not?

Grammar

Articles

A Read the sentences 1–6 and look at the nouns in bold. Which words come before 1–4?

1 The **water** in this pond is dirty.
2 A **cave** can be a dangerous place.
3 The **trees** in this forest are very old.
4 A **scientist** at this university has discovered a new species. The **scientist** has worked here for many years.
5 **Pollution** is a very serious problem.
6 Have you ever seen **whales** in the sea?

B Match the sentences in A with the descriptions below. Which sentence has …

a a noun used for the first time and then mentioned again? ☐
b a specific plural noun? ☐
c a specific uncountable noun? ☐
d a plural noun with a general meaning? ☐
e a singular countable noun with a general meaning? ☐
f an uncountable noun with a general meaning? ☐

C Complete the rules with *a / an* or *the*.

- We use the indefinite article _____ with singular countable nouns with a general meaning or when we mention them for the first time.
- We use the definite article _____ with countable and uncountable nouns with a specific meaning or when the noun has already been mentioned.
- We don't use _____ or _____ with plural nouns or uncountable nouns with a general meaning.

Be careful
We always use:
● *a / an* with jobs.
She is a biologist.
the with instruments, unique nouns, names of rivers, deserts and mountain ranges.
She plays the violin.
The Earth is round.
He loves the Rockies.
No article with proper names.
Is James here?

▷ Grammar Focus p. 165 (3.7 & 3.8)

D Complete the sentences with *a, an, the* or -.

1 There is _____ elephant in the zoo. _____ elephant is nearly 40 years old.
2 John is _____ teacher.
3 _____ millions of people speak Chinese.
4 He plays _____ piano very well, so his parents want to buy him _____ piano for his birthday.
5 _____ Sahara Desert is huge.
6 In _____ 80s _____ Jacques Cousteau became famous for his expeditions.
7 _____ moon is round and it orbits _____ Earth.
8 I saw _____ octopus in the sea. _____ octopus had eight 'arms'.
9 Everyone should try to help _____ poor.
10 There is _____ article in _____ *Times* about _____ Alps.
11 I love _____ music, but _____ music I don't like at all is _____ jazz.

E Complete the text with *a, an, the* or -.

Angel Falls

At a height of 979 metres, Angel Falls is (**1**) _____ highest waterfall in the world. It is situated in (**2**) _____ Auyantepui Mountain in Venezuela.

Because of its location deep in the Venezuelan rainforest, nobody in (**3**) _____ outside world knew about Angel Falls until 1935. However, (**4**) _____ local people called, (**5**) _____ Pemones, knew about it for thousands of years before that. Its name in (**6**) _____ Pemon language is Kerepakupai Merú, which means 'waterfall of the deepest place'.

In 1935, (**7**) _____ American pilot, Jimmie Angel, was flying his plane along (**8**) _____ Carrao River when he discovered the falls. He went back in 1937 and tried to land his plane on top of the falls, but (**9**) _____ wheels of the plane got stuck in mud. Angel and the three other passengers had to walk down from (**10**) _____ top of the falls on foot. It took them 11 days, but (**11**) _____ people all over the world learnt of his adventure and the existence of (**12**) _____ waterfall. He became (**13**) _____ legend and the falls were named after him.

Thirty-three years later, (**14**) _____ helicopter lifted Jimmie Angel's plane from the mountain and today it is in front of (**15**) _____ airport at Cuidad Bolivar in Venezuela. Sadly, Jimmie Angel was hurt very badly while he was landing (**16**) _____ aeroplane on 17th April, 1956 in (**17**) _____ Panama. He died eight months later from his injuries. His ashes were scattered over Angel Falls.

Angel Falls, Venezuela, South America

Writing: an informal email

Learning Focus

Including useful expressions

- When you are writing an informal letter or email there are useful phrases and expressions that can help to make your writing natural. It's a good idea to learn these expressions so you can use some of them every time you write an informal letter or email.

- You can start your letter or email using friendly greetings and questions, e.g. *Hi!, Hello, How are you? How are things? How is it going?*

- You can end in a friendly way too, e.g. *Bye, Bye for now. See you soon. Speak to you later. That's all for now. Write soon!*

- There are other expressions you can use in informal letters and emails, e.g. *Sorry for not answering your last email. It's great to hear from you! I really miss you! Write back soon and tell me all about it. I love reading your emails. Good luck!*

A Read the example Email and <u>underline</u> the useful expressions the writer has used.

New message

To: Alice@hotmail.com   **From:** charlotte@hotmail.com   **Subject:** Hi

Hi Alice!

How are things? It's great to hear from you. I really miss you!

That's an interesting project your teacher has given you. Why don't you write about the special day we had at school a month ago? Everyone made or gave things to sell. There were cupcakes, bread, pizza, books, pictures and clothes. Our families came and we had a party. It was fantastic. We made £1,600!

We gave all the money to help protect honeybees. A lot of the natural habitat for bees has gone because people have built houses and roads on it. We need to save the bees!

Good luck with your project. Please write back and tell me about it.

Bye!

Charlotte

B Read the writing task below and then answer the questions about it in your notebook.

This is part of an email you got from a friend in England.

> Our teacher has asked the class to write about the things people do to help protect the planet around the world. I want to write about what people do in your country. Can you send me some information?

Now write an email to your friend. (100 words)

1 What type of text do you have to write?
2 What will it be about?
3 What does your friend need?
4 Will it be formal or informal?

C Read the example email again and write T (True) or F (False).

The writer …

1 likes the person she is writing to. ☐
2 hasn't written about the environment. ☐
3 describes an event in the past. ☐
4 gives information about how people help to protect the planet. ☐

D Match the correct paragraph number in the example email with these descriptions.

a Information about the things people do to help protect the planet. ☐
b Information about the environment. ☐
c Friendly ending with informal expressions. ☐
d Friendly opening, asking about the reader. ☐

E Read the *Exam Close-up* and the *Exam Task*. Underline all the information you need to include in your email.

F Complete the *Exam Task*. Remember to make a plan before you start.

Exam Task

This is part of an email you get from a friend in England.

> We are all making posters at school about renewable energy around the world. I want to make mine about renewable energy in your country. Can you send me some information about it?

Now write an **email** to your friend giving some information about renewable energy in your country. (100 words)

Planning your work

- Before you start writing in the exam, think about the information you need to include.
- Read the exam question carefully and underline the key points.
- Decide what information you are going to write in each paragraph – make notes.
- Check you have included all the points in the exam question in a logical order.

Useful Expressions

Friendly openings

Hi!
Hello
How are you?
How are things?
How is it going?
It's good to hear from you!

Useful phrases

I really miss you!
I love reading your emails.
Good luck!
Sorry for not answering your last email.

Friendly endings

Write back soon and tell me all about it.
Bye!
Bye for now.
See you soon.
Speak to you later.
That's all for now.
Write soon!

Penguins on melting ice

3 Swimming with Sharks

Florida Keys   Bahamas

Before you watch

A **Look at the photo and discuss these questions with a partner.**

- Would you pay money to dive with sharks?
- Do you think feeding sharks should be banned?
- Which animals do you think bite more people every year: dogs or sharks?

While you watch

B **Watch the video and decide if these statements are T (True) or F (False).**

1 People don't want to pay a lot of money to dive with sharks. ☐
2 Kathy enjoyed diving with sharks. ☐
3 Jeff Torode encourages the tourists to feed the sharks. ☐
4 You are more likely to be killed by a bee than by a shark. ☐
5 Bob Dimond is worried that sharks are becoming afraid of people. ☐
6 Trista was surprised by how calm the sharks were. ☐

After you watch

C **Complete the summary of the video below using these words.**

| bite confuse creatures horror inaccurate negative realise think |

Many tourists go to places like Florida, Hawaii and the Bahamas to dive with sharks. Of all the
(**1**) _____ in the sea, they are the most interesting to some people. Attracting sharks by
feeding them used to be common. However, in 2002, there were a large number of shark attacks
on humans. Many people felt (**2**) _____ at these attacks, and they gave sharks a very
(**3**) _____ image. Feeding sharks was then made illegal in Florida and other places.

Nonetheless, the idea that sharks kill a lot of people is (**4**) _____. Each year snakes kill
more people and dogs attack more people than sharks do. Most shark attacks are just one quick
(**5**) _____. The shark rarely tries to eat the person. Researchers
(**6**) _____ that sharks sometimes
(**7**) _____ humans with the other
types of animals they usually eat, such as seals and
fish. The shark will (**8**) _____ that it
has made a mistake and leave.

Tourists diving
with sharks

Ideas Focus
- Do you think shark tourism should be encouraged in places that have sharks? Why? / Why not?
- Do you think it's important to protect the sea and the animals in it? If so, what can people do to help preserve them? Why? / Why not?

42

Special Relationships

Reading:	true/false, worrying about new words
Vocabulary:	relationship-related words, phrasal verbs
Grammar:	relative clauses: defining & non-defining, temporals
Listening:	true/false, listening for similar words
Speaking:	relationships, problem solving, considering advantages & disadvantages, giving advice
Writing:	story (1), thinking of ideas, organising a story / ideas, describing people

A young, hand-raised raccoon playing with his best friend, the family dog, in a meadow near their home in Germany

Reading

A Look at the dogs in photos 1–3. Which ones do you think are 'working'?

B What sort of work can dogs do? Work in pairs and list as many jobs as you can think of in your notebook.

C Read the article about the relationships between humans and dogs. What reason does the writer give for the growing number of domestic dogs?

Word Focus

suspicious: describes an action that makes you feel that something is wrong or illegal
sniff: to smell something
physical disability: a physical illness or injury that makes it difficult for someone to do the things that other people do
rubble: the broken bricks, stone, etc that are left when a building falls down

Dogs in a human world

The friendship between humans and dogs possibly began 14,000 years ago. Perhaps wild dogs became interested in human rubbish, or humans took the puppies of wild dogs and trained them to be obedient pets and helpers. When humans choose the parents of dogs, they can create a wonderful variety of dogs with plenty of talents and many different looks. Here are four examples of 'a dog's life' in the human world.

A Food sniffer dogs

Jacques is one member of the Beagle Brigade, a group of beagles that work at international airports in the United States. Their job is to smell and find illegal fruits, vegetables and other foods in luggage and mail. These foods sometimes bring insects and diseases which could be <u>dangerous</u> for plants and animals. The beagle calmly sits down next to anything that smells suspicious. The dog's human partner then checks for illegal foods. Why beagles? They're friendly and cute, so they don't scare people as they sniff through the crowds. More importantly, beagles have an <u>astonishing</u> nose for food. The Beagle Brigade can find food in luggage and packages 84% of the time!

B Treated like a queen

Some dogs live in luxury. Tiffy, a <u>lovely</u> Maltese, is one of these. Her owner, Nancy Jane Loewy, treats her like a queen. She carefully prepares Tiffy's meals of meat, fish, chicken and a variety of fresh vegetables. Tiffy also eats yoghurt and biscuits after dinner.

Loewy's husband has a very good job and her two sons are away at university, so she has the time and money to treat Tiffy extremely well, and she truly enjoys doing it. 'I want to give her the healthiest, most wonderful life possible for as long as possible,' she says.

D Read the *Exam Close-up*. Then read the *Exam Task* below and underline the key words.

Exam Task

Look at the sentences below about dogs. Read the text to decide if each sentence is correct or incorrect. Write T (True) or F (False).

1   Wild dogs have existed for approximately 14,000 years. ☐
2   Humans are responsible for the different kinds of dogs in the world. ☐
3   All airports in the United States use beagles to check for food. ☐
4   Some foods are not safe because they can carry sicknesses. ☐
5   Tiffy eats home-cooked meals, not normal dog food. ☐
6   Jessie doesn't help the patients in hospital. ☐
7   Service dogs can do simple tasks for people who cannot walk. ☐
8   SAR dogs use their sense of smell to find people who are lost. ☐
9   Dogs that love to chase a tennis ball do not need rewards. ☐
10 It is possible that one day there will be no more wolves. ☐

Exam Close-up

Worrying about new words

- When you are reading a text, don't worry when you see vocabulary that you don't know.
- Remember that it isn't necessary for you to understand every word to find the answers to the questions.
- In your own language, when you see a new word, you can find the meaning by looking at the words around it. Do the same with English.

E Find the adjectives below in the text and then match them with the meanings 1–6.

dangerous   astonishing   lovely   strong   obedient   beneficial

1   _____: listens and does what you say
2   _____: not good for you
3   _____: can move heavy things
4   _____: very nice, beautiful
5   _____: good for you
6   _____: very surprising

C Animal carers

Jessie is a whippet that visits very sick children in hospital. She shows them her love and gives the children a chance to exercise. When they feel down, Jessie makes them happy. Jessie helps patients like young Lukas Parks to stay strong during their time in hospital.

There are many different kinds of animals that help people. We train 'service dogs' to help people with physical disabilities. The best known service dogs are guides for the blind. But four-legged friends perform other roles too. They can learn to open and close doors, turn lights on and off, pick up objects from the floor and even pull wheelchairs.

D Doggie detectives

Search-and-rescue (SAR) dogs use their amazing noses to find people. Hercules, an Alsatian, can smell tiny clues that people leave wherever they go. These include bacteria, small pieces of clothing and hairs. He has found missing hikers and has searched through rubble after earthquakes and other disasters. SAR dogs must be strong, obedient, athletic and smart. Most of all, they must love to play. Trainers look for dogs that go crazy over a favourite toy, such as a tennis ball. Those dogs will do any job if the reward afterwards is playtime.

As workers or pets, dogs are certainly beneficial to humans in many ways. They have a special place as 'man's best friend' and this has helped dogs to survive in our world. Wolves and wild dogs have nearly disappeared from the earth, but the number of pets and working dogs continues to increase, because of their special relationship with humans.

- Do you know anyone who has an animal helper?
- Do you think it's right to let animals work for humans? Why / Why not?

Ideas Focus

Vocabulary

A Match *to*, *with*, *of* and *on* with the words below.

in love / agree / angry: _____

rely / keen / concentrate: _____

jealous / ashamed / proud: _____

listen / similar / belong: _____

B Complete the table with words in A.

Verb + preposition	Adjective + preposition

C Complete the text with some of the words from A.

A relationship that breaks the ice

Explorers started to go to Everest in the early 20th century and needed to (**1**) _____ on local people to give them information about the mountain. The Sherpas live on and around the Himalayas and are very (**2**) _____ of the mountains. They can also breath the thin air because they live so high up. Many explorers are very (**3**) _____ of this ability because Sherpas can climb Everest more easily than most Western climbers. However, Western climbers (**4**) _____ to what the Sherpas say about the mountain because they want to get to the top and back down again safely. If a Sherpa says it's not a good day to climb then explorers usually (**5**) _____ with them. Even though mountain explorers aren't (**6**) _____ to their Sherpa guides and they don't have much in common, they often become life-long friends after a climb because know they couldn't have done it without them.

A Sherpa guide pictured at the foot of Mount Everest in the Himalayas, Nepal

D Complete the sentences with a verb or adjective from B.

1 Jamie is really _____ to his sister Louisa. They both have blonde hair and blue eyes.

2 "Be quiet! I can't _____ on my homework with so much noise!"

3 We're very _____ of our son Daniel. He's done very well in his exams.

4 I think Susie is really _____ on Alex. She's always smiling at him in class.

5 "Do these shoes _____ to you?"

6 My uncle is very _____ of his car. It's very old and dirty.

7 My grandmother has to _____ on my mum to help her with the housework.

8 She doesn't _____ with making animals work. She thinks it's unkind.

Ideas Focus

- Do you ever get jealous of other people? Why? / Why not?
- Do you think it's good to rely on other people for help? Why? / Why not?
- Do you agree that people should never be ashamed of their family? Why? / Why not?

Grammar

Relative Clauses: defining & non-defining

A **Read the sentences and underline the relative pronouns (*who*, *whose*, *which*, *that*, *where* and *when*) in each.**

1 My grandparents remember the day when they first met.
2 That's the shop where my neighbour works.
3 I think people who/that speak three languages are clever.
4 Is that the man whose dog saved the little girl?
5 Did you like the poster which/that I bought you?

B **Complete the questions below with the words you underlined in A.**

Which of the words you underlined in A …

a refers to people? _____
b refers to things? _____
c shows possession? _____
d refers to a period of time? _____
e refers to a place? _____

C **Read the sentences below. How is the meaning different?**

1 The ball which/that is over there is mine.
2 The ball, which is over there, is mine.

D **Match the sentences in C with the rules below.**

a Defining relative clauses give essential information about who or what we are talking about. ☐
b Non-defining relative clauses give extra information about who or what we are talking about. This information isn't necessary for the sentence to make sense. It is separated from the rest of the sentence by commas. ☐

> **Be careful**
> Remember that in a defining relative clause *that* can be used instead of *who* or *which*, but in a non-defining relative clause *that* cannot be used instead of *who* or *which*.

> ▷ Grammar Focus p.165 (4.1 to 4.3)

E **Circle the correct words.**

1 That's the woman whose / who son won a prize.
2 Have you seen Dad's keys where / which I left on the sofa?
3 Can you remember the name of the hotel when / where we stayed last year?
4 Summer is the time when / who everybody likes to relax by the sea.
5 The teacher is talking to the boy whose / that always looks scruffy at school.
6 Where is the girl which / whose computer is broken?

F **Use the prompts to write sentences in your notebooks. Use *who*, *which* or *where*.**

1 mobile phone / something / we use to call friends
2 cinema / place / we watch films
3 zoo / place / we see animals
4 teacher / person / teach young people
5 gorilla / animal / live in Africa
6 doctor / person / make people feel better
7 pool / place / we go swimming
8 camera / something / we use to take photos.

G **Complete the text with *which*, *when*, *where* and *whose*. Use one of the words twice.**

An unusual relationship

Most people love dogs, but you don't often find orangutans that are in love with them too! However, Suryia the orangutan is the exception. He and his dog friend, Roscoe, are two animals (1) _____ friendship is unique.

Suryia and Roscoe live at the Myrtle Beach Safari, (2) _____ is a 50-acre nature park, in South Carolina, USA. In 2008, (3) _____ Suryia was riding on an elephant with the director of the safari, a lost dog suddenly came out of the woods. Suryia jumped off the elephant and ran to the dog. They started playing together and have been best friends ever since. Now they go to the pool in the the park, (4) _____ they swim and play around. Suryia holds Roscoe by the tail and Roscoe pulls him around the water. Suryia takes Roscoe for walks around the park and even gives him his monkey biscuits.

This friendship, (5) _____ is very unusual, has made many people around the world smile.

Suryia the orangutan with his best friend, Roscoe.

Listening

A Do these words express positive or negative emotions? Write P (positive) or N (negative).

respect someone ☐ be jealous ☐
feel ashamed ☐ argue with ☐
trust someone ☐ feel let down ☐
be angry ☐ be impressed ☐
be proud ☐ be disappointed ☐

B 4.1 ▶❚❚ Listen to four people talking and match them to how they feel.

Speaker **1** ☐ **a** feels angry **b** feels let down
Speaker **2** ☐ **a** is disappointed **b** has argued with someone
Speaker **3** ☐ **a** respects someone **b** is proud of someone
Speaker **4** ☐ **a** feels ashamed **b** is jealous of someone

C Read the *Exam Close-up*. Then read the *Exam Task* below and think about the words you might hear.

D 4.2 ▶❚❚ Now listen and complete the *Exam Task*. Look at the six sentences.

Exam Task

You will hear a boy called Danny and a girl called Cathy talking about different people in their family. Decide if each sentence is correct or incorrect. Write **T** (True) or **F** (False).

1 Danny has a good relationship with his younger brother. ☐

2 Cathy identifies with Danny's problem. ☐

3 Danny's sister doesn't support him very much. ☐

4 Cathy's dad isn't interested in his children's problems. ☐

5 Cathy sometimes feels embarrassed when she talks about her problems. ☐

6 Cathy hasn't got very good maths exam results. ☐

Exam Close-up

Listening for similar words

• You won't hear the exact words that you'll read in the exam question.

• Try to listen for similar words and phrases that describe how people feel and think.

• Read the exam questions and try to think of some similar words before you start to listen.

E 4.2 ▶❚❚ Now listen again.

Speaking

A Work with a partner and answer these questions.

- Are you a sociable person?
- Do you make an effort to be popular?
- Do you have a good relationship with your friends / family / neighbours?

B **4.3** ▶❙❙ Read and listen to 1–6 below. Which gives advice, gives orders or makes suggestions? Write A (advice), O (order) or S (suggestion) for each one.

1 Don't stay up late! You've got an exam tomorrow at 8 am. ☐

2 If I were you, I'd talk to your mum. She usually knows what to do. ☐

3 They must clear up the room before they leave. ☐

4 I think it would be better if he said sorry to her. ☐

5 Shall we invite Marta to the party next week? ☐

6 He shouldn't waste so much time playing video games all day. ☐

C Read the *Exam Close-up*. Then look at the *Exam Task* below and decide what you think the problem is.

Useful Expressions

Giving advice
If I were him, I'd …
I think it would be better to … because …
Perhaps he should … then he …
He should also …
I really think it's best to … because
To be honest, I'd …

Exam Close-up

Considering advantages & disadvantages

- Look at the pictures and listen carefully to the examiner to find out as much information as you can about the situation.

- Think about the advantages and disadvantages and talk about each option before you decide on the best one.

- Remember, there are no right or wrong answers so you can say what you think.

Exam Task

Your friend Mark has been invited to a party the night before an exam.

- What is the problem?
- What are the options?
- What are the advantages and disadvantages of each option?

Talk together about what he should do then say which would be best.

- If you had a problem with one of your friends, would you speak to him / her about it? Why? / Why not?
- What's more important to you: your education or your friends? Why?
- Do you ask for advice when you have a problem? Why? / Why not?

Ideas Focus

Vocabulary

Phrasal verbs

A **Match the phrasal verbs 1–8 to their meanings a–h.**

1 look up to someone ☐	**a**	invite on a date
2 hang out ☐	**b**	have respect for
3 make up ☐	**c**	stop being a girl or boy friend
4 ask someone out ☐	**d**	like, be friends
5 break up ☐	**e**	forgive each other
6 put someone down ☐	**f**	disappoint someone
7 let someone down ☐	**g**	spend time relaxing
8 get on ☐	**h**	be critical of someone

B **Use the phrasal verbs in A to complete the second sentences below. Use no more than three words.**

1 He wants to invite Julia on a date.

He wants to _____.

2 Billy stopped being Helen's boyfriend because he moved to another city.

Billy moved to another city so he _____ with Helen.

3 I have respect for my father because he's reliable, honest and very clever.

My father is reliable, honest and very clever so I _____. him.

4 Everyone is friends with her, but I'm not.

She's friends with everyone, but I don't _____. with her.

5 I spend a lot of time relaxing in the park with my friends.

I _____. in the park with my friends a lot.

6 After the argument, it took Joe and Fran a long time to forgive each other.

It took Joe and Fran a long time _____. after the argument.

7 Why do you always say I'm stupid and lazy? You criticize me all the time!

Why do you _____. all the time? You always say I'm stupid and lazy.

8 I won't ever disappoint you again, Dad. I'm very sorry.

I'm so sorry I _____. Dad. It'll never happen again.

C **Complete the blogs about teen problems with phrasal verbs from A.**

🔙 ▶ 🏠 www.teentalk.com

Lonelygirl56 – Missing my friend

My friend and I used to (**1**) _____
really well, but last week, she told me that
she wanted to make new friends. We used
to (**2**) _____ together all the
time at my house, but now she's just unkind
and wants to (**3**) _____ me
_____ all the time by saying I
look scruffy and I'm overweight.

Dreamyboy23 – Nobody to talk to

I always try to talk to my older brother
about my problems because I really
(**4**) _____ him. When I ask him
something, though, he always says he's busy
and I feel like he's (**5**) _____
me _____ because I don't
have anyone else to talk to. What should
I do?

Shyguy100 – New girl in town

I (**6**) _____ with my girlfriend
last week and now she keeps texting me
and asking to (**7**) _____. The
problem is, I met a girl at karate class and I
think I'd like to (**8**) _____ her
_____. What should I tell
my ex-girlfriend?

Ideas Focus

- Do you think it's important to make up after an argument? Why? / Why not?
- Who do you look up to? Why?
- Do you think it's important not to let people down? Why? / Why not?

Grammar

Temporals

A Read the sentences and underline the verbs after the words in bold.

1 Michael will call **as soon as** he has any news.
2 **When** we go to Italy, we'll visit our cousins.
3 I'll wait **until** you have finished your dinner.
4 Check that you have your passport **before** you leave.
5 Please call me **the moment** the manager arrives.

B Read the sentences again and answer the question below.

The sentences above all talk about the future. Are the words in bold (temporals) followed by future tenses or present tenses?

_____

C Complete the rules.

Temporals are time expressions. When we use them to talk about the future, they are followed by a _____ tense, not a future form.

> **Be careful**
> When we want to emphasise that one action finishes before another starts, we use the Present Perfect Simple.
>
> *You can go out and play when you've tidied your room.* (You'll tidy your room first and then you'll go out and play.)

▶ Grammar Focus p.165 (4.4)

The Colosseum in Rome, Italy

D Circle the correct words.

1 I'll clean as soon as / until the painters have left.
2 When I finish / will finish university, I'll travel the world.
3 By the time / After Jenny arrives, the birthday party will be over.
4 I'll text you the moment the postman will deliver / delivers the parcel.
5 I won't come home until / the moment I've found my best friend a present!
6 Harry's parents will buy a new car after they will save / have saved up enough money.

E Complete the sentences with *before*, *by the time*, *until*, or *as soon as*. Use each temporal twice.

1 _____ Janet gets home, the flowers will be there.
2 _____ he goes on Facebook, he'll turn on the computer.
3 _____ I get home, I'll walk the dog.
4 He'll buy a new game _____ he gets his pocket money.
5 The food will be all gone _____ your father gets home from work.
6 You can watch TV _____ it's time for lunch.
7 I'll turn off all the lights _____ I leave the house.
8 _____ you get another bike, I'll drive you to school.

F Complete the sentences so that they are true for you.

1 I'll buy a new laptop when _____.
2 I'll learn a new sport as soon as _____.
3 I'll go on holiday after _____.
4 I'll do my homework before _____.
5 I'll go out as soon as _____.
6 I'll call you the moment _____.

writing: a story (1)

Learning Focus

Organising a story
- Most stories have a beginning, middle and end.
- The beginning of a story introduces and describes the people, place and time of a story.
- The middle section of a story usually describes the action or the things that happen to the people or in the place in a story.
- The middle section of a story can have several paragraphs so the writer can describe more action. This is where the writer sometimes includes something surprising or unexpected.
- The end of a story explains the action or events in a story or it can leave the reader with a question or mystery.

A Use the words to complete the sentences.

Suddenly... / In the end... / Meanwhile... / Once upon a time... / At first... / It all started...

1 _____ there was a beautiful princess named Louise.
2 _____ a few years ago, on the first day of Summer.
3 _____ , she thought she was still asleep.
4 _____ , there was a bang!
5 _____ , the others were still looking for a way out.
6 _____ nobody won the prize.

B Read the writing task below and answer the questions about it in your notebooks.

> Your English teacher has asked you to write a story. Your story must have this title:
> *A true mystery* (100 words)

1 Has the teacher given the first line of the story?
2 What does your story need to be about?

C Read the paragraphs of the example story and put them in the correct order.

1 _____
2 _____
3 _____
4 _____

D Read the example story again and write T (True) or F (False).

The girl …
1 is scared of cats. ☐
2 hasn't written about a mystery. ☐
3 knew that Toby was dead. ☐
4 Toby was ten when he died. ☐

a Molly looked at the cat and read the name on its collar. Yes, it was Toby! The cat that belonged to her when she was six years old. Her old phone number was on the collar.

b Molly was walking home from school one day. It was a bright sunny day and Molly, a tall clever girl from Manchester, was relaxed and she was thinking about the weekend.

c Suddenly, Molly started to run. She was scared. Toby can't be here! No, because Toby is dead. He died 10 years ago.

d Before Molly turned into her street, a cat suddenly appeared in front of her. It was a beautiful black cat.

E Complete the sentences by using the words in the *Useful Expressions* box.

1 It is so _____ . Winter is definitely here.
2 Sorry, I'm so _____ . The traffic was awful.
3 My friend is very _____ . She could be a model.
4 My audition is tomorrow. I am _____ .
5 I can't wait for my party this _____ .

F Read the *Exam Task* below. What has your teacher already given you?

Exam Task

Your English teacher has asked you to write a **story**.
Your story must begin with this sentence:

A girl was walking home one day.

(100 words)

G Read the *Exam Close-up* and think of some ideas for a beginning, middle and end for your story. Read the *Useful Expressions*. Are there any words you can use in your story? Add them to your notes.

H Now complete the *Exam Task*.

Useful Expressions

Describing people
tall /short
slim / overweight
kind / unkind
friendly / unfriendly
clever / stupid
young / old
easy-going / nervous
scared /happy
Describing place/time
morning / lunchtime / afternoon / evening
dark / bright
clean / dirty
cold / hot
early / late

Exam Close-up

Thinking of ideas
- Before you start writing a story in the exam, it's a good idea to think of lots of ideas first.
- Write notes about who could be in your story and the place he / she could be in.
- Think about the words you can use to describe the people and the place in your story.
- Note down some ideas for the middle of the story. What happens? Is there something surprising and unexpected?
- Think about how you can end your story with an explanation or a mystery.

4 Man's Best Friend

Before you watch

A Match each dog to one of the statements below.

1 This dog pulls people through the snow. ☐
2 This is the animal that all dogs come from. ☐
3 This dog finds illegal items in luggage. ☐
4 This dog herds sheep. ☐

While you watch

B Watch the video to see if your answers in A are correct.

C Watch the video again and circle the words you hear.

1 The story of man and dog is a complicated / complex story that goes back thousands of years.
2 Dogs interact with / relate to humans in a variety of ways.
3 Dogs have a sense of smell 1,000 / 10,000 times more powerful than our own.
4 Over the years, the wolf became the gifted / talented domestic pet we know as the dog.
5 Was it a hunting partnership / relationship?
6 It's a partnership that's likely to carry on / continue for many years to come.

After you watch

D Complete the summary of the video below using these words.

| beneficial | domestic | illegal | obedient |
| partnership | talent | unknown | variety |

Dogs and humans have had a(n) (**1**) _____ for thousands of years. Dogs have many skills, which they use to help humans in a(n) (**2**) _____ of ways.

Dogs have very powerful noses and they have a great (**3**) _____ for smelling things. This makes them good at finding lost people and also (**4**) _____ items in people's luggage. The most important thing about dogs is that they are very (**5**) _____, rarely failing to do as they are told.

How and why humans and dogs first began interacting is still (**6**) _____. However, we do know that over thousands of years, the wolf has slowly changed into the (**7**) _____ dog we have today. However the relationship began, nowadays, it is clearly (**8**) _____ to both humans and dogs.

a a border collie

b a husky

c a beagle

d a wolf

Ideas Focus

- Did you grow up with a dog in the home? Why? / Why not?
- Do you consider yourself an animal lover? Why? / Why not?

Review 2 — Units 3 & 4

Vocabulary

A Circle the correct words.

1 The Chinese government is giving more land for conservation / endangered areas for pandas.
2 This book is a great source / research of information on polar expeditions.
3 Archaeologists found a cave / glacier with ancient paintings on the walls.
4 Wind and solar power are forms of renewable / beneficial energy.
5 The wide use of fossil / endangered fuels is causing them to run out.
6 They are building a new solar / power station not far from my house.
7 If we want to save the panda, we must focus on the conservation / pollution of its natural habitat.
8 Many endangered / conservation species will eventually become extinct.
9 Water flows down this stream / coast in spring after the snow has melted.
10 New ideas / threats are being considered to protect our wildlife.
11 Many coral reefs have damaged / survived for millions of years.
12 My grandfather has a physical / suspicious disability.

B Complete the sentences using these words.

| ashamed | astonishing | beneficial | complicated | domesticated |
| embarrassed | obedient | protected | suspicious | talented |

1 Our dog is not always as _____ as we would like him to be.
2 I always get _____ when my grandmother starts kissing me all the time.
3 It is _____ how many new species have been found in these deep waters.
4 Molly is a very _____ singer and dancer, but she wants to be a conservationist.
5 The Bald Eagle in America used to be a _____ species, but now it is doing well.
6 The situation is _____ by the fact that they haven't spoken to each other for years.
7 Dogs and cats have been _____ for so long, that no one knows when it happened.
8 Malcolm was _____ of himself for destroying the bird's nest.
9 Jeremy's behaviour is a bit _____ lately. What do you think he's up to?
10 Planting trees can be very _____ to the environment.

C Complete the sentences with the correct preposition.

1 My teacher is a wonderful person and we all look _____ to him.
2 I argued _____ my mum this morning and now I wish I hadn't.
3 Don't forget to turn _____ the heating when you leave.
4 Simon decided to ask his classmate _____ on a date.
5 She asked her family for help, but they let her _____.
6 You should apologise and make _____ after the argument you had.
7 They must be friends as they hang _____ together all the time.
8 You shouldn't rely _____ other people all the time. Be more independent.
9 They argued when they first met, but now they get _____ really well.
10 Jason thinks he's cleverer than everybody else and is always putting us _____.

Grammar

A Complete the sentences with the Present Perfect Simple, the Present Perfect Continuous or the Past Simple of these verbs.

| begin   cause   do   finish   increase   rise   study   take |

1 The team of biologists _____ the effects of pollution on plants for years.

2 The government _____ measures to limit sea pollution by passing new laws in 2000.

3 Overfishing _____ some species to become extinct over the years.

4 Ecotourism _____ to become popular when I was at university.

5 The use of fossil fuels _____ the amounts of carbon dioxide in the atmosphere in the past few years.

6 The scientist _____ research on coral reefs since he left university.

7 Sea levels _____ gradually in the last 10 years.

8 The journalist _____ writing an article on the Amazon a month ago.

B Circle the correct words.

1 A / The / - North Pole is located in the middle of the Arctic Ocean.

2 He can speak many languages, but he can't speak the / - / an Arabic.

3 It's very important to eat - / a / the breakfast in the morning.

4 I don't know why - / a / the people like ice climbing. It's very dangerous.

5 There is a volcano on the island. A / - / The volcano is not active.

6 Bill is a / an / the architect who built that modern hotel.

7 It was his dream to go to a / the / - Himalayas.

8 They didn't go by a / - / the bus. They used their car.

9 Hopefully, an / - / the environment will be saved from any more damage.

10 Nowadays, the / a / - computers help significantly with scientific research.

C Choose the correct answers.

1 My best friend, ____ parents travel a lot, feels very lonely at home.
   a who her   **b** who   **c** whose

2 Turning 21 is the time ____ people should think about their future.
   a which   **b** that   **c** when

3 We can't continue our research until he ____ us some information.
   a has given   **b** will give   **c** is giving

4 The doctors won't tell us anything about Grandma's health ____ they see the test results.
   a until   **b** when   **c** by the time

5 Please call me as soon as the babysitter ____.
   a leaves   **b** will leave   **c** is leaving

6 ____ people realise the damage we have done to our planet, it will be too late.
   a After   **b** By the time   **c** Until

7 The dog ____ we found on the street is very friendly, so we took it home.
   a where   **b** that   **c** who

8 This is the restaurant ____ the wedding reception was held.
   a which   **b** where   **c** that

Reading:	short texts, multiple-choice questions, eliminating answers
Vocabulary:	home-related words, collocations & expressions
Grammar:	*will*, *be going to*, future plans & events, future predictions
Listening:	multiple-choice questions, understanding technical or specific words
Speaking:	talking about homes, general conversations, expanding on the topic, talking about a topic
Writing:	informal letter, replying to a letter, using informal language , accepting/rejecting invitations, responding to news, making suggestions

A hill showing Uchisar Castle cave houses. Cappadocia, central Turkey

Reading

A What kind of problems can buildings have? Who fixes them? Match the problem (1–5) with the person (a–e).

1 the bathroom light doesn't work
2 there is water under the kitchen sink
3 a storm damaged the roof
4 the house is really dirty
5 the walls are a boring colour

a builder
b cleaner
c electrician
d painter
e plumber

B Work with a partner. You have a problem in your home. Tell your partner what the problem is. Your partner tells you who to call for help.

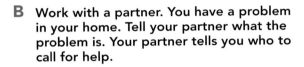

The living room ceiling is wet.

You need a plumber!

C Quickly read the adverts 1–5 below and decide where you might find each one.

D Read the *Exam Close-up*. Then read the *Exam Task* below and underline the key words.

Exam Close-up

Eliminating answers

- Read all the texts first and think about where they are from.
- Then read and underline the key words in the answer options.
- Look for similar information to the words you underlined in the text.
- If you can't find any similar information for one of the answer options in the text, you can eliminate it.
- Check the information for the options you didn't eliminate and choose the one which answers the question.

Exam Task

Look at each of the texts. What do they say? Choose the correct letter **a**, **b** or **c**.

1 The advert says that
  a the lift in the building doesn't work.
  b the bus stop is next to the shops.
  c you can't have animals in the flat.

2 a Helen doesn't want to buy a brown sofa.
  b Helen isn't sure if Tim will like the sofa.
  c Helen has got half of the money for the sofa.

3 a All areas of the gym are open from Monday.
  b Members should not go to the gym at the weekend.
  c The problem with the swimming pool is not serious.

4 Why has Judy written the email?
  a to get Dina's opinion about the hotel
  b to check if Dina is going to Dublin
  c to ask Dina to book rooms for them

5 What must Robby do?
  a Show the plumber where the money is.
  b Ask the plumber to fix the bowl in the sink.
  c Check the plumber's work before he gives him the money.

Word Focus

urgent: needs attention very soon before anything else
inconvenience: a situation that causes problems or a delay
historic: important in history

1

To Let
New 2-bedroom 3rd floor flat next to bus stop and close to shops
$200 a week
Available from 1st July
No lift
No pets
Carl: 0401276894

2

16:57

Helen
04-Aug 16:55

Tim,
I'm at the furniture shop. They've got the sofa we've been looking for at half price, but not in black. Is brown OK with you? I don't mind.

Reply   More

3
Joe's Gym

Important notice for members!

The swimming pool will be closed on Saturday and Sunday for urgent repairs.

All other areas of the gym are open as usual.

We apologise for any inconvenience.

R. Smith
Manager

4 email

From: Judy   To: Dina

Hi. Are you still interested in going to Dublin with us? I need to book the rooms tomorrow.

We're staying in this beautiful historic building. Here's the link:

www.princesshotel.com

It's great, isn't it?

5
Robby,
The plumber will be there at four o'clock to fix the sink. I have left the money for him on the kitchen table under the bowl. Please make sure the sink is OK before you pay him!
Dad

Ideas Focus

- Do you get on well with your neighbours? Why? / Why not?
- Do you think the city or the countryside is a better place for a teenager to grow up in? Why? / Why not?

Vocabulary

A Label the pictures with these words.

| block of flats | bungalow | castle | cottage | detached house | semi-detached house | tent | terraced house |

B Circle the odd ones out.

1 bedroom   garden   bathroom   **4** ceiling   roof   keys
2 lift   3rd floor   ground floor   **5** garage   sofa   bed
3 toilet   sink   fridge   **6** living room   kitchen   wall

C Choose the correct answers to complete the sentences.

1 When we go camping, I'll rely on you to put up the _____.
   a tent   **b** ceiling   **c** terraced house

2 My sister's going to move into a _____ of flats in the West End.
   a lift   **b** block   **c** garage

3 The great thing about a _____ house is that you don't share any walls with anyone.
   a terraced   **b** semi-detached   **c** detached

4 You can see the castle on the cliff out of my bathroom _____.
   a sink   **b** window   **c** bungalow

5 When I get older, I'm going to buy a lovely _____ with a stream in the garden.
   a cottage   **b** kitchen   **c** 3rd floor

6 Mum, you look tired; I'll tidy the _____ for you.
   a fridge   **b** ceiling   **c** living room

7 "Dad! Can you help? I can't open the _____ door!"
   a keys   **b** garage   **c** bed

8 Your plumber did a great job. Your new _____ looks lovely.
   a roof   **b** garden   **c** sink

Ideas Focus

- What would your ideal home be like?
- Would you want to live in a house with all of your friends? Why? / Why not?

Grammar

will

A Read the sentences and look at the future forms. Write (A) for affirmative, (N) negative or (Q) for question.

1 The architect believes he **will finish** the new building next month. ☐
2 Tidy your room or I **won't let** you go out. ☐
3 He **will become** rich one day. ☐
4 You can rest. I**'ll do** the dishes. ☐
5 Her son **will be** 21 tomorrow. ☐
6 **Will** you please **open** the window? ☐
7 I'm sorry! I **won't** ever **lie** again! ☐

B Match the sentences in A with the uses of the Future Simple below.

a to ask someone to do something ☐
b to offer to do something ☐
c for promises ☐
d for threats ☐
e for future facts ☐
f for predictions (when we don't have proof) ☐
g after verbs of opinion (*think, believe, expect, suppose, be sure,* etc) and with words like *probably* and *maybe* ☐

> **Be careful**
> Remember, a future tense cannot be used with temporals such as *when, after, until, the moment* and *as soon as,* even if the main clause contains a future tense. Instead, we use a present tense.

be going to

C Read the sentences below. How can you make them negative?

1 They**'re going to** build a block of flats here next year.
2 That wall is very safe. It**'s going to** fall down.

D Match the sentences in C with the uses of *going to* below.
a future plans. ☐
b predictions based on present evidence. ☐

▶ Grammar Focus p.166 (5.1 & 5.2)

E Use forms of *will* or *be going to* to write an example sentence for each of the points below.

1 a future prediction
2 a promise
3 a threat
4 an offer to do something
5 an opinion about the future
6 a sudden decision

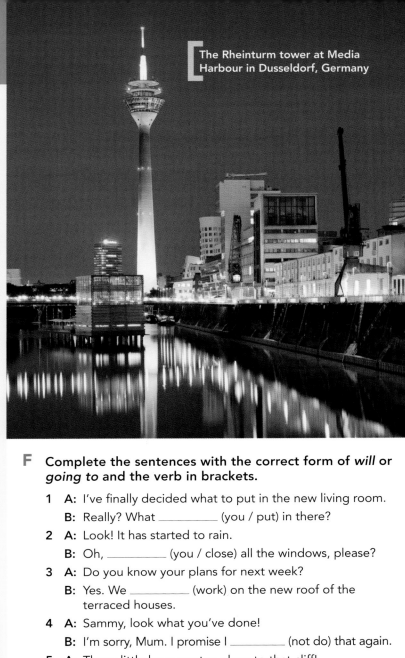

E The Rheinturm tower at Media Harbour in Dusseldorf, Germany

F Complete the sentences with the correct form of *will* or *going to* and the verb in brackets.

1 **A:** I've finally decided what to put in the new living room.
   B: Really? What _____ (you / put) in there?
2 **A:** Look! It has started to rain.
   B: Oh, _____ (you / close) all the windows, please?
3 **A:** Do you know your plans for next week?
   B: Yes. We _____ (work) on the new roof of the terraced houses.
4 **A:** Sammy, look what you've done!
   B: I'm sorry, Mum. I promise I _____ (not do) that again.
5 **A:** Those little boys are too close to that cliff!
   B: Yes, they _____ (fall) off the edge!
6 **A:** Have you finished decorating your new cottage yet?
   B: No, but I'm sure I _____ (finish) very soon.
7 **A:** Did you clean the floor for me?
   B: No, we forgot but we _____ (clean) it this afternoon.
8 **A:** How old is your brother?
   B: Tom _____ (turn) nine next Sunday.

G Complete the sentences using ideas of your own. Use *will* or *be going to*.

1 I think _____.
2 Be careful! That door _____ _____.
3 'Oh no! I've broken a glass.' 'Don't worry. I _____ _____.'
4 We've got plans for the weekend. We _____ _____.
5 I promise _____.
6 Tidy your bedroom now or I _____ _____.

Listening

A Label the pictures with these words.

bamboo   brick   concrete   netting   steel   straw

_____   _____

_____   _____

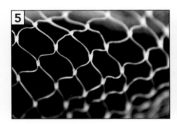

_____   _____

B 5.1 ▶|| **Listen and read sentences 1–5 and choose the best definition for the underlined words.**

1 Many buildings came down, <u>crushing and trapping people.</u>
   a people were pushed and fell out of buildings
   b things fell on top of people and they couldn't escape
2 One technique is to <u>reinforce</u> concrete with steel.
   a make stronger
   b make longer
3 Buildings made of light materials are <u>less likely</u> to come down in an earthquake.
   a not as possible
   b impossible
4 Some bricks are cheap and walls made from them <u>crack and collapse</u> very easily.
   a get bigger and fall off
   b break a bit and fall to pieces
5 Cheaper materials are better than nothing for poorer countries that <u>can't afford</u> anything else.
   a to not have enough money to pay for something
   b to not be able to use something

C 5.1 ▶|| **Listen again and check your answers. How did you know which option to choose?**

D Read the *Exam Close-up*. Then read the *Exam Task* and think about what the listening is going to be about.

E 5.2 ▶|| Now listen and complete the *Exam Task*.

Exam Close-up

Understanding technical or specific words
- In the exam, if you hear technical or difficult words that you don't understand – try not to panic.
- Think about the words you do know and what the listening is about and try to use the context to help you understand.

Exam Task

You will hear some students interviewing engineer, Robert Weston. For questions **1–6**, circle the best answer, **a**, **b** or **c**.

1 Robert is interested in
   a recording the numbers of deaths in earthquakes.
   b how to rescue people from collapsed buildings.
   c how to construct buildings that won't fall down.
2 Modern building methods
   a don't use steel or concrete.
   b offer cheap solutions.
   c are too expensive for poor countries.
3 Roofs are stronger when they're made from
   a concrete.
   b metal.
   c straw.
4 Plastic netting is used to
   a hold roofs in place.
   b hold walls together.
   c protect houses from underneath.
5 What are engineers testing in Indonesia?
   a How to build with bamboo instead of metal.
   b How to protect houses from below the structure.
   c How to construct walls with sand.
6 Robert thinks that using cheap or local materials
   a is completely useless.
   b is better than using expensive materials.
   c may not produce the best results.

F 5.2 ▶|| Listen again and check your answers.

Speaking

A **Work with a partner and answer these questions.**

- Is your home big or small?
- What do you like the most about your home?

B **Look at the list of features that a house or neighbourhood might have. Decide if they are A (advantages) or D (disadvantages).**

1 attic ☐
2 modern kitchen ☐
3 large park ☐
4 busy roads ☐
5 garage ☐

6 garden ☐
7 good public transport ☐
8 shops nearby ☐
9 pollution ☐
10 central heating ☐

Useful Expressions

Talking about a topic

My favourite room is …. because … and / but …

If I could change something about my house / flat, it would be / I'd … because …

Do you like the … in your house / flat?

How much time do you spend in … ?

Would you change the same things as me in … ?

What about your … ?

C **Work with a partner. Student A describes photo 1 and Student B describes photo 2. Remember to listen to each other's descriptions.**

D **Read the *Exam Close-up* and the *Exam Task* below. Think of three different questions to ask your partner about their house, flat or neighbourhood.**

Exam Task

Work with a partner. Talk together about the different rooms in your house or flat and say which is your favourite room. Then say what you would change about your house or flat if you could.

Exam Close-up

Expanding on the topic

- After you have described the photos you will talk together about the topic.
- Try to expand on your ideas and give reasons for your answers.
- Ask your partner for more information and try to keep the conversation going!

E **Now complete the *Exam Task*.**

- Would you ever design and build your own house? Why? / Why not?
- If you could live anywhere in the world, where would you live and why?

Ideas Focus

5 A Place to Call Home

Vocabulary

Collocations & Expressions

A In the following exercise, two of the options given are used with each verb in bold to make a collocation. For each question, cross out the option that cannot be used with the verb in bold.

1 **make:** a rest / a mess / your bed
2 **move:** house / with the times / dinner

3 **do:** the housework / a lot of noise / the dishes
4 **take:** a bath / a break / a coffee

B Complete sentences 1–8 with collocations and expressions from A. You will use some of the expressions more than once.

1 You aren't going anywhere until you get in your room and _____.
2 I'm hot and dirty from working in the garden. I need to _____; a hot one!
3 I don't mind if you cook, but make sure you don't _____ in the kitchen.
4 We didn't want to _____, but my wife got a really good job offer in London.
5 The only thing I hate about _____ is cleaning the toilet.
6 Your uncle has _____ because his detached house was too expensive!
7 Your furniture is ancient! _____, Carol, go buy some modern things.
8 Celia _____ every morning before she goes to work; she doesn't like to have a shower.
9 Vince broke his mother's favourite plate while he was _____.
10 We've been painting for hours; let's _____.

C Cover Exercises A and B and complete the collocations and expressions. Don't look! You will need to use the verbs more than once.

| do   make   move   take |

1 _____ a bath
2 _____ a break
3 _____ a mess
4 _____ house

5 _____ with the times
6 _____ your bed
7 _____ the dishes
8 _____ the housework

Ideas Focus
- It's fine if you make a mess at home - somebody else will tidy it up. Do you agree? Why? / Why not?
- Would you live in a mobile home? Why? / Why not?

Grammar

Future Plans and Events

A Read the sentences below. What forms are used for future plans or events?

1 The cleaner is coming tomorrow afternoon at 3pm.
2 I'm going to paint this wall blue next week.
3 My exams start on Tuesday 3rd June.

B Match the sentences in A with the uses below.

a We use the Present Simple for future events which are set because of a timetable or schedule. ☐
b We use the Present Continuous for future plans which are already fixed or arranged. ☐
c We use *be going to* for things we want or intend to do in the future but haven't made definite plans for yet. ☐

Future Predictions

C Read the sentences and underline the forms used to make predictions.

1 The plumber will finish the bathroom by Friday, I think.
2 The painter is working very hard. I think he's going to finish by lunchtime.
3 Be careful! You might / could break the window.

D Complete the uses with the forms for making predictions in C.

• We use _____ when there is evidence for the prediction in the present situation.
• We use _____ for future predictions we can't be sure of.
• We use _____ for predictions we believe but don't have any evidence for.

▶ **Grammar Focus p.166 & 167 (5.3 & 5.4)**

E Match 1–6 with a–f.

1 The Homes of the Future exhibition opens in ☐
2 The builders phoned ☐
3 The cleaner is going to do ☐
4 We're going to buy a ☐
5 I'm going to bed. My train leaves ☐
6 I'm very excited! We're moving ☐

a and they'll be here in the morning.
b house next week.
c new sofa at the weekend.
d at 7.30am tomorrow morning.
e the kitchen next.
f Edinburgh next month.

F Complete the second sentence so it means the same as the first. Use no more than three words.

1 I've finally decided to change the kitchen sink.
   I'm _____ change the kitchen sink.
2 Sam and Sophie have planned to meet in the library this afternoon.
   Sam and Sophie _____ in the library this afternoon.
3 I'm catching the 7.45 train.
   The train _____ at 7.45.
4 Mr Brown has arranged to show us the bungalow today.
   Mr Brown _____ us the bungalow today.
5 The first day of the school holidays is Thursday 16th July.
   The school holidays _____ on Thursday 16th July.
6 Jenny intends to use the lift.
   Jenny _____ use the lift.

G Answer the questions in your notebook. Use *will, be going to, might* or *could* so the answers are true for you when you write them.

1 What will you have for lunch today?
2 Who will you live with when you're an adult?
3 Where will you be at five o'clock tomorrow evening?
4 When will you move out of your parents' house?
5 What kind of house will you buy when you're older?
6 Where will you go on holiday this summer?
7 When will you next visit relatives?
8 What will you get your mum or dad for his or her birthday?

Writing: an informal letter

Learning Focus

Replying to a letter
- When you're replying to a letter, remember to react to what the writer has said.
- Read it carefully to see if you have to apologise, give an explanation, express enthusiasm, ask for or give information, thank the sender, accept / decline a request or accept / reject an invitation.
- You can organise your letter by replying to the writer's comments in a similar order.

A Look at these questions and notes and then write a reply to the questions in your notebook.

1 Can you help us do some packing next week?
   Sorry, but ...

2 Have you heard we've just bought a houseboat?
   Yes! ...

3 I hear you are moving house. Is there anything I can help with?
   Yes, can you ...

4 Would you rather come to visit on Saturday or Sunday?
   Saturday, because ...

5 Is now a good time to move house?
   No, because ...

6 Have you any idea how I can get my sister to help tidy our room?
   Have you tried ...?

B Read the writing task and underline the sections you need to respond to.

C Think of ways you could respond to your underlined sections and write notes. Compare with a partner. Did you write the same?

Hi Kirk,

How are you?

Guess what, we're moving house next week! Our new house is a cottage. It's really old and interesting and I like it but I'm a bit worried I won't like being in the countryside. I also don't know if there are any people my age who live nearby.

By the way, Mum says we're having a housewarming party at the end of August. Can you come?

I really hope you can – we'll need help with the music! Maybe you could bring some of your amazing collection? Do you want to be DJ?

Bye for now,

Robbie

You have received a letter from your friend, Robbie, who is moving house. Write a letter in reply to Robbie. (100 words)

D Read the example letter. Did Kirk include any similar responses to the ones you and your partner talked about?

Hi Robbie,

It's good to hear from you.

What exciting news! I've always wanted to live in the countryside. You'll be able to cycle around without any traffic and camp out at night. It will be great!

Don't worry about making new friends. You've always been very popular. Why don't you see if there's a local football team or youth club?

I'd love to come to your party. It will be great fun. And of course I'd love to be the DJ! I'll bring lots of different types of music so everyone can have a good time. Have you decided on a date yet?

Bye for now,

Kirk

Useful Expressions

1 _____

If I were you, I'd / I wouldn't …

Why don't you …?

How / What about …?

2 _____

I'd love to come …

I'll definitely be there.

I'm sorry, I can't make it.

Unfortunately, I won't be able to come.

3 _____

What exciting / sad / great … news!

I'm really pleased for / proud of you.

It'll be fun / great … !

E Read the example letter again and answer these questions.

1 Does Kirk respond to all of Robbie's letter?

2 Does he copy large parts of Robbie's letter?

3 Does Kirk write in an appropriate style?

F Match 1–5 with a–e to complete the plan that Kirk made before writing the letter in B.

1 Greeting and opening ☐

2 Paragraph 1 ☐

3 Paragraph 2 ☐

4 Paragraph 3 ☐

5 Signing off ☐

a Accept the invitation, ask about the date, agree to be DJ

b Bye for now, Kirk

c Suggest things Robbie can do to find new friends.

d Say good things about the move to make him feel better.

e Hi Robbie, It's good to hear …

G Read the *Exam Close-up*. Then complete the *Useful Expressions* with the words below.

Accepting / Rejecting invitations
Responding to news
Making suggestions

H Now complete the *Exam Task*. Remember to make a plan before you start.

Exam Close-up

Using informal language

- In the exam, your letters will always need to be informal so remember to use friendly expressions and informal language.

- Try to use contractions and include useful expressions we usually use in informal letters and emails.

Exam Task

This is part of a letter you receive from an Australian friend.

> I start at my new school after the holidays. I don't know anyone there. Do you think I'll get on with everyone? How can I make new friends?

Now write a **letter** to your friend giving some advice. (100 words)

5 Living in Venice

Venice, Italy

Before you watch

A Look at the photo and read the sentence. Label the picture with the words in pink.

A gondolier rows a gondola along a Venice canal.

While you watch

B Watch the video and decide if these statements are T (True) or F (False).

1 Early evening is the best time to shop in outdoor markets. ☐

2 Fabrizio Copano thinks Venice is the most beautiful city in the world. ☐

3 Gino Penzo's son doesn't live in Venice. ☐

4 The average age of people living in Venice is increasing. ☐

5 Venice is the only expensive city. ☐

6 Lots of people enjoy living in Venice. ☐

After you watch

C Complete the summary of the video below using these words.

annually   challenges   children
particularly   property   residents
tourists   welcomes

Today this city has a problem. Increasingly, many Venice locals – (1) _____ the young – are leaving and moving to other places. Why? For one thing, (2) _____ in Venice is very expensive. Parents want their (3) _____ to stay, but for many young people, it's difficult to buy their own homes. Venice (4) _____ visitors from all over the world – millions (5) _____. At times, the large number of people in the streets can be very difficult for (6) _____. Jobs are another problem. If one doesn't want to be a gondolier or do other work with (7) _____, it can be hard to find a job.

Giovanni dal Missier lives in Venice. He wants to stay in his home town. 'I know that it's a very special gift … to live in a city such as Venice,' he says. Despite all of the (8) _____, Giovanni can't imagine living anywhere else.

1

2

3

Ideas Focus

• Do people in your city or town face challenges like the ones mentioned in this video? Why? / Why not?

• Do they face any other challenges? What can be done to help?

68

6 Ready, Steady, Go!

Reading:	matching, matching descriptions
Vocabulary:	sport-related words, word formation
Grammar:	conditionals: zero & first, second conditional, *if*
Listening:	multiple-choice questions (pictures), identifying emotions
Speaking:	talking about sport, decision-making, giving opinions, agreeing & disagreeing, asking if someone agrees, giving your opinions
Writing:	sentence transformation (1), clauses of purpose, transforming sentences

A tortoise rolling on a skateboard

Reading

A Are you fit? Have you ever done any watersports or do you prefer to be on land?

B Work with a partner. Why do people do sport? Make a list of the reasons in your notebooks.

C Quickly read the descriptions of the people 1–5 in the *Exam Task* and underline any reasons they give for wanting to do sport.

Sport
with a difference

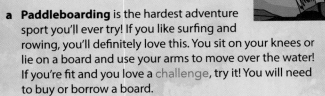

Word Focus

challenge: something difficult that tests your ability
equipment: things you need to do a particular sport
coordination: the ability to make your arms, legs and other body parts move in a controlled way
ice rink: an area inside a building with ice for people to skate on

a **Paddleboarding** is the hardest adventure sport you'll ever try! If you like surfing and rowing, you'll definitely love this. You sit on your knees or lie on a board and use your arms to move over the water! If you're fit and you love a challenge, try it! You will need to buy or borrow a board.

b For an underwater challenge, try **scuba diving**. There are courses for all levels, including beginners. <u>Instructors</u> with years of experience can teach you, so you'll be in safe hands. Lessons are available all year at local swimming pools. The bad news? Lessons are expensive and you have to pay extra to hire the equipment.

c **Judo** could be the right sport for you if you like reaching your goals. It uses coloured belts to show your level. There are seven levels, from white to black. When students get their first belt, it shows them that they can <u>succeed</u>. It gives them <u>confidence</u> and makes them want to go higher.

d **Cycling** is an activity you can enjoy alone, or you can train and enter <u>competitions</u>. Who knows? You could be a future winner of the Tour de France! Whether you ride for health, <u>enjoyment</u> or competition, you must wear special equipment. Never cycle without a helmet to protect your head.

e If your coordination is good and you aren't afraid of falling over, **figure skating** (dancing on ice) is an excellent way to get exercise and have some fun. You only need a pair of skates. If you'd like to try it, ask about figure skating programmes at your nearest ice rink.

f You have heard of surfing, but what about … **skurfing**? It's an exciting new sport that combines water-skiing and surfing. A fast motorboat pulls you along; you stand on a surfboard instead of skis, and ride the waves that the boat creates. You need to hold on tight and not fall. Don't forget your life jacket.

D Read the *Exam Close-up*. Then read the first description in the *Exam Task* again and underline any other key words.

E Now complete the *Exam Task*. Remember to check your answers when you have finished.

Exam Task

The teenagers below are all looking for a sport to do. There are eight descriptions of sports for young people. Decide which sport would be the most suitable for the teenagers. For questions **1–5**, mark the correct letter **a–h**.

1 Juan is very interested in the environment and would like to study the oceans when he's older. He'd like to do an activity that will help him to explore the seas. ☐

2 Inga has been doing snow sports all her life, so she wants to try something else. She wants to spend time exploring the countryside around her village. ☐

3 Mario is new to the area and wants to meet people his age. He's a good athlete who loves basketball and football but he'd like to try something a bit different. ☐

Exam Close-up

Matching descriptions

Exam Close-up

Matching descriptions

- When you match descriptions of people with texts in the exam, it's important to look for similar words and expressions.
- Read the description of the first person and underline the key words.
- Then read all the texts and look for words and expressions that are similar to the words you underlined in the first description.
- Do the same for each description until you have matched all the people to the texts.
- You will only need to match five of the eight longer texts, so check your answers carefully.

4 Cheryl really enjoys discovering new things, so she doesn't want to do any of the usual sports. She's fit and wants to do something that will push her body. ☐

5 Nigel is shy and isn't really interested in sports, but his doctor has told him he needs to get fit. Nigel wants to see results for his hard work. ☐

g Fast and exciting, **snowboarding** is one of the coolest winter sports. The baggy hip-hop clothing that snowboarders wear make it trendy. It's also an extreme sport, and that means it can be dangerous. If you've never done snow sports before and are trying snowboarding for the first time, make sure your instructor is experienced.

h **Handball** is one of the fastest team sports, so if you want to play it, make sure you have great coordination and are athletic. Good ball skills are important, too; you must be able to catch, throw and shoot a ball very quickly. Indoors or outdoors, it's a fantastic way to make friends and keep fit.

- In 2010, Jessica Watson became the youngest person to sail around the world on her own.
- Would you do it? Why? / Why not?
- Do you enjoy doing sports? Why? / Why not?

F Find the words with the form in brackets in the text. Then complete each sentence below with the correct word.

athlete – (adj)   compete – (n)   confident – (n)
enjoy – (n)   instruct – (n)   success – (v)

1 The most popular sports _____ in the world are the Olympics and the World Cup.

2 My judo _____ learnt the sport in Japan and has been teaching it for many years.

3 Nick can run fast, swim like a fish and play tennis like a champion! He's very

   _____.

4 Luke's coach always encourages him and this gives him the _____ to win races.

5 Harry only plays basketball for

   _____, but he is very good and should play for a team.

6 Work hard, listen to your coach, don't stop trying – this advice will help you to

   _____.

Ideas Focus

Vocabulary

A Complete the table with the sports below.

volleyball running judo skiing tennis gymnastics swimming aerobics weightlifting basketball cycling snowboarding

Do you ever … ?

go	play	do

B Work with a partner and find out which sports you both take part in.

C Complete the word groups with these words.

net cap referee stick team tournament track

1 umpire, line judge, _____
2 pitch, pool, _____
3 racket, bat, _____
4 helmet, glove, _____

5 basket, goal post, _____
6 individual sports, indoor sports, _____ sports
7 match, game, _____

D Choose the correct answers.

1 The _____ didn't see the ball and said it was in but actually it was out.
   a line judge   **b** umpire   **c** referee

2 If he runs around the race _____ more than once, I'll be astonished!
   a pool   **b** pitch   **c** track

3 You can't play tennis if you haven't got a _____.
   a stick   **b** racket   **c** bat

4 It was a good thing Tony was wearing his _____ when he fell off or he could have got a nasty head injury.
   a cap   **b** helmet   **c** glove

5 We're not really keen on _____ sports like basketball; we prefer sports where we play one-on-one.
   a indoor   **b** individual   **c** team

6 The football _____ went into extra time but Germany won in the end.
   a game   **b** match   **c** tournament

7 He didn't score because the ball hit the _____.
   a net   **b** goal post   **c** basket

Ideas Focus

- Do you think referees and umpires are always fair? Why? / Why not?
- Do you think individual sports are more interesting than team sports to watch? Why? / Why not?

Grammar

Conditionals: Zero & First

A Look at these conditional sentences and answer the questions below.

Zero conditional
- If you **exercise** regularly, you **stay** in shape.
- When a player **gets** the ball in the net, he **scores** a point.

First conditional
- If Josh **plays** football all today, he**'ll be** too tired to go to the party.
- My parents **might / may** buy me a present if I **win** the tournament.
- If Tabitha **does** that again, she **could** get a red card.

1 Which conditional is used to talk about something that is likely to happen in the present or in the future?

   _____

2 Which conditional is used to talk about facts and general truths?

   _____

3 Which conditional can you use *when* instead of *if*?

   _____

4 Which conditional can we also use *may*, *might* or *could* with?

   _____

> **Be careful!**
> When the *if* or *when* clause comes before the main clause, remember to use a comma.

▶ Grammar Focus pp.167 (6.1 & 6.2)

B Use the prompts to write Zero Conditional sentences in your notebook.

1 you / hit the ball past the other player – you / get a point
2 you / boil water – it / evaporate
3 you / mix orange and brown – you / get yellow
4 you / sunbathe for hours – you / burn
5 you / get to the end first – you / win the race
6 you / eat too much – you / get fat

C Match and then write sentences in your notebook using the First Conditional.

1 be thirsty ☐   a catch the bus on time
2 feel cold ☐   b eat something nutritious
3 be hungry ☐   c put on a sweatshirt
4 be tired ☐   d drink some water
5 want to win ☐   e try your hardest
6 not want to be late for the race ☐   f take a short break

D Complete the text with the correct form of the verbs in brackets.

Virtual sports

If you (1) _____ (not know) what virtual sports are, could you guess from the name? Well, virtual sports are like real sports only you do them in front of a screen in your own home. They're very popular because they're part of our high-tech world and most people love anything that is connected with technology. When something new (2) _____ (come) onto the market, everybody wants to buy it.

Virtual sports certainly have their advantages. If you (3) _____ (not have) enough time to go to a sports club, you can exercise at home. Moreover, you can play a game of tennis or football when it (4) _____ (rain) outside. Another great advantage is that you can play anything you like without paying for expensive equipment.

However, there is one disadvantage. When you (5) _____ (do) virtual sports, you don't have an experienced instructor to give you advice.

So, if you are one of those people who doesn't want to leave the comfort of their own home, you (6) _____ (love) virtual sports.

A possible future for virtual sports

6 Ready, Steady, Go!

Listening

A Work with a partner. Look at the picture carefully and answer the questions below.

1 What do you think the people are watching?
2 How do you think the people feel?
3 How long do you think the people have been there for?

B Match the feelings to the sentences.

> afraid   angry   disappointed   excited   relieved

1 'Oh, no! What a shame!': _____
2 'Oh, thank goodness! Phew!': _____
3 'Your behaviour is completely unacceptable. Get out of my sight!': _____
4 'Are you sure it'll be OK? I'm not confident about this … .': _____
5 'I can't wait! This is going to be amazing!':
_____

C Read the *Exam Close-up*. Then read the *Exam Task* and identify the emotions in the pictures.

D 6.1 ▶❙❙ Now complete the *Exam Task*. Remember to underline the key words in the questions before you start.

Exam Close-up

Identifying emotions
- When there are questions about people's feelings, look at the pictures and identify the emotions before you listen.
- Think about the words you might hear and how the speaker might sound.

Exam Task

There are six questions in this part. For each question, there are three pictures and a short recording. Circle the correct answer **a**, **b** or **c**.

1 You hear a girl talking. Which sport does she do?

a    b    c

2 You hear a coach talking to a basketball team. How does he feel about the team?

a    b    c

3 You hear two boys talking at a sports match. How do they both feel?

a    b    c

4 You hear radio commentary on a cycling race. Which team wins?

a    b 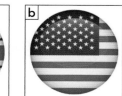   c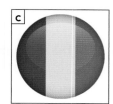

5 You hear two teenagers talking about their plans for after school. How does the girl feel?

a 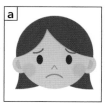   b 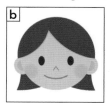   c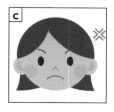

6 You hear an interviewer talking to a tennis player. Where are they?

a 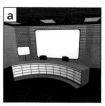   b 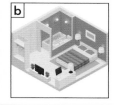   c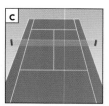

E 6.1 ▶❙❙ Now listen again.

Speaking

A Work with a partner and answer these questions.

- What do you do to keep fit?
- Do you enjoy watching major sports events like the Olympics or the football World Cup? Why? / Why not?
- What is your favourite sport? Why?

B Look at the list of things that describe certain sports. Tick (✓) those that you think would help a student choose a sport to take up.

1 helps you meet new people ☐
2 lasts a long time ☐
3 needs specialist equipment ☐
4 is challenging ☐
5 is cheap ☐
6 is dangerous ☐

C Compare with a partner. Do you have the same opinions?

D Read the *Exam Close-up*. Then read the *Exam Task* and note what you think about each picture and why.

E Work with a partner and complete the *Exam Task*. Use the *Useful Expressions* to help you.

Exam Close-up

Giving opinions

- When you are discussing the different options with your partner in the exam, remember it is OK to disagree and give your own opinion.
- If your partner says something which you don't agree with, politely say why you don't agree and suggest something different.

Exam Task

A friend of yours wants to take up a new sport to get fit and meet new people, but she hasn't got much time. Talk together about the different activities she could do.

going to the gym

hiking

playing football

kayaking

Which sport is best?

running

Now decide which would be best.

Useful Expressions

Giving your opinion
I think … is a good idea because …
Well, I don't think he / she should …
But if he / she … , he / she'll … !

Asking if someone agrees
Do you agree (with me)?
Would you agree that …?
Do you think so, too?

Agreeing
I agree.
Yes, I totally / quite agree with you.
I think you're (quite / absolutely) right.

Disagreeing
Actually, I don't really agree.
I'm afraid I don't agree.
I don't think that's a very good idea because …

Ideas Focus

- Would you prefer to play indoor or outdoor sports? Why? / Why not?
- Do you agree that a 'healthy body means a healthy mind'? Why? / Why not?

Vocabulary
Word formation

A Complete the table.

noun	verb	adjective	adverb
(1) _____	define	defined	definitely
competition / compete	(2) _____	competitor	competitively
(3) _____ /assistant	assist	assistant	–
(4) _____	free	free	freely
follower	(5) _____	following	–
(6) _____	concentrate	concentrated	–
depth	deepen	(7) _____	deeply
(8) _____ / supervisor	supervise	supervised	–
danger	(9) _____	dangerous	dangerously
–	–	proper	(10) _____

B Complete the text with the correct form of the words.

Free-diving: the big blue

The (1) _____ of free-diving is any underwater activity which people do by holding their breath for a long time. People (2) _____ to dive down as far as possible on one single breath, without the (3) _____ of air tanks.

Many divers say the experience of free-diving gives them a feeling of (4) _____ while they are underwater.

Also, many of the sport's (5) _____ regularly use yoga to help them (6) _____ and hold their breath for longer so they can dive to a much greater (7) _____ than normal.

Before you decide to try free-diving, you must go through a lot of training first under the (8) _____ of a professional.

This is because it can be a very (9) _____ sport if it's not done (10) _____.

DEFINE

COMPETITION
ASSIST

FREE
FOLLOW
CONCENTRATION
DEEP

SUPERVISE
DANGER
PROPER

C Complete the sentences with the correct form of the words from the table in A.

1 My trainer always says if you're going to do something, you should always do it _____.
2 That man is a great yoga teacher; he's got thousands of _____ who listen to his every word.
3 You'll have to improve your level of _____ if you want to take up tennis.
4 Kids, do not do this at home! You should only do this sport under the _____ of an adult.
5 I believe free-diving is one of the most _____ sports in the world – I wouldn't try it.
6 I wish I'd been a(n) _____ in that race! I know I could have won!
7 What is your _____ of a great athlete? Mine is someone who excels at sport.
8 Is anyone mad enough to jump from a plane without the _____ of a parachute?
9 Who knows what strange creatures live in the _____ of the ocean!
10 Don't you love the sense of _____ you get when you're skiing?

Ideas Focus

- Do you think you would like to try free-diving? Why? / Why not?
- Do you think it's important to do sports? Why? / Why not?

Grammar

Second Conditional

A **Read the sentences below. What tense is used with *if*?**

1 You would be more relaxed if you did yoga.
2 If I won Wimbledon, I'd be famous!
3 If I were you, I'd eat healthier food.

B **Match the sentences in A with the uses of the Second Conditional below.**

We use the second conditional

a for things we know will not happen now or in the future. _____
b to give advice _____
c for things that probably won't happen now or in the future. _____

C **Read the sentences and answer the questions below.**

1 Jack could win the race if he had better running shoes.
2 You might not win the match unless you get another tennis racket.

a What other words can we use instead of *would*?
b What word can we use that means the same as *if not*?

▶ Grammar Focus p.167 (6.3 & 6.4)

D **Rewrite the sentences in your notebook using the Second Conditional.**

1 I don't have a bike, so I get the bus to the football club.
2 He doesn't get any exercise, so he's overweight.
3 She's not good at running, so she doesn't get chosen for teams.
4 We don't have money, so we can't buy new team uniforms.
5 We don't have enough players, so we might have to cancel the match.
6 The people don't have tickets, so they can't come into the stadium.

E **Complete the second sentence so it means the same as the first. Use as many words as you need.**

1 You might be off the team unless you say sorry for hitting the referee.
Unless you _____
2 If Stella doesn't start practising, she won't play in the match.
Unless Stella _____
3 Unless you get lots of exercise, you might get fat.
If you don't _____
4 They'll miss the start of the competition unless they leave right now.
If they don't _____
5 If James doesn't score soon, we'll take him off the pitch.
Unless James _____

F **Complete the sentences with the correct form of the verbs in brackets. Add commas where necessary.**

1 **A:** Should I play basketball or football this evening?

   B: If I _____ (be) you, I _____ (not play) either!

2 **A:** If he gets one more point, _____ (he / win) the tournament?

   B: No. He needs to win another game.

3 **A:** I'm hungry. Do we have anything to eat?

   B: Yes. If you _____ (open) the cupboard door, you _____ (see) lots of food.

4 **A:** We're going to be late for the match!

   B: Calm down. If we get Dad to drive us, we _____ (make) it on time.

5 **A:** What _____ (you / do) if you won an Olympic medal?

   B: I _____ (run) around the track for hours!

Writing: sentence transformation (1)

Learning Focus

Clauses of purpose

We use clauses of purpose to explain why someone does something or why something happens.

- infinitive:
  She went running <u>to get fit</u>.

- because + subject and verb:
  She went running because <u>she wanted to get fit</u>.

- so that + subject and verb:
  She went running <u>so that she could get fit</u>.

- so as to + infinitive (without *to*):
  She went running <u>so as to get fit</u>.

- in order to + infinitive (without *to*):
  She went running <u>in order to get fit</u>.

- for + noun:
  She went running <u>for her fitness</u>.

A Choose the correct answers.

1 He did weightlifting _____ get stronger.
   a for   b to   c because

2 We waited for hours _____ buy tickets for the race.
   a in order to   b so that   c for

3 She was asked to wear a number _____ the race.
   a to   b for   c so as to

4 They watched the tennis match so as to _____.
   a they relax   b relaxation c relax

5 Call the teacher _____ you need some help.
   a because   b so that   c in order

6 The runners warmed up _____ they wouldn't hurt themselves.
   a because   b so as to   c so that

B Read the instructions for the writing task and write T (True) or F (False) for each of the statements that follow.

> Here are some sentences about sport. For each question 1–5, complete the second sentence so that it means the same as the first. Use no more than three words.

1 All the sentences are on the same topic. ☐
2 There are 15 questions. ☐
3 Each question has two sentences. ☐
4 You have to fill the gap in the second question. ☐
5 You can only use three words. ☐

C Read the first three sentences that a student has completed for the task in B. Did he follow the instructions correctly?

1 The cyclists in the race all wore helmets.
   The _competitors_ in the cycling race all wore helmets.

2 She did aerobics to make new friends.
   In _order to_ make new friends, she did aerobics.

3 The team collapsed after an hour.
   The team _fall_ to pieces after an hour.

D Correct the student's mistakes in your notebooks.

E Choose the correct words to complete the sentences below. How did you know which words to choose?

1 He started playing basketball three years ago.
   He has played basketball _____ three years.
   a started   **b** during   **c** ago   **d** for

2 There was a swimming competition at my school last week
   Last week my school _____ a swimming competition.
   a have   **b** at   **c** had   **d** there was

F Read the *Exam Close-up*. Then read the *Exam Task* and underline the key words in the sentences.

G Now complete the *Exam Task*. Remember to check your answers when you have finished.

Exam Task

Here are some sentences about sport. For each question 1–5, complete the second sentence so that it means the same as the first. **Use no more than three words.**

1 She started playing volleyball for her health.
   She started playing volleyball to get _____.

2 Does this bat belong to you?
   Is this _____ bat?

3 Alice liked team sports a lot.
   Alice was very keen _____ team sports.

4 David skied for 21 years before he hurt his back.
   David skied for _____ 20 years before he hurt his back.

5 She wanted a drink after the race.
   She was _____ after the race.

Exam Close-up

Transforming sentences

- Read the first sentence and see if it is in the present, past or future.
- Underline the verb and any other key words.
- Then read the second sentence and look at the gap. What type of word is missing?
- Complete each with a verb, noun, preposition, adverb or adjective.
- Remember, you may need more than one word but don't write more than three.

Cyclists in the women's road race at the London 2012 Olympic Games

6 Water Sports Adventure

Oregon and Washington, USA

Before you watch

A **Work with a partner and answer these questions.**

- Why do you think spectator sports are so popular?
- Would you like to be a professional sportsperson? Why? / Why not?

While you watch

B **Watch the video and circle the words you hear.**

1 To most people, the cold wind would feel uncomfortable / comfortable.
2 Roeseler says that the power of the wind / waves in a kite can be like a bird moving its wings.
3 Wind power is something that's easily found in the gorge which divides / connects Washington and Oregon.
4 In recent years, more and more people have started using towers for kiteboarding / wakeboarding.
5 Roeseler's tower is 17 / 70 feet off the water.
6 It's got to go on a small / big wakeboard boat and get tested in the right environment.

After you watch

C **Complete the summary of the video below using these words.**

behind	fly	higher	invent	kite	launched	power	than

Cory Roeseler is a mechanical engineer who likes to (1) _____ things. He came up with the idea of kiteboarding in the 1990s. He used a(n) (2) _____ to catch the power of the wind and to allow the board to launch off the water for a few seconds and (3) _____. When Roeseler was a teenager, he was the first person to try kite-skiing. He didn't water-ski (4) _____ a boat like other people, he decided to use wind (5) _____ to ski below a kite. More recently, Roeseler invented a new kind of wakeboarding boat that has a sail on the back. Roeseler's boat also has a tower which is six feet higher (6) _____ other wakeboarding boat towers, so the wakeboarding rope is placed (7) _____. This allows the wakeboarder to jump higher in the air. Roeseler's friend, Jeff, was a bit worried before testing the new equipment because he hadn't seen anything like it before. He needn't have worried; as the boat went faster he started moving quickly across the water and then (8) _____ high into the air.

[A young man wakeboarding

Ideas Focus

- Would you like to try kiteboarding or wakeboarding? Why? / Why not?
- Do you think that it takes a special type of person to do these sports? Why? / Why not?

Review 3 — Units 5 & 6

Vocabulary

A Circle the odd ones out.

1	referee	plumber	builder
2	cottage	attic	garage
3	hire	sofa	bed
4	pitch	track	wall
5	helmet	racket	bat
6	lift	course	court
7	gymnastics	tournament	race
8	win	succeed	achieve

B Complete the sentences with these words.

> do   get   go   hold   make   move   play   take

1 Louise has to _____ the bus to school every morning.
2 They _____ every weekend in a basketball team.
3 It's difficult for older people to _____ with the times.
4 If you cook dinner, I'll _____ the dishes.
5 Jess likes to _____ a bath before going to bed.
6 The instructor told me to _____ on tight to the windsurfing board.
7 Jamie will _____ skiing in January.
8 All members of our family _____ their beds themselves.

C Choose the correct answers.

1 Most houses in Europe are made of ___ .
   a brick   **b** steel   **c** bamboo

2 I think we should ___ the bedroom white.
   a roof   **b** paint   **c** clean

3 The ___ around the house needs to be repaired.
   a cottage   **b** attic   **c** wall

4 I met my new ___ yesterday. They were very friendly.
   a resident   **b** builder   **c** neighbours

5 William fell ___ his bike and into the road.
   a of   **b** off   **c** up

6 Please don't ___ a mess in the living room. We're expecting guests.
   a do   **b** make   **c** have

7 We're not sure of the ___ of the river here.
   a deep   **b** depth   **c** deepen

8 If the new player scores today, we ___ win the league this year.
   a would   **b** might   **c** have

9 The goalkeeper pulled on his ___ and walked out onto the pitch.
   a gloves   **b** net   **c** helmet

10 His brother doesn't like ___ sports. He prefers jogging on his own.
   a competition   **b** compete   **c** competitive

Grammar

A Complete the sentences with *will*, *the*, *be going to* or the Future Perfect Simple of these verbs.

> arrive　be　clean　finish　fix　instal　live　not let　stay　try

1 This time next week, we _____ in a flat in a huge block of flats.
2 I think it _____ great to see the Rheinturm tower in Germany.
3 _____ the technician _____ the new central heating system by the time the cold weather begins?
4 I'm sorry! I _____ to be more careful when doing the dishes.
5 Would you like to relax for a while? I _____ the kitchen for you.
6 He's not sure he _____ building his house by next year.
7 _____ tourists _____ in the castle during the holidays?
8 Our new neighbours' furniture _____ this afternoon.
9 Dad _____ the broken plumbing all day tomorrow.
10 Please tidy your room or I _____ you go out with your friends.

B Match the first part of the sentences 1–6 with the second part a–f.

1 Would you try doing an extreme sport ☐
2 You would be healthier ☐
3 If we ran in marathons, ☐
4 When you exercise too much, ☐
5 If you want to learn how to ski, ☐
6 If I were you, ☐

a you should find an experienced instructor.
b if you didn't eat so many sweets.
c if you had the chance?
d your body reacts badly.
e we would know how challenging they are.
f I wouldn't try fixing the roof myself.

C Complete the sentences with the correct form of the verbs in brackets.

1 If I _____ (be / you), I would use solar energy in my house.
2 What kind of house _____ (you / buy) if you had the money?
3 If you had to move house, which area _____ (you / choose)?
4 If only he _____ (listen) to his coach during yesterday's match.
5 If it's still snowing later, we _____ (not / play) football.
6 If you're free tonight _____ (come) to my house for dinner.
7 Don't use the lift when you _____ (get) home tomorrow.
8 Unless you _____ (arrive) early, we won't be able to go shopping.
9 I wish I _____ (not / have to do) the housework every day.
10 If we used modern building methods, then our houses _____ (not / fall) down during earthquakes.

Reading:	multiple-choice questions, reading for general understanding
Vocabulary:	words related to extreme situations, prepositions, collocations & expressions
Grammar:	past perfect simple, past perfect continuous, question tags, subject & object questions, negative questions
Listening:	gap-fill, checking spelling
Speaking:	describing photos, talking about extreme situations, paraphrasing
Writing:	story (2), using narrative tenses, creating suspense, reviewing your writing

A man rope jumping, a new extreme sport which combines the thrill of rock climbing, bungee jumping and sky diving into one

Reading

A Read the breaking news about a real-life story. Who are the people in the story and where were they? Where were they going? What do you think happened next?

BREAKING NEWS

Thursday, October 12, 1972: Flight 571 carrying Uruguay's championship rugby team took off from Montevideo, Uruguay, heading to Santiago, Chile. On the plane were 45 people: the crew, the Uruguayan players, and their friends and relatives. Soon after take off, the plane had to stop in Mendoza, Argentina, because of bad weather.

Friday, October 13, 2.18 pm: Flight 571 took off again, heading for Santiago.

Friday, October 13, 3.20 pm: About an hour into the flight, the pilots began the descent into Santiago, not realising the plane was still close to the high peaks of the Andes Mountains ...

B You are going to read an article about what happened to the passengers on Flight 571. Quickly scan the article to check your predictions about what happened next.

Survival in the Andes

On Friday, October 13, 1972, a plane that had been flying from Uruguay to Chile with 45 people on board <u>crashed</u> into a mountain in the Andes. How some of the passengers managed to live is one of the great <u>survival</u> stories.

Twenty-nine people died in the crash and in the weeks following it. On the mountain, it was freezing cold and the survivors stayed inside the crashed plane to stay warm. They had very little food and were in very great danger while they waited for a rescue team. After 11 days on the mountain, they found a small radio on the plane and they heard the news that the rescue teams had stopped <u>searching</u> for them. All hope was gone. They were alone and terrified.

Days became weeks. Two months after the crash, after they had waited for summer to arrive, three of the passengers, Roberto Canessa, Nando Parrado and Antonio Vizintin, left to search for help. Each man wore three pairs of socks, with a plastic bag around each foot to keep the water out, boots, four pairs of trousers and four jumpers. Many of the clothes were from the people who had died in the crash. They also took with them a large sleeping bag that they had made. Only they could <u>save</u> the others now.

How did these brave young men <u>cope with</u> the journey? None of them had climbed mountains before and it was hard. They climbed very dangerous, icy peaks, trying to reach the top of the mountain. Some days later, exhausted and cold, they <u>reached</u> it. They had imagined this moment for days. On the other side of the mountain, they wanted to see a valley below that would take them out of the mountains. But instead of a valley, they saw more of the same snowy peaks. Lots of them. They weren't near the end of the mountains; they were in the middle of them. What could they do now?

Word Focus

peak: the top of a mountain
exhausted: very tired
valley: an area of low land between mountains, often with a river through it
ordeal: a very painful or difficult thing

But there was still hope. Parrado saw two low peaks about 65 kilometres away that didn't have snow on them. If they could get there, they would be out of the high Andes. But to reach the peaks, they would need to walk for more days and they didn't have enough food. But Parrado had a solution: Vizintin could return to the plane and he and Canessa would take his food. They agreed on the plan, and Canessa and Parrado continued their journey.

As they walked, the area around them slowly began to change. The men discovered a small river; the sun was warmer. After a few days of walking, the snow had disappeared completely and flowers were everywhere. 'This is the valley,' Canessa said excitedly. 'This is the way out!'

Soon, they saw a few cans on the ground and some farm animals

C Read the *Exam Close-up*. Then read the *Exam Task* and underline the key words.

Exam Task

Read the text and questions below. For each question, choose the correct letter **a**, **b**, **c** or **d**.

1 What is the writer doing in this text?
   a giving advice on how to survive
   b explaining incredible past events
   c showing that air travel is dangerous
   d writing an imaginative story

2 Why were the three men disappointed?
   a The view from the mountain was not very good.
   b They didn't know how to return to the plane.
   c They realised they had more problems.
   d They had not brought enough warm clothes.

3 Vizintin returned to the crash site because
   a he had lost hope.
   b he didn't agree with Parrado's solution.
   c he didn't want to walk any further.
   d there wasn't enough food for three people.

4 Parrado and Canessa knew they were close to safety because
   a they saw things that belonged to people.
   b they discovered a river.
   c they had been walking for ten days.
   d there were flowers in the snow.

Exam Close-up

Reading for general understanding

- It's a good idea to get a general understanding of the message of the text before you complete the exam task.
- Read the text carefully from beginning to end without worrying about new vocabulary. This will give you a good idea of what the text is about.
- Go back to each paragraph and make notes about the main idea in each one.
- Then take some time to think about all the ideas in the text before starting the exam task.

5 Which best describes what happened to the people on Flight 571?
   a The survivors of the crash waited for many weeks in the plane for someone to find and rescue them.
   b Tragically, 29 people died when the plane they were travelling in crashed into a mountain in the Andes.
   c In a terrible situation, and with no hope at all, the survivors found a way to save themselves.
   d To stay warm in the freezing cold, they wore the clothes of the people who had died in the crash.

The Andes mountains, near Santiago, Chile

D Find the meaning of the words below in the text. Then complete the sentences below.

> cope with   search   survive   save   crash   reach

1 You will _____ the car if you don't know how to drive it properly.

2 It is possible to _____ in the jungle if you know how to find food.

3 There were many problems and Harry didn't _____ them very well.

4 They were in the middle of the desert so nobody could _____ them.

5 After we _____ the river, we'll rest before we cross to the other side.

6 Rescue teams will continue to _____ for the missing mountain climbers.

E Write some more sentences in your notebook, using the words in D.

in a field. They knew there must be people somewhere nearby. On December 21st, after ten days, the exhausted men reached the town of Los Maitenes in Chile, and a rescue team went to save the other passengers high up in the Andes.

What had happened to them? Fortunately, they had all survived as they waited for the others to get help. The memories of the crash in the Andes would be with them forever, but their ordeal was over. They had made it out – alive.

- Do you think you would cope with the situation if you got lost in a foreign country? Why? / Why not?
- What one thing could you not survive without?

Ideas Focus

Vocabulary

A Match the words with their definitions.

> destination strength conditions companion
> expedition limit explorer journey

1 _____ : A person or friend you travel or live with.
2 _____ : Someone who goes to places not many people have ever been to.
3 _____ : A trip to find or see something that is a long way away.
4 _____ : A physical power or energy.
5 _____ : A trip; travelling from one place to another.
6 _____ : The final place you want to get to when you go on a journey or trip.
7 _____ : The maximum point or level of something or someone.
8 _____ : The way things are around you; your circumstances.

B Complete the text with the words in A.

Truly extraordinary: Ed Stafford

Some people call Ed Stafford an amazing (**1**) _____, but others think he's crazy! How can this be? Well, Ed Stafford has recently completed an incredible (**2**) _____.
He has become the first man to walk the length of the Amazon river. He reached his (**3**) _____, a beach on the Atlantic coast, after walking for 860 days in dangerous and extreme (**4**) _____. His journey required both mental and physical (**5**) _____ as he had to deal with heat, hunger, thirst and some very unfriendly people who wanted to kill him! The walk tested Stafford to his (**6**) _____ every step of the way.

Ed Stafford's success was partly due to his travelling (**7**) _____, Cho Sanchez Rivera, who he relied on to help him when things got very bad. It seems that the final part of the (**8**) _____ was the most difficult and Ed collapsed at the side of the road. Luckily, however, Cho was there to with him to help.

Let's see what adventure this extraordinary man will think of next! For more information see www.edstafford.org

C Circle the odd ones out.

1	survive	die	live
2	give up	carry on	continue
3	get better	get well	get on

4	deal with	panic	cope with
5	go along	go away	disappear
6	injure	hurt	help

D Choose the correct answers.

1 If I _____ this expedition, I'll never go on another adventure!
   a survive   **b** die   **c** live

2 It was so cold we had to _____ and go home.
   a get on   **b** give up   **c** deal with

3 Practice, practice and more practice! Then you'll _____.
   a go along   **b** get well   **c** get better

4 She had been very badly _____ and doctors didn't expect her to live.
   a hurt   **b** injure   **c** survive

5 Helen had been swimming for years, so she _____ well when she fell from the boat.
   a lived   **b** helped   **c** coped

6 If you don't want to get lost, don't _____ from the group.
   a go away   **b** get on   **c** carry on

7 Many climbers _____ their backs.
   a panic   **b** deal with   **c** injure

8 The divers were calm and didn't _____ when they saw the sharks.
   a go along   **b** carry on   **c** panic

Ideas Focus

- What's the most exciting thing you've ever done?
- Would you like to go on a journey like Ed Stafford's? Why? / Why not?

Grammar

Past Perfect Simple

A **Read the sentences. Then make them negative.**

1 We **had forgotten** our passports, so we went home to get them
2 He **had travelled** all over the world by his 30th birthday.

B **Answer the questions.**

1 In sentence 1, what happened first?
2 In sentence 2, what happened before his 30th birthday?

C **Is the sentence below T (True) or F (False)?**

We use the Past Perfect Simple for an action or situation that finished before another action, situation or time in the past. ☐

Past Perfect Continuous

D **Read the sentences and underline the verbs.**

1 They had been walking in the desert for days, so they were exhausted.
2 We had been driving for a few hours before we realised that we were lost.

E **Match the uses of the Past Perfect Continuous with the sentences in D.**

We use the Past Perfect Continuous for actions

a that started in the past and were still in progress when another action occurred in the past. ☐
b that were in progress in the past and had an effect on a later action in the past. ☐

▶ Grammar Focus p.167 & 168 (7.1 to 7.3)

F **Complete the sentences with the correct form of the Past Perfect Simple of the verbs in brackets.**

1 The skier _____ (return) to the hotel before the storm started.
2 Shelley _____ (never / play) golf in her life, but she realised she was very good at it.
3 _____ (they / already / call) a taxi by the time you arrived?
4 Until 2008, we _____ (never / be) sailing.
5 I _____ (work) as an instructor for ages and was a bit bored with my job.
6 Dean and Fran _____ (walk) in the Alps once and really enjoyed themselves.

G **Complete the sentences with the correct form of the Past Perfect Continuous of the verbs in brackets.**

1 My grandfather _____ (live) in his old house for ages before he moved in with us.
2 I _____ (cope) with my problem for weeks before I found a solution.
3 _____ (she / fight) against the disease for long before she died?
4 They _____ (not fly) for long when they lost radio contact.
5 How long _____ (you / dig) before you found the buried treasure?
6 We _____ (play) in the rain since midday, so we were very wet.

H **Complete the sentences with the correct form of the Past Perfect Simple or the Past Perfect Continuous of the verbs in brackets.**

1 The survivors _____ (finally / reach) a village after days of walking.
2 The students _____ (prepare) for their excursion for months.
3 We _____ (hope) to find some water for days.
4 The man _____ (manage) to stay alive for 5 days before he was rescued.
5 The explorer _____ (not / imagine) that it would be so difficult to cross the river.
6 The young man _____ (surf) since he was a child.

Listening

A Read the sentences below about a race. Two of the options given fill the gap correctly. For each question, cross (X) out the option that does not fit the gap.

1   competitors   limits   athletes

In this race, the ___ must be extremely fit and strong.

2   most challenging   toughest   incredible

The event is one of the ___ in the world.

3   deal with   carry on   cope with

Competitors must ___ some very difficult conditions.

4   hot   dry   windiest

Most deserts are extremely ___ places.

5   event   success   competition

Only a small number of people can enter this ___.

Exam Task

You will hear some information about a race in extreme parts of the world. For each question, fill in the missing information in the numbered space.

The Four Deserts Race

The race starts in the (**1**) _____ Desert, in Chile.

Length of each part of the race: (**2**) _____ km.

Gobi Desert: problems include strong (**3**) _____ and snow in the mountains.

Sahara desert: competitors find it difficult to (**4**) _____ because of sandstorms.

The final part of the race is in the (**5**) _____ desert.

Competitors can see penguins, seals and (**6**) _____.

Competitors sleep on a (**7**) _____.

Competitors run in very (**8**) _____ conditions.

B 🔊 **7.1** Practise saying the alphabet with your partner. Then listen and write down the words that are spelt.

1   _____

2   _____

3   _____

4   _____

C Read the *Exam-Close-up* and the *Exam Task*. Then look at each gap carefully and think about what information might fit.

Exam Close-up

Checking spelling

- Remember to think about what words might be missing in the gaps.
- Be careful with spelling. It's important to spell the words correctly to get a correct answer.
- If there is a repeated letter in a word, you will hear the word 'double', e.g. difficult, D- I double F- I- C- U- L- T.

D 🔊 **7.2** Now complete the *Exam Task*.

E 🔊 **7.2** Listen again and check your answers.

Participants walk across a sandy pass during the Marathon des Sables. An endurance race across the Sahara Desert in Morocco

Speaking

A Work with a partner and answer these questions.

- Have you ever done an extreme sport? If not, would you like to?
- Have you ever been to any extreme places?

B Put a tick (✓) next to the statements that describe extreme sports and a cross (✗) next to those that do not.

1 They're dangerous. ☐
2 In the end, you get a sense of achievement. ☐
3 They're relaxing. ☐
4 They're very exciting. ☐
5 You need a good instructor. ☐

C Read the *Exam Close-up*. Then work with a partner and take it in turns to explain the words below. Use the *Useful Expressions* to help you.

Student A	Student B
bungee-jumping	windsurfing
scuba diving	free-diving
skurfing	paddleboarding

D Now complete the *Exam Task*.

Useful Expressions

Paraphrasing

It's a sort of …
It's a kind of …
It's a an activity that … / a place where … / a person who …
I think it's a …
It could be / might be a ….
It's similar to …
It's dangerous because …
You need … to do it.
You shouldn't do it on your own because …
You have to be careful of …
Some equipment, such as … is necessary to …

Exam Close-up

Paraphrasing

- Don't worry if you don't know or can't remember a word in the exam. Try not to waste time trying to remember it.
- Think of another way of saying the same thing. This is called 'paraphrasing'.

Exam Task

Student A looks at photograph 1 and describes what he or she can see. Student B listens.
Then student B describes photograph 2 and Student A listens.

- Do you know anyone that does an extreme sport?
- Are extreme sports appropriate for all ages? Why? / Why not?

Ideas Focus

Vocabulary

Prepositions

A Circle the correct prepositions to complete the phrases.

1 **between** / **about** the same size
2 the top **of** / **to** the mountain
3 **over** / **along** 32 degrees Celsius
4 **onto** / **in** a desert
5 **below** / **under** freezing
6 **in** / **on** the planet
7 runs **across** / **of**
8 **over** / **above** sea level
9 **during** / **over** the years
10 **behind** / **in** the water

B Choose the correct answers.

River deep, mountain high!

From the top of the highest mountain to the bottom of the sea, the world is full of extremes. Let's take a look at some of the most amazing ones.

With temperatures well (**1**) ___ freezing and very strong winds, a mountain top is an extreme place to be! The tallest mountain (**2**) ___ the planet is, of course, Mount Everest. Its peak rises 8,850 metres (**3**) ___ sea level. (**4**) ___ the years, 1,200 people have made the long, lonely climb to the top of Everest!

The Sahara Desert is in North Africa and is (**5**) ___ the same size as the USA! With so much sun and very little rain, summer temperatures there are often (**6**) ___ 32° Celsius. The hottest temperature ever recorded on earth was in the Sahara, when the temperature reached 58° Celsius!

The Amazon is one of the longest rivers in the world. It begins in the mountains of Peru, goes (**7**) ___ South America and ends at the Atlantic Ocean. If you ever go on a journey to the Amazon, be very careful! As well as the lovely pink dolphins there are also some horrible creatures (**8**) ___ the water, including flesh-eating piranha!

Collocations & Expressions

C Match the words to make collocations.

1	keep	a	lost
2	do	b	missing
3	get	c	calm
4	go	d	someone's life
5	save	e	on a journey
6	go	f	your best

D Complete sentences 1–6 with collocations from C.

1 Everyone should _____ their _____ at school.

2 You must wear a lifejacket when you're on a boat. It might _____ your _____.

3 Try to _____ if you are in a dangerous situation.

4 Take a map with you. You don't want to _____.

5 Many people _____ every year while out walking in the mountains.

6 I'll _____ to the Amazon next year when I've saved up enough money.

1	a	after	b	below	c	besides
2	a	on	b	at	c	of
3	a	among	b	along	c	above
4	a	In	b	Over	c	Down
5	a	about	b	between	c	opposite
6	a	toward	b	outside	c	over
7	a	behind	b	across	c	onto
8	a	in	b	outside	c	above

Ideas Focus

- Do you agree with these statements? Why? / Why not?
  - It's always better to keep calm in extreme situations.
  - I think climbing Mount Everest would be easy.
  - Life in the desert must be quite difficult.

Grammar

Question Tags

A Read the sentences and underline all the verbs. What do you notice?

1 All the passengers in the train crash were rescued, **weren't they**?
2 The climbers haven't reached the summit yet, **have they**?

B Complete the rules.

Question tags are short questions that we add at the _____ of a sentence.
We use a(n) _____ question tag with an affirmative sentence and a(n) _____ question tag with a negative sentence.

Subject & Object Questions

C Underline the verbs in the sentences.

1 **Who** climbed Mount Everest for the first time?
2 **Who** will the rescue team try to find?

D Read the examples in C again. Then write T (True) or F (False) for sentences 1–4 below.

1 In sentence 1, the word **who** asks about the object of the sentence. ☐
2 In sentence 1, the words are in the order that we usually use for statements. ☐
3 In sentence 2, the word **who** asks about the subject of the sentence. ☐
4 In sentence 2, the words are in the order we usually use for statements. ☐

Negative Questions

E Match each sentence with one use of negative questions.

1 Didn't you hear about the flood? It was on the news! ☐
2 Isn't that one of the most amazing survival stories you've ever heard? ☐

We can use negative questions

a to express surprise.
b when we expect the listener to agree with us.

▶ Grammar Focus p.168 (7.4 to 7.6)

Demonstration of alpaca weaving by the women of Chincheros, Peru

F Match the sentences with the question tags.

1 He's never been to Peru, ☐
2 She's a top athlete, ☐
3 Let's go mountain biking, ☐
4 Peter can deep-sea dive, ☐
5 I'm fit enough to go windsurfing, ☐
6 Don't do anything silly, ☐
7 Harriet booked her extreme holiday, ☐
8 Everyone had a great time, ☐
9 Those people aren't here for the competition, ☐
10 You've paid for the boat rental, ☐

a can't he?
b didn't she?
c didn't they?
d will you?
e isn't she?
f aren't I?
g are they?
h shall we?
i has he?
j haven't you?

G Write subject questions for the answers below in your notebooks.

1 James plays tennis with Malcolm.
2 The instructor was teaching basketball skills.
3 Francis went fishing with Dad.
4 Jan borrowed the blue racket.
5 The coach asked Petra to join the team.
6 The fisherman is fixing Jack's net.
7 Ted took up the most dangerous sport.
8 The boy decided to get the little black puppy.

H Write negative questions in reply to these sentences using the prompts given.

1 **A:** You won't see Sue on the skiing trip.
B: Why not? _____ (she / not come / with us)
2 **A:** I got lost in the mountains last week.
B: Oh no! _____ (you / not be / scared)
3 **A:** I haven't slept since we came back.
B: Why not? _____ (you / not tired)
4 **A:** Where are you going?
B: _____ (anyone / not tell you / about the trip today)
5 **A:** You seem familiar to me.
B: Yes. _____ (we / have not met / somewhere before) 91

Writing: a story (2)

Using narrative tenses

To write stories based in the past, we use narrative tenses. The most common narrative tenses are the Past Simple, the Past Continuous, the Past Perfect Simple and the Past Perfect Continuous.

- Use the Past Simple to talk about a completed action / state in the past, a series of actions that happened one after the other in the past or to take the action of the story further.
- Use the Past Continuous to set the scene of the story and to talk about an action that was in progress in the past when another action interrupted it.
- Use the Past Perfect Simple to talk about an action that happened before the time of the narrative or another past action.
- Use the Past Perfect Continuous to talk about an action that was in progress for some time in the past which was interrupted by another past action, or which had an effect on a later event in the past.

A Complete the sentences with the correct form of the verbs in brackets. Sometimes more than one answer is possible.

1 He stopped running, took the mobile phone out of his pocket and _____ (throw) it into the river.
2 The family _____ (sit) in the garden when they heard the blast.
3 Jane couldn't believe that she _____ (make) such a dangerous journey on her own.
4 Everyone was exhausted because they _____ (run) for miles.
5 She jumped up and _____ (chase) the thief down the street.
6 It was the perfect location. Palm trees _____ (sway) gently and the sun _____ (shine) brightly.
7 They were getting ready for bed when they _____ (hear) a knock at the door.
8 Throughout their ordeal, they _____ (keep) calm.

B Read the writing task below. Write T (True) or F (False) for each of the statements that follow.

> Write a story which begins with this sentence: *Everyone was scared to death.* (100 words)

1 The story will involve several people. ☐
2 It will be about a frightening situation. ☐
3 Someone must die in the story. ☐
4 You can begin the story any way you like. ☐
5 The story will probably have suspense. ☐

C Read the example story and circle the correct words.

Everyone was scared to death. They were trapped in the darkest cave they (**1**) had ever seen / ever seen after getting lost on a school trip.

The students (**2**) had screamed / were screaming loudly as pieces of rock fell to the ground. Luckily, no one (**3**) was / was being injured.

Toby had never been in such an extreme situation before, but he (**4**) had been keeping / kept very calm.

All of a sudden, he (**5**) remembered / was remembering that he had his mobile phone. His teacher (**6**) had told / told everyone to leave their phones in the tent but Toby (**7**) decided / had decided to secretly bring his.

As quick as lightening, Toby (**8**) was running / ran to his bag and found the phone. He called his mum and (**9**) explained / had explained the situation. 'Don't worry,' she said 'Rescue teams are already looking for you.' Toby smiled and immediately (**10**) told / was telling everyone the good news.

D Read the model story again and write T (True) or F (False).

1 The writer hasn't used the given sentence properly. ☐
2 The story describes why everyone was so scared. ☐
3 Narrative tenses have been used. ☐
4 The writer uses special phrases to create suspense. ☐
5 By the end of the story the students are completely safe. ☐

E Complete the plan for the example story with these sentences.

Paragraph 1   **a** Describe how the plan is carried out and what happens next. ☐

Paragraph 2   **b** Describe the scene and give more details. ☐

Paragraph 3   **c** Introduce the main character and a plan of action. ☐

Paragraph 4   **d** Use the sentence you were given and say where the story is set. ☐

> ## Useful Expressions
>
> **Creating suspense**
>
> At that point …
> During the minutes / hours / days that followed …
> All of a sudden …
> As quick as lightning, / As fast as he could, …
> He'd never been in such an extreme situation.
> Without thinking, …
> There was no sign of …
> He thought of a plan.
> To make things worse, …
> They were just about to give up when …

F Match 1–6 with a–f to make sentences using some of the *Useful Expressions*.

1 As quick as
2 Without
3 From that
4 There was no
5 Then, she thought of a
6 At that

a sign of a rescue team.
b time on, they knew they only had each other.
c lightning, she ran to the car.
d plan that would save them.
e point the ambulance turned up.
f thinking, he went to the injured man.

G Read the *Exam Close-up* and the *Exam Task* below. Then make a plan for your story.

H Now complete the *Exam Task*. Remember to use the *Useful Expressions* to help you and to check your story carefully when you have finished.

Exam Close-up

Reviewing your writing

- When you have finished your story, it's important to read it and check it carefully.
- Does the story make sense?
- Does it have a beginning, middle and ending?
- Have you used the correct narrative tenses?
- Remember to leave yourself enough time in the exam to check your story before you finish.

Exam Task

Your English teacher has asked you to write a **story**. Your story must begin with this sentence:

> *Nobody knew where they were.*

(100 words)

Before you watch

A Match the words with their meanings.

1 adrenaline ☐
2 anticipation ☐
3 limitation ☐
4 pulse rate ☐

a a feeling of excitement about something nice that is going to happen
b how often your heart beats
c something that prevents you going past a certain point
d something your body produces when you are scared, angry or excited that makes your heart beat faster and gives you energy

While you watch

B Watch the video and decide if these statements are T (True) or F (False).

1 Many ships sink in the rough waters where the Columbia River empties into the ocean. ☐
2 The skills taught at the Coast Guard's national motor lifeboat school can't be used to drive any other boat. ☐
3 Aaron Ferguson has been a driver here for over two years. ☐
4 For students only, pulse rates accelerate and heart rates rise as soon as the sea becomes more dangerous. ☐
5 Student, Ralph Johnston, needs to learn to control the elements. ☐
6 If drivers are comfortable in bad weather, then the crew is also more comfortable, and they'll be more effective. ☐

After you watch

C Complete the summary of the video below using these words.

| convinced | mercy | missions | prove | satisfaction | tragedy | training | violent |

In the US Coast Guard's national motor lifeboat school, trainee boat drivers often find themselves at the (1) _____ of waves that can kill them. They must face some of the most (2) _____ and unpredictable seas. In an area known as the 'Graveyard of the Pacific', drivers learn how to cope with the kind of rough conditions that they will frequently face in their job, battling against severe weather.

The (3) _____ is important as these skills will help them to perform their dangerous life-saving (4) _____. Instructor Aaron Ferguson is (5) _____ that the motor lifeboat school gives the students the best kind of training.

The two-week class ends with the students ready to do the 'man-overboard drill'. For student, Ralph Johnston, this is the chance to (6) _____ that he can move the lifeboat through huge waves while keeping it steady. The rescue attempt succeeds and he passes the test. For the instructors, there is (7) _____ in knowing that the skills students learn here might one day prevent a terrible (8) _____.

Rough seas crash over the ship *National Geographic Endeavour* in the Atlantic

Ideas Focus
- Do you think you could do this job? Why? / Why not?
- Whose story of survival in this unit do you think is the most incredible? Why?

Reading: multiple-choice questions, reading around the gap
Vocabulary: words related to free time, phrasal verbs
Grammar: modals & semi-modals (1 & 2)
Listening: multiple-choice questions (pictures), predicting from pictures
Speaking: talking about free-time activities, decision making, talking about all the options, talking about possibility
Writing: postcard, linking words & phrases, writing the correct amount, writing a postcard

Reading

A What do people do in their free time? Below is a list of popular free-time activities for young people in the UK. Put them in the order of popularity from 1 (most popular) to 10 (least popular).

- ☐ Listening to music
- ☐ Shopping
- ☐ Reading
- ☐ Watching TV
- ☐ Eating out
- ☐ Going for a day out
- ☐ Exercising
- ☐ Going to after school clubs
- ☐ Going to the cinema
- ☐ Spending time with friends / family

Your teacher will give you the correct answers.

B Work with a partner. Think of some activities people enjoy that can be very dangerous. What makes them dangerous?

C Read the title of the text. Where do you think this activity is taking place?

Stormchaser Herb Stein of the Center for Severe Weather Research with DOW 7, a specially-equipped research vehicle

---

Word Focus

headlamp: a large, powerful light that you wear on your forehead
victim: someone who has been hurt or killed
threat: something that can cause damage or danger

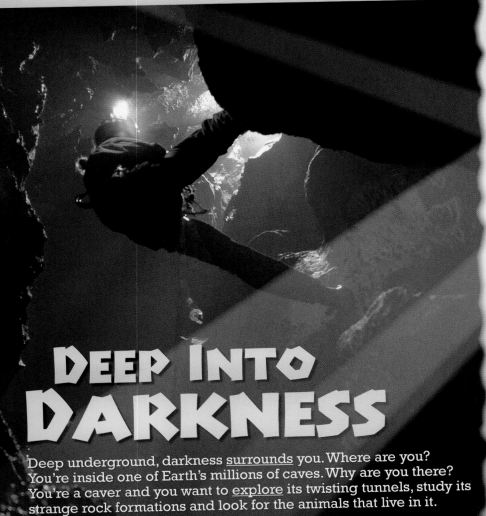

DEEP INTO DARKNESS

Deep underground, darkness <u>surrounds</u> you. Where are you? You're inside one of Earth's millions of caves. Why are you there? You're a caver and you want to <u>explore</u> its twisting tunnels, study its strange rock formations and look for the animals that live in it.

MEET A CAVER

Stephen Alvarez is a caver. He travels the world exploring and photographing caves. He (**1**) _____ to climb mountains to reach some caves or dive deep down to search for underwater caves. He has photographed some very impressive caves including the longest in the world, Mammoth Cave in the USA, (**2**) _____ has 580 kilometres of tunnels.

UNDERGROUND DANGER

People sometimes ask Alvarez (**3**) _____ caving is dangerous. It is. 'Caves are dangerous if you don't know what you're doing,' he says. Staying safe is important. Alvarez goes into caves with other cavers, never by himself. That way, team members can look out for each other.

Cavers carry the right (**4**) _____ for all situations. Knee pads and gloves are important, and they must wear a (**5**) _____ to protect the head. Most cavers use headlamps to provide light. This leaves their hands free to climb and <u>crawl</u>. They also carry extra torches and they know how to use ropes.

D Read the *Exam Close-up*. Then read the text again and think of words which could go in each gap.

E Now complete the *Exam Task*. Remember to check if each word fits in the gap before choosing the correct one. Your teacher will give you the words.

F Find these words in the text and use them to complete the definitions below.

| capture | crawl | destroy | explore | flow | surround |

1 To _____ means to be all around something or someone.

2 To _____ means to damage something completely.

3 To _____ means to catch someone or something.

4 To _____ means to travel around an area to learn about it.

5 To _____ means to move slowly along the ground on hands and knees.

6 To _____ means to move easily in one direction.

Exam Close-up

Reading around the gap

- Read the text quickly to get a general understanding of it.
- Then re-read the sentences with gaps and try to think of a word that could fit before you look at the answer options.
- Read the answer options, start by eliminating the obviously wrong answers, and then focus on the options that are left.
- Sometimes, two answers seem possible, so read 'around' the gap so you understand the complete sentence.

Exam Task

Read the text and choose the correct word for each space. For each question, mark the correct letter **a**, **b**, **c**, or **d**. Your teacher will give you the words.

DECORATIONS

There are fantastic shapes to see in caves. These shapes are called decorations and they form when rainwater drips onto stone. Examples of these are stalactites, which hang down from a cave ceiling, and stalagmites, which grow upwards from the cave floor. But Alvarez says there are many (**6**) _____, including some that look like popcorn and some that look like a nest of eggs.

CAVE CREATURES

Beautiful cave decorations are not all that you'll see in caves. Animals live in caves, too. Many of (**7**) _____ are eyeless. They don't need eyes because there is no light in the cave. Alvarez has seen fish and spiders without eyes. Because they can't see, these creatures can hear, touch or smell very well. They can move around and they know what's nearby. They can capture their food without ever seeing the victim!

CAVE THREATS

Explorers like Alvarez know how important it is to (**8**) _____ caves. Pollution is one threat. Polluted water from farms or businesses can flow into caves, destroying decorations and killing animals. Human visitors can also be a threat. A (**9**) _____ caver can destroy in minutes what took thousands of years to form. That's (**10**) _____ responsible cavers say, 'Take nothing but pictures. Leave nothing but footprints. Kill nothing but time!'

Ben Caddell descends into Majlis al Jinn cave in Oman

Cavers light the entrance passage of Ora Cave. New Britain Island, Papua New Guinea

Ideas Focus

- Would you like to try caving? Why? / Why not?
- Do you enjoy doing all of the activities in Exercise A? Why? / Why not?

Vocabulary

A Match the free-time activities 1–8 with pictures a–h

1 photography ☐   3 martial arts ☐   5 sculpture ☐   7 ballet ☐
2 cookery ☐   4 drama ☐   6 painting ☐   8 gaming ☐

B Complete the sentences with some of the words in A.

1 Ben teaches _____ to primary school students. Some of them want to become actors now.
2 "I don't understand this _____. The colours are bright but I can't see what it is".
3 The _____ course I went on was excellent. I know a lot more about my camera now.
4 He's done Judo since he was four. He's always preferred _____ to team sports.
5 Tom loves _____. He's always got his nose in a recipe book.
6 She's a very talented artist; her _____ stands in many famous art galleries.

C Work with a partner. Use the words below to talk about the activities in A.
Give your opinion of each and a reason why you like it or why not.

adore   love   really like / like a lot   quite like   like ... a bit   don't like   really don't like   hate   can't stand

I really like cookery because I love eating!

So do I!

Ideas Focus
- Are there any hobbies you do with your family? If yes, what are they?
- Do you think hobbies should be educational as well as entertaining? Why / Why not?

Grammar

Modals & Semi-modals (1)

A Read the example sentences carefully. What do the modal verbs in bold in each group have in common?

Group 1
Harry **could** be in the library.
I **may** travel abroad next year.
We **might** go to the cinema tonight.
You **must** be tired. You've been exercising all morning. You **can't** be hungry. You just had lunch.
The modal verbs refer to _____
_____.

Group 2
My grandad **can** speak seven languages.
Karen **could** run very fast when she was at school.
Francis **was able to** go mountain climbing at the weekend.

The modal verbs refer to _____
_____.

Group 3
You **should** eat more fruit and vegetables.
We **shouldn't** spend so much money on magazines.
You **ought to** make an appointment to see the doctor.
The modal verbs refer to _____
_____.

B Work with a partner and complete the meanings of each group in A with the words below.

- ability
- advice and suggestions
- possibility and certainty

▶ Grammar Focus p.168 & 169 (8.1 to 8.9)

C Choose the correct answers.

1 Is it OK if I borrow your pencil for a minute?
_____ I borrow your pencil for a minute?

   a Should   **b** Can   **c** Am I able

2 I'm certain he's in the park because his football boots aren't here.
His football boots aren't here so he _____ in the park.

   a must be   **b** can't be   **c** might be

3 You are able to join the photography club.
You _____ join the photography club.

   a must   **b** can   **c** mustn't

4 You ought not to go swimming today.
You _____ go swimming today.

   a mustn't   **b** aren't able to   **c** shouldn't

5 He was able to play the piano very well when he was younger.
When he was younger, he _____ play the piano very well.

   a wasn't able   **b** can   **c** could

6 It's possible that he will have an art exhibition next spring.
He _____ have an art exhibition next spring.

   a should   **b** must   **c** may

7 I think it's a good idea for you to go outside more.
You _____ go outside more.

   a might   **b** must   **c** ought to

8 They weren't able to open the window.
They _____ open the window.

   a couldn't   **b** can't   **c** did not

D Work with a partner. Decide on the advice you would give your friend for each point below and suggest things that could help in each situation.

Your friend wants to …

1 get fit and lose weight
2 learn bungee-jumping
3 start a recycling campaign at school

4 change schools because she has broken up with her boy / girlfriend

Listening

A Look at the pictures below and write a word or phrase to describe the connection between the pictures in each set.

1

2
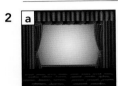 

B Imagine the pictures in A (a, b or c) are the answer choices to a listening task. Discuss with a partner what the people might talk about and any words they might say.

C [8.1] ▶‖ Now listen to the conversations and see if you were right. Choose the pictures in A (a, b or c) that answer the questions below.

1 How is the girl going to travel to Scotland?
2 What has the woman planned to do first?

D Read the *Exam Close-up*. Then read the *Exam Task* and note down what you might hear for each set of pictures.

E [8.2] ▶‖ Now complete the *Exam Task*.

Exam Close-up

Predicting from pictures
- Before you listen, it's important to read the questions and look at the pictures carefully.
- When you look at the pictures, try to imagine what the listening could be about.
- Think about the differences and the words you could hear for each picture.

Exam Task

There are seven questions in this part. For each question, there are three pictures and a short recording. Circle the correct picture **a**, **b** or **c**.

1 What time does the girl's music lesson start tonight?

2 Which sport did Tom try?

3 Which concert is the boy NOT going to buy a ticket for?

4 Which bikini does the young woman prefer?

5 Where is the tennis racket?

6 How much does the woman pay per month for her gym?

a	b	c
£20	£30	£50

7 What has the grandmother done this afternoon?

F [8.2] ▶‖ Now listen again.

Speaking

A **Work with a partner and answer these questions.**

- Which type of transport do you prefer to use on a long journey?
- What could you do to stop getting bored when you go on a long journey?

B **Write A (advantages) or D (disadvantages) after the statements 1–6 about going on a journey by car.**

1 You feel sick. ☐
2 You can look out of the window and enjoy the view. ☐
3 There are traffic jams. ☐
4 You can't stand up and walk around. ☐
5 It's a fast way to travel and can be comfortable. ☐
6 You can stop and get out when you want to. ☐

C **Read the *Exam Close-up*. Then read the *Exam Task* and think about the advantages and disadvantages of each option.**

D **Now work with a partner to complete the *Exam Task*. Use the *Useful Expressions* to help you.**

Exam Task

A boy and a girl are going on holiday by coach. It's a long journey and they might get bored so they want to take some things to do while they are travelling. Talk together about the things they could do.

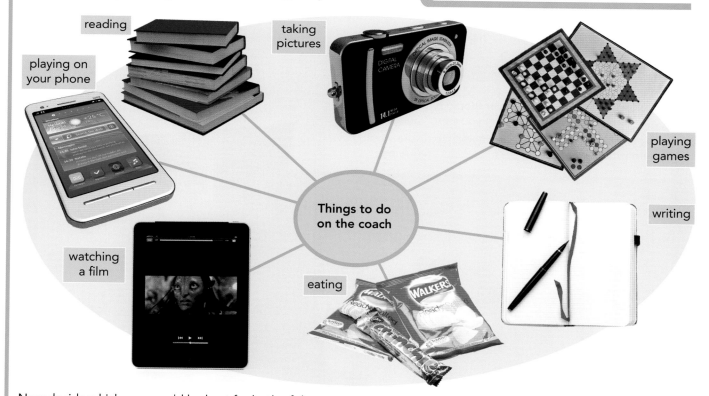

reading

taking pictures

playing on your phone

playing games

Things to do on the coach

writing

watching a film

eating

Now decide which one would be best for both of them.

- Do you normally have free time during the week? Why? / Why not?
- Is travelling a waste of time? Why? / Why not?
- If you could spend more time with someone, who would it be and why?

Vocabulary

Phrasal Verbs

A Match the phrasal verbs with their meanings.

1	call for	☐	a	to audition
2	cut out for	☐	b	to behave boastfully
3	find out	☐	c	to announce
4	show off	☐	d	to start to like
5	take to	☐	e	to discover
6	take up	☐	f	to begin
7	call out	☐	g	to be suited to
8	try out for	☐	h	to require

B Complete the sentences with the correct form of the phrasal verbs from A.

1 You could have looked online if you had wanted to _____ about the different martial arts.

2 Are you really going to _____ the main role in the school play?

3 So you're a top athlete – you still shouldn't _____ about the fact that you're super rich.

4 I didn't like ballet in the beginning, but I'm really beginning to _____ it now.

5 You won an Olympic gold medal; this _____ a celebration!

6 I could have been a rock star, but I wasn't _____ life on the road.

7 You're overweight and unfit – you should have _____ a sport when you were younger.

8 Mary Jane can't have been in the audience or she would have come on stage when I _____ her name.

C Rewrite the sentences below in your notebook replacing the words in bold with some of the phrasal verbs in A.

1 I wish Pete wouldn't **behave in a boastful way** about his iPod all the time.

2 I didn't use to like tap dancing, but I'm beginning to **start to like** it now!

3 I want to **begin** ballroom dancing, but I'm scared my friends will laugh at me!

4 Martial arts **requires** great strength and stamina.

5 I'm not **suited to** drama classes. I'm too shy!

6 I'll **discover** what time the art classes start when I'm surfing the Net later.

D Discuss these questions with a partner.

- Are there any hobbies you would like to **take up** in the future?
- Have you ever had to **try out** for something? What happened?
- Have you ever **shown off**? What happened?

Teenagers perform in a production of *A Very Potter Musical*

Grammar

Modals & Semi-modals (2)

A **Read the example sentences carefully. What do the modal verbs in bold in each group have in common?**

Group 1

Can I go to the party, please?
You **can** borrow my new game if you like.
Could you get me a glass of water, please?
May we have another ice cream, please?
You **may** leave when you finish the test.
The modal verbs refer to _____

_____.

Group 2

I **must** make some snacks for the party.
You **have to** be at the sports club by seven o'clock.
You **mustn't** park your car here.
The modal verbs refer to _____
_____.

Group 3

You **needn't** buy any milk because there's some in
the fridge.
We **don't have to** go to the festival if you don't want to.
The modal verbs refer to _____
_____.

B **Work with a partner and complete the meanings of each group with the words below.**

- lack of obligation or necessity
- necessity, obligation and prohibition
- permission and request

▶ **Grammar Focus p.168 & 169 (8.1 to 8.9)**

C **Choose the correct answers.**

1 Don't forget you ____ do your maths homework by 10 tomorrow. Mr King will be angry if you don't do it!
   a have to   **b** don't have to   **c** could

2 We ____ buy any materials for the arts and crafts class. It's all provided by the school.
   a need   **b** must   **c** don't have to

3 Mum told me I ____ stay up so late watching TV.
   a ought not   **b** shouldn't   **c** must

4 Excuse me? ____ you help me with this suitcase? Thanks very much.
   a Must   **b** Can't   **c** Could

5 Members _____ use the school theatre without asking Mrs Devon.
   a mustn't   **b** needn't   **c** have to

6 It's OK. You _____ come early; I'll have lots of helpers so come a bit later.
   a needn't   **b** have to   **c** mustn't

7 She hurt her ankle but, luckily, she _____ go to hospital.
   a doesn't have to **b** might   **c** must

8 We ____ bring your passport here tomorrow so we can check it.
   a need   **b** must   **c** ought

D **Complete the sentences with these words or phrases, then match them to the responses.**

Can	Could	Do we have to	He doesn't have to	may	must	mustn't	shouldn't

1 You _____ work all the time; get a hobby. ☐
2 You _____ shout at your teammates! It's wrong! ☐
3 _____ go to summer camp? ☐
4 Excuse me, Mr Jenkins. _____ you help me with my sculpture? ☐
5 You _____ wear a helmet when you go cycling or you'll get a fine ☐
6 Hey, Dad! _____ you give me a lift to the gym? ☐
7 _____ take a racket; I've got an extra one. ☐
8 I _____ start weightlifting again, but I'm not sure if I have time. ☐

a Okay, I'll tell him.
b What? Again? Why don't you walk?
c Let me know when you're sure and I'll join you
d Yes, of course. Give me a minute, please.
e No, only if you want to.
f I know. I'll put it on right now.
g Sorry, Coach. It won't happen again.
h You know, that's very good advice.

Writing: a postcard

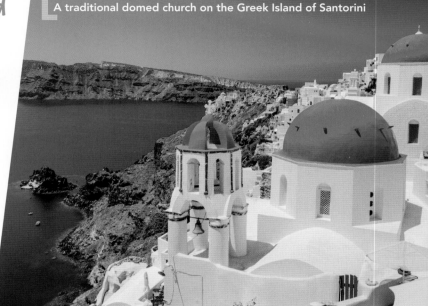

A traditional domed church on the Greek Island of Santorini

Learning Focus

Linking words and phrases

Linking words and phrases can make your writing flow better.

- Use *also*, *as well*, *and*, *too* and *as well as* to join ideas that are similar in some way or to add information.
- Use *as*, *since* and *because* to say why something happens.
- Use *like*, *such as*, *for instance* and *for example* to give examples. You can use *for example* and *for instance* at the beginning of a sentence, but you can't begin with *like* or *such as*.

A Circle the correct words.

1 I've got three sisters as well / as well as a brother.
2 We're making a cake because / and it's my best friend's birthday.
3 Tell me more about your family. For example / Such as, where does everyone live?
4 I'm going to art college like / since painting and sculpture are my favourite pastimes.
5 They went to Peru in 2010 and / too again in 2012.
6 Activities also / like ice hockey, skiing and snowboarding are very popular in Canada.
7 Aunt Meg will help us as / for instance she's very reliable.
8 They invited their relatives and their in-laws as well / because to the party.

B Read the writing task below and then answer the questions about it in your notebook.

> *You are on holiday with your family. Write a postcard to your friend Jo in America. In your card you should:*
>
> - tell Jo about your holiday
> - say what you are going to do tomorrow
> - ask Jo about his holiday
>
> Write 35–45 words.

1 What will you write?
2 Who will read it?
3 What information should you include?
4 What question do you need to include?
5 How many words do you have to write?

C Read the example postcard and circle the linking words and phrases that Luke has used.

Hi Jo!

We're having a lovely time. The food is delicious. We've had grilled fish, as well as tasty starters like Greek salad and calamari.

We're going water-skiing tomorrow afternoon.

When are you going on holiday? Send me a postcard!

Bye!

Luke

0085

Jo Denman
42 Acacia Ave.
Denton
California 802543
USA

D Read the example postcard again and tick (✓) the things the writer has done.

1 included a question ☐
2 described negative things about the holiday ☐
3 used different adjectives ☐
4 included the plan for the next day ☐

5 described the weather ☐
6 used informal language ☐
7 explained the positive points about the holiday ☐
8 included a greeting and ending ☐

E Read the *Exam Task* below. Then work with a partner and complete the sentences with your ideas.

1 We're on holiday in …
2 The weather is …
3 The hotel / campsite / apartment is …
4 The food is … . We've had …
5 We've been to … and seen …

F Now read the *Exam Close-up* and complete the *Exam Task*. Remember to check your postcard when you have finished.

Exam Close-up

Writing the correct amount
- Remember to read the number of words you can write before you plan your writing.
- If you write too many words, remember not to cross out the information the exam question asked you to include.

Exam Task

You are on holiday with your family.
Write a **postcard** to your friend Ed in England. In your card you should:

- say where you are
- say what you have done
- ask Ed about his holiday

Write 35–45 words.

Useful Expressions

Writing a postcard

We're having a lovely time.
The weather is …
The hotel / campsite / apartment is …
The beach is …
The food is …
We've had …

We've been to …
We've seen …
We've done some sightseeing.
See you soon!
Miss you!

8 Young Adventurers

Virginia, USA→

Before you watch

A Look at the photo and label it with these words.

caver   ledge   ropes   waterfall

A caver prepares to climb a waterfall in a cave. New Britain Island, Papua New Guinea

1 _____
2 _____
4 _____
3 _____

While you watch

B Watch the video and circle the words you hear.

1 But this is no ordinary / normal camping trip.
2 Using ropes to rappel into the cave is the only real choice / option for going underground.
3 Lights and warm clothes are both necessities / requirements for the cavers.
4 After only a few feet, they're at a very tight spot called 'the chimney'. It's a fall / drop of nine metres.
5 But she says, in the cave, everyone encourages / supports each other.
6 Nature is better / bigger than we are, and it will be here, the caves will be here, even if we aren't.

After you watch

C Complete the summary of the video below using these words.

choice   confidence   descend   exhilarating   huge   narrow   techniques   underground

Jessica Fagan has been caving since she was very young. She learnt many of her caving (**1**) _____ from her father, Joey, an experienced caver. Today, Jessica and her fellow Girl Scout cavers have decided to (**2**) _____ into a difficult cave in the hills of Virginia.

To get access to the cave, the girls use ropes to gently lower themselves through the cave entrance. Once (**3**) _____, the girls continue on through the tunnels. Sometimes the only (**4**) _____ the girls have is to squeeze their way through the (**5**) _____ passages on their hands and knees. It can be a frightening experience, which is why Jessica feels that (**6**) _____, not strength, is the main requirement for being a caver. Eventually the girls arrive at a(n) (**7**) _____ 18-metre waterfall, a(n) (**8**) _____ sight at the end of their long journey.

Ideas Focus
• What qualities does a person need to be a caver?
• Would you like to spend your free time caving, or doing a less extreme kind of activity? Why / Why not?

Vocabulary

A   Complete the sentences with the correct form of the words in bold.

1   Despite the weather, the woman took her dog for an _____ walk in the park. **EXHILARATE**
2   The archaeologists discovered two huge _____, at the entrance to the tomb. **SCULPT**
3   Jane wanted to take up _____ classes as a hobby. **COOK**
4   Jo has been good at _____ since she was two years old. **PAINT**
5   The climber just didn't have the _____ to go any further that day. **STRONG**
6   Mark has made a career out of _____, selling most of his pictures to online news sites. **PHOTO**
7   The _____ of the climbers was the rescue team's main concern. **SURVIVE**
8   He's Dutch and works in the _____ industry. He gets to try out all the new games. **GAME**
9   Roger is very _____ about how much money his family has. **BOAST**
10   The explorer was _____ after walking through the desert for thirty days. **EXHAUST**

B   Circle the correct words.

1   My brother likes to show up / off about his sports car.
2   Rock climbing calls for / about great concentration and strength.
3   The village is situated between / among two rivers.
4   She didn't like cooking at first, but now she has taken by / to it.
5   Peter has decided to try out with / for the long-jump team.
6   The hikers managed to cope at / with the extreme heat.
7   Are you cut out in / for being the leader on an expedition?
8   I'm thinking of taking up / off salsa dancing in my free time.
9   The temperature in Sweden can go below / under freezing.
10   Some islands in the Pacific rise just a few metres above / on sea level.

C   Match the opposites.

1   survive   ☐   a   healthy
2   give up   ☐   b   physical
3   cope with   ☐   c   continue
4   hurt   ☐   d   go away
5   mental   ☐   e   die
6   go along   ☐   f   panic

D   Complete the sentences with these words.

> adapt   collapse   do   go   prevent   companion

1   He was lucky he had a great travelling _____ with him.
2   A climber may _____ from lack of oxygen while climbing Mount Everest.
3   We decided to _____ on a journey to the mountains.
4   I will _____ my best when I take part in the competition.
5   If you live in a warm climate, it's difficult to _____ to a cold climate.
6   You must follow the safety rules to _____ accidents from happening.

Review 4
Units 7 & 8

Grammar

A Complete the text with the Past Simple, the Past Perfect Simple or the Past Perfect Continuous of these verbs. Sometimes more than one answer is possible.

> be climb decide explore have manage not tell try

An amazing survival

Aron Lee Ralston (**1**) _____ to climb the red rocks near the Canyonlands National Park on Saturday, 26 April, 2003. Aron, who was an athletic 27-year-old and a very experienced climber, (**2**) _____ Colorado's peaks for years, before that fateful Saturday.

That day, he was dressed in a T-shirt and shorts. He also had a backpack with a few supplies. At some point while he (**3**) _____ over a huge rock that filled a narrow slot in the canyon, it came loose and crashed down trapping his right forearm against the rock wall. He (**4**) _____ to free his arm, but without success. He knew there was little hope of getting help as he (**5**) _____ anyone about his plans for that day.

Aron's condition was becoming worse and worse every day because he (**6**) _____ very little food or water for days. He knew that if he didn't do something soon, he would die. Then on Thursday morning, his fifth day in the canyon, he decided that the only chance he had to survive was to cut off his arm! He did it using a multi-tool he had with him. Even though he (**7**) _____ in terrible pain, he (**8**) _____ to walk out of the canyon. He was spotted by some hikers and eventually rescued by helicopter. The rescuers were amazed at Aron's will to live and the brave thing he had done.

B Choose the correct answers.

1 Let's keep on walking for a while, ___ ?
   a should we   b shall we   c do we

2 Who ___ the equipment for the expedition?
   a did prepare   b prepared   c prepare

3 You haven't realised that we're lost, ___ ?
   a have you   b haven't you   c did you

4 What ___ to land the plane safely?
   a the pilot did   b did the pilot   c did the pilot do

5 ___ invited Jane to the party?
   a You didn't   b Haven't you   c You

6 The climbers' adventure was on the news, ___ ?
   a weren't they   b wasn't it   c were they

7 I am going to adapt to this weather, ___ ?
   a am I   b I'm not   c aren't I

8 ___ enjoying your holiday?
   a Not are you   b Aren't you   c You aren't

C Complete the second sentences so that they have a similar meaning to the first sentences. Use the words in bold.

1 Perhaps the climbers are lost. Let's call the police. **may**
   The climbers _____ . Let's call the police.

2 They had the ability to go on holiday last summer. **able**
   They _____ go on holiday last summer.

3 My advice is to ask for your parents' permission. **ask**
   You _____ for your parents' permission.

4 All rescuers are obliged to wear special clothes. **had**
   All rescuers _____ special clothes.

5 It wasn't necessary for them to find a hotel because they camped every night. **need**
   They _____ a hotel because they camped every night.

6 I'm sure the explorers have reached their destination by now. **reached**
   The explorers _____ their destination by now.

7 The hiker took a raincoat with him, but it didn't rain. **have**
   The hiker _____ a raincoat with him, as it didn't rain.

9 High-Tech World

Reading:	true/false, finding the answers
Vocabulary:	technology-related words, prepositions
Grammar:	passive voice: tenses, *by* & *with*, the passive voice: gerunds, infinitives & modal verbs
Listening:	multiple-choice questions (pictures), listening again
Speaking:	talking about technology, decision making, making a decision, deciding
Writing:	sentence transformation (2), using collocations, checking the meaning

Robotic fish developed at Massachusetts Institute of Technology. Cambridge, Massachusetts

Reading

A These devices can be used to spy on people. What kind of information do you think people doing surveillance could get from these devices?

- a surveillance camera
- a video camera
- a computer
- a mobile phone
- a satnav

B Quickly read the text and write T (True) or F (False).

What does the text tell us about surveillance?

1 We are being watched all the time. ☐

2 It should only be used on criminals. ☐

3 Surveillance equipment can be more effective than people at detecting some things. ☐

The view from one of four million surveillance cameras in the United Kingdom; this one, in London, includes tiny wipers to clear the rain.

They're watching you

In the novel 1984, which was published in 1949, British author George Orwell wrote about a time in the future when it is impossible to hide from surveillance by the government. In the novel, people are always reminded that the government can see them by the phrase, 'Big Brother is watching you'.

Police check cars using cameras and optical licence tag recognition in London

The world that Orwell predicted is already here. Video systems that watch people are now used in many cities around the world. In Paris, France, for example, there are road cameras nearly everywhere to help control traffic and approximately 2,000 cameras on city buses to prevent crime. In Britain, there are cameras that watch streets and parks, public transport, stadiums and shopping areas. With nearly five million cameras – one camera for every 14 people – Britain has more surveillance cameras than anywhere else in Europe.

So who's watching? The police, certainly. There is nothing a criminal can say when the crime he has committed has been caught on video. For example, in 2009, 95 per cent of Scotland Yard murder cases used video surveillance as evidence. But even when criminals are not actually caught on video, just seeing a video camera can make an area safer. For this reason, some people put up signs that say 'Video Surveillance Is In Operation' even where there are no video cameras.

Video surveillance has also been used to save lives. One day in France, 18-year-old Jean-François LeRoy was swimming in a public swimming pool. While he was under water, he lost consciousness. The lifeguards who were watching the pool didn't realise

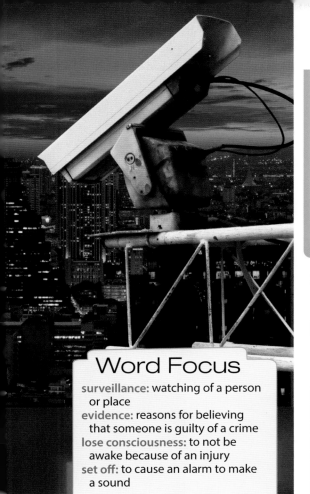

Exam Close-up

Finding the answers

- Before you read the text, make sure you underline the key words in the questions.
- As you read the text, write short notes about the content or topic of each paragraph.
- Go back to the questions and work out which paragraph the information is in.
- The content of the questions is in the same order as the information in the text.
- As you read through the paragraph, look for words or expressions that are similar to the key words you underlined.

C Read the *Exam Close-up*. Then read the *Exam Task* below and underline the key words.

D Now complete the *Exam Task*. Remember to check your answers carefully when you have finished.

Exam Task

Look at the sentences below about surveillance. Read the text to decide if each sentence is correct or incorrect. Write T (True) or F (False).

1 The author refers to the book 1984 to recommend we read it. ☐
2 In 1984, the government knows everything that everyone does. ☐
3 Each surveillance camera in Britain can watch 14 people. ☐
4 Britain has fewer surveillance cameras than France. ☐
5 There are surveillance cameras at sports events in Britain. ☐
6 Criminals say nothing when they are caught by the police. ☐
7 British police have used surveillance cameras to find killers. ☐
8 A sign on a house about video cameras might not be true. ☐
9 The Poseidon system had been working in the pool for less than a year. ☐
10 Norman Siegel is concerned because nobody wants to vote. ☐

E Find the meaning of the red words below in the text. Then circle the correct words in the sentences.

1 When there are many police officers on the streets, it can prevent / commit crime.
2 Can you predict / remind what will happen in five years?
3 The police must catch / control the fans at a football game.
4 Public / People transport is very expensive in some cities.
5 She threw the stick into the river and it drowned / sank to the bottom.
6 Dad put in / put up a car alarm so that no one could steal his taxi.

Word Focus

surveillance: watching of a person or place
evidence: reasons for believing that someone is guilty of a crime
lose consciousness: to not be awake because of an injury
set off: to cause an alarm to make a sound

what was happening. LeRoy sank slowly and quietly to the bottom of the pool. Without help, he would have died in four minutes.

Although no lifeguard saw LeRoy drowning, 12 large machine eyes under the water noticed it. Nine months earlier, a surveillance system called Poseidon had been put in the pool. Poseidon can understand when swimmers are not moving normally, and it sets off an alarm for the lifeguards. Just 16 seconds after Poseidon noticed that LeRoy was sinking, the lifeguards pulled him from the pool. Poseidon had saved his life.

Although it is useful for fighting crime, many people are still concerned about public surveillance. Norman Siegel, an American lawyer, says that there has been a huge increase in video cameras in public places, but there hasn't been a lot of discussion about the advantages and disadvantages. He believes that people should vote to show if they agree or disagree with public surveillance.

Whether you agree with it or not, the fact is that we live in a world where we are surrounded by surveillance.

Ideas Focus

- Generally, do you agree or disagree with public surveillance? Why? / Why not?
- Is there video camera surveillance in your area? Where?
- How would you feel if there were cameras at your school?

Vocabulary

A Label the pictures with these words.

| batteries | laptop | tablet | camera | satnav | microchip | remote control | USB stick |

_____   _____   _____   _____

_____   _____   _____   _____

B Complete the sentences using two of the words in each group.

1   install   crash   log in

I've just bought this game for my computer and I want to _____ it, but I'm worried that it's going to make my computer _____ again.

2   design   instructions   gadget

I don't understand how this _____ works – where's the _____ for it?

3   revolutionised   developed   experimented

Home computers _____ the world when they first came out and most of us can't remember what life was like before they were _____.

4   research   engineer   process

The _____ who works in my department is doing _____ on a new kind of technology.

5   progress   lab   test

The scientists in the _____ realised that they had to do a different _____ to find the answer to their question.

C Choose the correct answers.

1   What size _____ do I need for the camera, dad?
   a   microchips   b   batteries   c   gadgets

2   _____ are better than tablets for word processing.
   a   Satnavs   b   Laptops   c   USB sticks

3   I love uploading pictures from my _____ onto my laptop and then editing them.
   a   remote control   b   camera   c   satnav

4   He couldn't _____ the game because his laptop had crashed.
   a   install   b   process   c   log in

5   A lot of _____ has been made in the development of computer technology.
   a   protest   b   progress   c   process

6   Tony _____ with different designs for the website on his laptop.
   a   developed   b   experimented   c   installed

7   We have a science _____ at school, but I don't like doing experiments, I prefer maths.
   a   engineer   b   research   c   lab

8   What's my password? I need to _____ to Facebook.
   a   crash   b   log in   c   install

Ideas Focus

- Do you think satnavs are annoying? Why? / Why not?
- Do you enjoy using new gadgets? Why? / Why not?

Grammar

The Passive Voice: Tenses

A **Look at this sentence and notice the verb in bold. Then answer the questions below.**

They **use** cameras in shops to help prevent crime.

1 Is the verb in the active or the passive voice? _____

2 What tense is the verb in? _____

3 What is the subject of the verb? _____

4 What is the object of the verb? _____

B **The sentence in A can also be written in the passive voice. Look at the verb in bold and answer the questions below.**

Cameras **are used** in shops to help prevent crime.

1 What is the subject of the passive verb? _____

2 What tense is the verb *be* in? _____

3 What form of the verb *use* appears? _____

C **Now complete the rules.**
We use the passive voice when we want to emphasise the action or event, or when we don't know the agent (the person/thing who did the action). We form the passive voice by using the auxiliary verb _____ in the correct tense and the past participle of the main verb. The _____ of the active sentence becomes the subject of the passive sentence.

by and *with*

D **Look at the use of *by* and *with* in these sentences and then answer the questions below.**

The laboratory was filled **with** smoke.
The new worker will be shown around the factory **by** the manager.
The computer has been cleaned **with** a special brush.

1 Which word do we use when we want to mention the agent? _____

2 Which word do we use when we want to mention the tool or material that is used? _____

▷ **Grammar Focus pp.169 & 170 (9.1 & 9.2)**

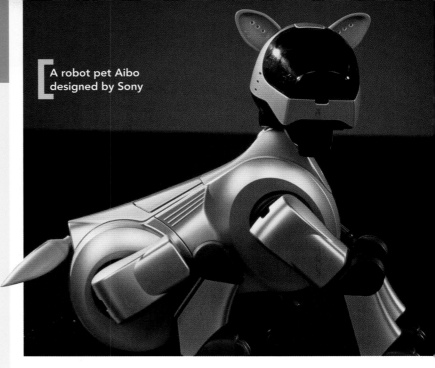

[A robot pet Aibo designed by Sony

E **Complete the sentences with the correct passive form of the verbs in brackets.**

1 My computer _____ (check) for viruses twice a day. It's very practical.

2 _____ (the food / deliver) to the house by lunch time?

3 The USB stick _____ (not need) yet.

4 Her tablet _____ (steal) last week.

5 While the songs _____ (download), I was watching a film online.

6 The young children _____ (teach) how to log in at the moment.

7 It was noon and all the emails _____ (already / send).

8 The new CCTV camera _____ (install) next week

F **Complete the second sentences with the passive voice.**

1 Manufacturers are developing a new type of mobile phone.
A new type of mobile phone _____ _____ manufacturers.

2 Technology has changed our lives dramatically.
Our lives _____ technology.

3 The scientist sent the lab some blood samples.
Some blood samples _____ _____ the scientist.

4 NASA will have designed a new robot for space exploration by 2035.
A new robot for space exploration _____ _____ NASA by 2035.

5 We will give Maria instructions on what to do.
Maria _____ on what to do.

6 Will science ever answer people's questions about the universe?
Will people's questions about the universe _____ science?

Listening

A Circle the odd ones out.

1	toy	laser	model
2	gadget	device	battery
3	fossil fuel	ecofriendly	recycled
4	interactive	individual	participate
5	try out	test	attach
6	exhibition	prediction	presentation

B 9.1 ▶️ **Listen to these people talking and write T (True) or F (False).**

1 The man wants to become a professional engineer.

2 The boy is going to try out a mountain bike before he gets one.

3 The man can't understand how to make the gadget work.

4 The girl doesn't like science and technology at school.

5 The boy made a solar-powered model boat first.

Exam Task

You will hear part of an interview about a technology exhibition. For each question, circle the correct option **a**, **b** or **c**.

1 When is the exhibition?
   a Saturday and Sunday, 10 am – 6 pm
   b Saturday and Sunday, 10.30 am – 6 pm
   c Saturday only, 10 am – 6 pm

2 Who is the exhibition for?
   a only engineers
   b only people who like science and technology
   c families and young people

3 What is true about the models that Julia describes?
   a They are all solar-powered.
   b They are all powered by batteries.
   c They are made by professional engineers.

4 What are the competitions for?
   a The craziest design.
   b The fastest battery-powered car.
   c The most unusual design.

5 What does Julia say about new technology at the exhibition?
   a that it is not usually eco-friendly
   b that some devices are designed to protect the environment
   c that green technology is very exensive

6 Julie says…
   a you can test gadgets and devices before you buy them.
   b entertainment and music gadgets are the most popular.
   c shops don't often sell eco-friendly gadgets.

C Read the *Exam Close-up*. Then read the *Exam Task* and underline all the key words. What do you think you will hear for each question?

D 9.2 ▶️ Now complete the *Exam Task*.

E 9.2 ▶️ Listen again and check your answers carefully.

Exam Close-up

Listening again
- Remember, you will hear the recording twice so the first time you listen, note down any answers you are not sure about.
- The second time you listen, check the answers you are happy with and concentrate on the questions you haven't answered yet.
- Don't leave any blank answers. Guess if you have to.

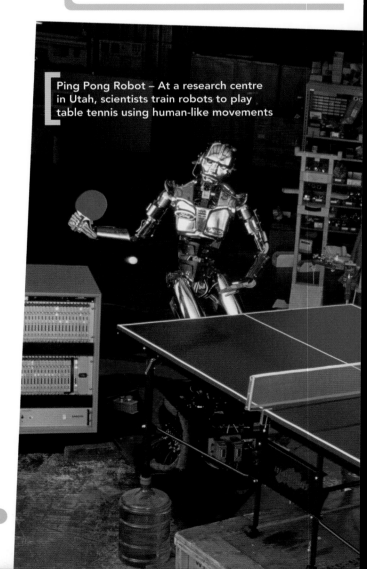

Ping Pong Robot – At a research centre in Utah, scientists train robots to play table tennis using human-like movements

Speaking

A **Work with a partner and answer these questions.**

- What kind of gadgets do you use on a daily basis?
- What are the advantages and disadvantages of having a mobile phone?
- Are there any electronic devices that you would like to have, but you don't own?

B **Look at the list of electronic devices a school might have. Order them from 1 (most important) to 8 (least important).**

- ☐ camera
- ☐ headphones
- ☐ alarm system
- ☐ air conditioning
- ☐ laptop
- ☐ microwave oven
- ☐ TV
- ☐ security doors

C **Read the *Exam Close-up*. Then work with a partner and discuss your lists in B and make a decision on the final list.**

D **Now work with a partner and complete the *Exam Task*. Use the *Useful Expressions* to help you.**

Exam Task

Imagine that your school wants to buy new equipment for their media centre. Talk together about the different things they could buy.

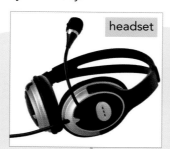
headset

camera

laptop

tablet

Buying new equipment

television

Now decide which one would be best for the students.

Vocabulary

Prepositions

A Complete the phrases with these prepositions. You will need to use some prepositions more than once.

about	for	in	of	on	to	under	with

1 communicate _____ somebody
2 be successful _____ doing something
3 come _____ threat
4 look _____ answers
5 be an expert _____ something
6 go _____ safari
7 concerned _____ something
8 lead _____ something
9 rely _____ something/somebody
10 use something instead _____ something else

An elephant on the Sabi Sand Reserve

B Circle the correct words.

CyberTracker

If you ever go (**1**) on / at safari, you may see huge herds of zebras, elephants and giraffes. But people are beginning to get concerned (**2**) about / around many species, because their natural habitat is starting to disappear and this could lead (**3**) on / to them coming (**4**) into / under threat.

Conservationists are looking (**5**) for / from answers and have turned to animal trackers for their help. Animal trackers are experts (**6**) on / at the animals which live on their land. They know what they eat and drink and where they sleep. However, there is a problem with relying (**7**) on / in them for information: they aren't always able to communicate (**8**) with / from the conservationists because they often don't read or write.

This is where technology has been helping out. Software developed by CyberTracker Conservation in Africa allows animal trackers to record their observations using pictures instead (**9**) of / up words. This makes data collection much faster, so larger amounts of high quality information are collected over a shorter period of time.

Hopefully, with new inventions like this available, we will be successful (**10**) from / in helping to save endangered species and the environments they live in.

C Complete the sentences with correct prepositions from A.

1 The conservationists deal with species that come _____ threat from man.
2 People have many forms of technology that help them communicate _____ others.
3 With this new invention, we hope we'll be successful _____ stopping illegal poaching.
4 People are still looking _____ answers to solve the world's problems.
5 What will all this crime lead _____? It's a very worrying issue.
6 I don't like to rely _____ anyone; I'm very independent.
7 The scientist is an expert _____ endangered animals and habitats.
8 When we went _____ safari, we were driven around in a jeep.
9 Are you concerned _____ the number of closed-circuit TVs there are in the city?
10 Batteries were used instead _____ electricity to power the phone.

Ideas Focus

• Do you think gadgets help people to communicate with each other? Why? / Why not?

Grammar

The Passive Voice: Gerunds, Infinitives & Modal Verbs

A Read the sentences and note the passive verbs in bold. Then answer the questions below.

   a I imagine **being watched** by cameras is not pleasant.
   b The scientist decided **to be involved** in the project.
   c The public **should be told** about the dangers of mobile phones.

Which sentence uses
1 a modal verb and a bare infinitive? ☐
2 a full infinitive? ☐
3 a gerund? ☐

B Complete the rules.
We form the passive of a gerund with _____ + past participle. We form the passive of a full infinitive with _____ + past participle. We form the passive of a bare infinitive with _____ + past participle.

▶ Grammar Focus p.170 (9.3)

C Choose the correct answers.

Robots

The word 'robot' was introduced for the first time in 1921 by the Czech writer Karel Capek in his play *Rossum's Universal Robots*. These robots were like humans because they could think for themselves. When we hear the word 'robot' nowadays, we think of a machine that must (**1**) ____ what to do and that cannot think for itself.

But can a robot that shows emotions (**2**) ____? Actually, yes, and it's already been done! A robot called Kismet has been developed with eyes, lips and ears. These features move and allow emotions (**3**) ____. Kismet doesn't enjoy (**4**) ____, so when that happens he looks sad. He loves attention, though, so when he sees a human face, he smiles. Other expressions such as interest, calm, surprise, anger and happiness can also (**5**) ____ on his face.

At present, other robots are being made that will be able to play sports, so in the future people might not (**6**) ____ millions to play for the best teams. Everyone will be cheering on their robot heroes instead!

D Complete the second sentences in the passive voice.

1 They should deliver our new state of the art computers today.
   Our new state of the art computers should _____ today.
2 The government is going to build a modern science museum.
   A modern science museum is going to _____ by the government.
3 I remember somebody giving me a digital watch.
   I remember _____ a digital watch.
4 The scientist doesn't like his colleagues telling him lies.
   The scientist doesn't like _____ lies by his colleagues.
5 Can you repair the machine?
   Can the machine _____?
6 Does he have to hand in the project today?
   Does the project have to _____ today?

A robot design with human features

1   **a** be told   **b** to be told   **c** being told
2   **a** be created   **b** to be created   **c** being created
3   **a** be expressed   **b** to be expressed   **c** being expressed
4   **a** be left alone   **b** to be left alone   **c** being left alone
5   **a** be seen   **b** to be seen   **c** being seen
6   **a** be paid   **b** to be paid   **c** being paid

Writing: sentence transformation (2)

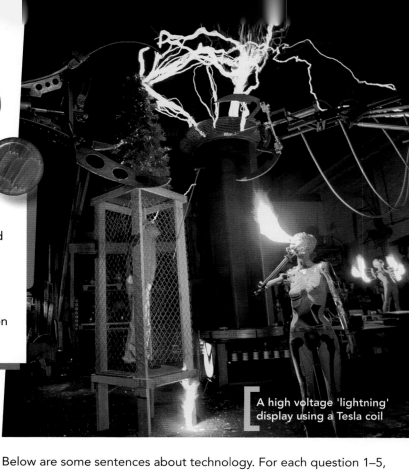

A high voltage 'lightning' display using a Tesla coil

Learning Focus

Using collocations

- Some words always go together, these are called 'collocations'.
- It's a good idea to keep a list of collocations and add to your list every time you learn a new one.
- Collocations in English can be grouped like this:

  verb + noun, e.g. keep a diary

  adjective + noun, e.g. natural habitat
- You can also list verbs + prepositions, e.g. rely on or adjectives + prepositions, e.g. angry with or phrasal verbs, e.g. hang out

A Match 1–8 with a–h.

1	break	☐	**a**	in love
2	renewable	☐	**b**	species
3	cope	☐	**c**	up
4	endangered	☐	**d**	with
5	proud	☐	**e**	judo
6	fall	☐	**f**	energy
7	do	☐	**g**	food
8	tasty	☐	**h**	of

B Write an example sentence for each of the collocations or phrasal verbs in A.

C Read the writing task on the right and answer the questions below.

1 What are all the sentences about?
2 How many exam questions are there?
3 Which sentence has the gap?
4 Do both sentences need to be the same?
5 How many words can you write?

D Read the writing task again. Why has the student underlined some of the words?

Below are some sentences about technology. For each question 1–5, complete the second sentence so that it means the same as the first. Use no more than three words.

GENERAL CERTIFICATE EXAM

SECTION A

Answer the questions below.

1. He started doing photography when he was ten years-old.
He was ten years-old when he took photography _____.

2. They should order new laptops because the ones we have now are too slow!
New laptops should _____ because the ones we have now are too slow!

3. You have to put batteries in before you can use the device.
This _____ doesn't work without batteries.

4. He isn't able to use the camera.
He _____ use the camera.

5. It isn't necessary for you to bring your laptop.
You don't _____ bring your laptop.

E Now look at the gaps in the writing task and see what word or words are missing. Then complete the sentences.

F Read the *Exam Close-up* and then check your answers carefully.

G Now read the *Exam Task* and underline all the key words. Try and identify what type of word is missing from each gap.

H Complete the *Exam Task*. Remember to check your answers carefully when you have finished.

Exam Task

Here are some sentences about technology. For each question 1–5, complete the second sentence so that it means the same as the first. **Use no more than three words.**

1 I remember that the teacher told us how to download this program.

I remember we _____ by the teacher how to download this program.

2 How about going to the technology exhibition?

_____ don't we go to the technology exhibition?

3 This shop sells all kinds of electrical devices; laptops, USB sticks and even microwave ovens!

This shop sells everything _____ laptops to microwave ovens!

4 You ought to try this game. It's fantastic!

This game is fantastic! You _____ try it.

5 He continued to use the laptop after class.

He _____ using the laptop after class.

Exam Close-up

Checking the meaning

- When you are transforming sentences in the exam, it is important to make sure your completed sentence means the same as the first sentence.

- Read each first sentence carefully and underline the key word or words.

- Read the second sentence, look back at the key words you have underlined in the first sentence, and think about what type of word or words are needed to complete the second sentence.

- If you have used a collocation or phrasal verb, make sure you have written the correct word and not repeated any by accident.

- Check that your second sentence makes sense and that you have not used too many words.

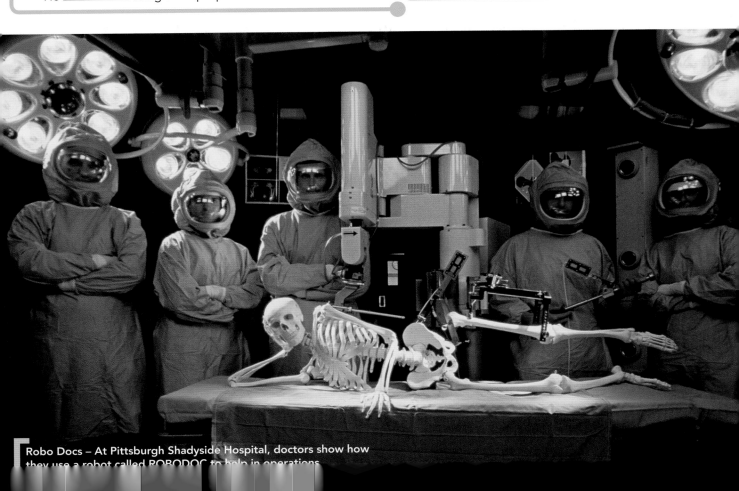

Robo Docs – At Pittsburgh Shadyside Hospital, doctors show how they use a robot called ROBODOC to help in operations.

9 Mars Rovers

Marfa, Texas

Before you watch

A Work with a partner and answer these questions.

- How has technology changed our lives?
- Do you think that we rely too much on technology? Why? / Why not?
- What technological advances do you think we'll see in the near future?

While you watch

B Watch the video and decide if these statements are T (True) or F (False).

1 Mars has so far been too far away and dangerous for humans to explore. ☐
2 Spirit landed first after a seventy-month trip. ☐
3 To look for water, the robots carried equipment to measure the water in the rocks. ☐
4 The rovers also carried special cameras for scientists to record images of the planet's rocks. ☐
5 Spirit moved on to an area that had been a volcano. ☐
6 The discoveries of the two Mars rovers answered some old questions, but they also brought up many new ones. ☐

After you watch

C Complete the summary of the video below using these words.

| alternative | find | existed | operate | patterns | rough | signs | whereas |

The planet Mars is very interesting to scientists because it is the closest and the most similar planet to Earth. For example, Mars has seasons with different weather, (1) _____ other planets have the same temperatures all year round. Did life exist on Mars?
To (2) _____ out, scientists need to know if Mars ever had water. In 2004, two robot explorers, or 'rovers', called Spirit and Opportunity were sent to Mars to look for (3) _____ of water. These rovers can drive over rocks and all kinds of (4) _____ ground. They can also (5) _____ cameras and send photos back to Earth. First, the two rovers found chemicals and (6) _____ in the rocks that were probably made by water. Then, they moved to a(n) (7) _____ area and found other rocks which may have been created by water. Now scientists think there was probably water on the planet long ago. They still don't know if life ever (8) _____ on Mars, but they received a lot of important information that will help them in the future.

Spirit and its twin robot Opportunity have travelled more than 20 km across the rocky surface of Mars and have given us a lot of new information about the planet

Ideas Focus

- Are you interested in space exploration? Why? / Why not?
- Do you think that space exploration is important? Why? / Why not?
- What has mankind gained from space exploration?

120

10 That's Entertainment

Reading:	short texts, multiple-choice questions, checking similar words
Vocabulary:	entertainment-related words, phrasal verbs
Grammar:	reported speech: statements, questions, commands & requests
Listening:	gap-fill, completing information
Speaking:	talking about entertainment, describing photos, talking about a photo, describing people, places & things
Writing:	letter or story, ordering ideas, choosing the right question, free-time activities

A girl break dancing

Reading

A Work in pairs. Match the instruments to these countries.

| Australia | Greece | Scotland | Trinidad & Tobago |

1 _____   3 _____

2 _____   4 _____

bouzouki

2 steel drum

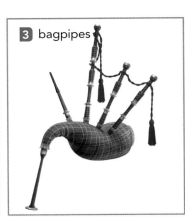

3 bagpipes

4 didgeridoo

B Quickly read the short texts below. Which ones are about music or instruments?

Word Focus

reschedule: change the time of a planned event
enquiry: an act of asking for information
attach: join something to something else
purchase: to buy

1

Becky

Mrs Potts rang to reschedule your singing lesson. She says she can see you at 5. Dad will collect you at 4.30. Please be ready and don't forget your sheet music.

Mum

2

< Back   **Inbox**

🔍 Search

Selfie Productions   16 January 2014 14:26
To: Kate Blankette
Other: Your enquiry

Thank you for your enquiry.

The next series of 'Glad!' will be filmed in May. Auditions for young actors will commence in February. Please fill in the attached application form and return it by 31st January.

3

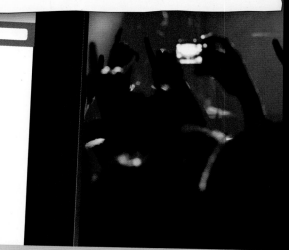

FOR SALE

ACOUSTIC GUITAR
Suitable for ages 12–14

Purchased new 2 years ago
No scratches or marks
Will exchange for drum kit
Phone Jim: 9563–8992

C Read the *Exam Close-up*. Then read the *Exam Task* and identify the different text types.

D Now complete the *Exam Task*. Remember to read the complete section with similar words to the answer options.

Exam Task

Look at each of the texts for each question. What do they say? Mark the correct letter **a**, **b** or **c**.

1 What should Harry do?
   a Buy tickets for him and Max.
   b Collect his ticket himself.
   c Meet Max outside the box office.

2 Why can adults not see The Smash live?
   a Their album can be bought at Festival Hall.
   b The concert on Saturday is only for students.
   c There are no more tickets left for the concert.

3 What must Becky do?
   a Get ready for her singing lesson before her dad arrives.
   b Ask her father for a lift to the singing lesson.
   c Collect her things for the singing lesson from her father.

4 Why has the email been written?
   a to make an appointment with Kate
   b to give Kate the information she requested
   c to tell Kate about a new TV show

5 The advert says the guitar
   a is in good condition.
   b comes with a drum set.
   c is almost 14 years old.

Exam Close-up

Checking similar words
- Be careful with words that are the same in the answer options and in the text; they often say something different.
- Read the answer option with the similar word(s) carefully. Then read the section in the text with the similar word and think about the meaning of that complete section or sentence. Does *is* mean the same as the answer option?

E Find the meaning of these words in the text. Then complete the sentences below.

audition	sheet music	scratch	box office	hit	drum kit

1 You can pay for tickets in cash or by credit card at the _____.

2 Here is the _____; you can read the musical notes on it.

3 He's a really good actor; I'm sure he will do well at the _____ and get the part in the film.

4 Tommy! Look at the piano! There's a huge _____ on it! Were you playing with your cars on it?

5 My son wants a _____ for his birthday but I don't like the idea of having a drummer in the house!

6 I don't like One Direction's new _____. Their last song was much better.

THE SMASH
Playing <u>hits</u> from their album
London Falling
Saturday 14th June, 8pm, Festival Hall
£50.00 / Students £30.00
Sorry, <u>SOLD OUT!</u>

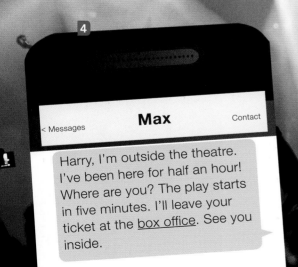

Max   Contact
< Messages

Harry, I'm outside the theatre. I've been here for half an hour! Where are you? The play starts in five minutes. I'll leave your ticket at the <u>box office</u>. See you inside.

- What is your favourite kind of music? Who is your favourite singer or group? Discuss with a partner.
- What do you think makes a good song?

Ideas Focus

Vocabulary

A Look at the words in 1–5 below and match them with the photos a–e.

1 reality show, soap opera, _____ ☐
2 producer, actor, _____ ☐
3 stage, dressing room, _____ ☐
4 play, lines, _____ ☐
5 lyrics, singer, _____ ☐

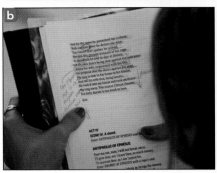

B Now complete the word groups in A with the words below.

director   box office   documentary   musician   script

C Work with a partner and add more verbs, nouns or adjectives to each word group in A.

D Choose the correct answers.

1 "Was Quentin Tarantino the _____ on this film?"
 "No! It was Martin Scorsese!"
 a director   **b** musician   **c** actor

2 Ken might not write or play music, but he's an amazing _____ .
 a singer   **b** musician   **c** play

3 I love the _____ of this song; they're sad, but wonderful!
 a lyrics   **b** producer   **c** script

4 All the _____ went on TV to talk about the film.
 a actors   **b** documentaries   **c** lines

5 They told us we could pick up our tickets at the _____ before the show.
 a stage   **b** dressing room   **c** box office

6 I can't imagine acting in the same _____ year after year.
 It must be boring!
 a reality show   **b** soap opera   **c** stage

7 I don't like _____ like Big Brother; I would never go on TV and show off like that!
 a reality shows   **b** soap operas   **c** documentaries

8 The actor couldn't remember his _____ so the director told him to go home and learn them.
 a script   **b** dressing room   **c** lines

9 The play was performed in an open-air theatre so the actors on _____ got wet when it rained.
 a musicians   **b** lines   **c** stage

10 A _____ is concerned with the money that is needed to make a film.
 a singer   **b** box office   **c** producer

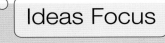

Ideas Focus

- Do you like soap operas? Why? / Why not?
- Do you think reality shows are good? Why? / Why not?

Grammar

Reported Speech: Statements

A Underline the verbs, pronouns and time expressions in these sentences. Notice what changes occur.

'**I went** to a great concert **last week**,' Kathy said.
Kathy said that **she had been** to a great concert **the week before**.

B Complete the rules.
We use reported speech to tell someone what another person has said. The main verb usually moves back one tense into the _____. We also change pronouns and possessive adjectives where necessary and there are often changes in words that show _____ and place.

C Underline the reporting verbs in these sentences. What is the difference in the structure of the sentences?

My piano teacher said that I had improved.
My piano teacher told me that I had improved.

D Complete the rules.
We can use the verbs *say* and *tell* to report speech. When we use _____, we follow it with an object.

▷ Grammar Focus p.170 & 171 (10.1 to 10.3)

E Circle the correct words.

1 My uncle told / said that *Conquest* was the best film he'd ever seen.
2 I couldn't believe it when my drama teacher said that she / I had acted on Broadway.
3 We told our parents that we would go to the opera with them the last week / next day.
4 David said he had given Jenny his music book the day before / yesterday.
5 The director said he was busy at the moment / at that moment.
6 Mrs Hill said her son's friend had scratched her / its violin.
7 Tina told me that you / I thought the song lyrics to *Mamma Mia* were great.
8 I told / said Jodie that she had an audition on Thursday afternoon.

F Change the direct speech into reported speech.

1 'I enjoyed the party last night,' Veronica said.
   Veronica said _____.
2 'My mum doesn't like this reality show,' Tom said.
   Tom said _____.
3 'We're going to visit the National Art Gallery tomorrow,' Mrs Jones told us.
   Mrs Jones told _____.
4 'Susan and Amanda will help me learn my lines,' said Natalie.
   Natalie said _____.
5 'I must finish my film review tonight,' Samantha said.
   Samantha said _____.
6 'I'm watching an interesting documentary at the moment,' Dad said.
   Dad said _____.
7 'Matthew joined the drama group last month,' Bill told me.
   Bill told _____.
8 'My grandmother has seen *The Phantom of the Opera*,' Vanessa told us.
   Vanessa told _____.

Listening

A Match the sections of a theatre a–e with the words below.

1 costumes ☐   2 backstage ☐   3 dressing room ☐   4 stage ☐

B Where would you find props in the theatre?

C 10.1 ▶❙❙ Listen to five people talking and write the words from A and B that they are talking about.

1 _____
2 _____
3 _____
4 _____
5 _____

D Read the *Exam Close-up*. Then read the *Exam Task* carefully and imagine the words which could complete the gaps.

E 10.2 ▶❙❙ Now listen and complete the *Exam Task*.

F 10.2 ▶❙❙ Listen again and check your answers.

Exam Close-up

Completing information

- Read and listen to the exam instructions carefully first.
- Then read the heading and the information and try to think of words that could fit in each gap.
- Remember you can write numbers as 10 or ten.
- It's important to fill in the exact words you hear and to write no more than three words.
- Check your answers and spelling carefully when you listen again.

Exam Task

You will hear some information about a school music and dance competition.
For each question, fill in the missing information in the numbered space.

School Music and Dance Competition

Length of performance: 20 to (**1**) _____ minutes.
Four main performers: one musician, one singer and two (**2**) _____
Subject this year: (**3**) _____
Dance teams should mix (**4**) _____ and _____ styles
Judges: Mark Wilson; contemporary dancer and

GGCoolK; rapper who has her first (**5**) _____ on the Internet.
First prize: visit to Westbeat International Academy
Other prizes: trip to a West End (**6**) _____ in London and set of sheet music.
Final performance: in Town Council Hall. Space for (**7**) _____ people.

Speaking

A Work with a partner and answer these questions.

- What is your favourite instrument? Why?
- Do you play any instruments?
- How many instruments do you know how to say in English? Make a list.

B Work with a partner. Student A looks at picture A and Student B looks at picture B.

> Take it in turns to describe your picture to your partner and then together identify two differences and two similarities between the two pictures.

C Read the *Exam Close-up*. Then read the *Exam Task* below. Are the photos similar?

D Work with a partner and complete the *Exam Task* below. Remember to describe your photo in detail. Use the *Useful Expressions* to help you.

Exam Close-up

Talking about a photo

- Remember to describe the people, places and things you can see in detail – imagine you are describing it to someone who can't see it.
- If you don't know a specific word, don't worry. Try to paraphrase and describe it in a different way.
- Remember you only have about one minute to describe the photo.

Exam Task

Student A looks at photograph 1 and describes what he or she can see. Student B listens. Then student B describes photograph 2 and Student A listens.

Useful Expressions

Describing people	**Describing places**	**Describing things**
She's got …	There are lots of …	It's a kind of …
He's wearing …	It looks like a …	I think it's a …
They're smiling …	I can see a … behind / in front of	It looks old / new / expensive …
He's sitting …	There's a … in the foreground / background	It could be …

- Is music important to you? Why? / Why not?
- Do you have to learn a musical instrument from a young age to be good at it? Why? / Why not?

Ideas Focus

Vocabulary

Phrasal verbs

A Rewrite the sentences below in your notebook replacing the words in bold with these phrasal verbs.

> turn away   turn down   turn off   turn on
> turn out   turn up

1 The documentary didn't **end in a particular way** to be very good.
2 The security guards might **refuse** me **admission** if I don't have a ticket for the concert.
3 Can you **switch on** the radio as my favourite programme is on in a minute?
4 Bob, **decrease the volume of** the music. It's too loud!
5 Could you **increase the volume of** the television, Mum? I can't hear a thing.
6 Make sure you **switch off** the electric guitar when you have finished using it.

B Match the phrasal verbs in bold 1–6 to their meanings a–f.

1 I'm not sure that type of music will **catch on**. It's too weird. ☐
2 I need you to **give out** these flyers about the rap competition. ☐
3 I must buy a ticket for the Madonna concert before they **sell out**. ☐
4 The drama group are going to **act out** the scene before they film it. ☐
5 I used to like magic shows but I've **grown out of** them now. ☐
6 I need to **get** these lyrics **down** on paper before I forget them. ☐

a run out of tickets for an event
b become too old for
c distribute
d become popular
e write down
f perform

C Complete the second sentence with the phrasal verbs from A and B so it means the same as the first. Use no more than three words.

1 'The play was very good in the end.'
She said that the play had _____ to be good.

2 He said that he didn't think hip-hop would ever become popular with older people.
'I don't think hip-hop will ever _____ with older people.'

3 'I think you should perform the scene a few more times before opening night.' the director said.
The director said they should _____ the scene a few more times before opening night.

4 The interviewer said that it was very interesting and she wanted to write it down.
'That's very interesting. Let me _____ that _____,' the interviewer said.

5 'We have to get the tickets now before they run out of them,' she said to me.
She said we had to get the tickets before they _____ .

6 My dad told us that he had loved reggae when he was younger, but that he's become too old for it now.
'I loved reggae when I was younger but I've _____ it now.'

7 'The club was full and they refused us admission at the door,' she said.
She said that the club had been full and that they _____ them _____ at the door.

8 They said they were distributing free concert tickets for that weekend.
'We're _____ free concert tickets for this weekend!'

Ideas Focus

- Have you ever been turned away from an event? What happened?
- Have you grown out of anything that you liked? Why do you think this is?

128

Grammar

Reported Speech: Questions, Commands & Requests

A Read the direct and reported questions and underline the verbs in each.

1 'Which instrument do you like the best?' Jason asked me. Jason asked me which instrument I liked the best.

2 'Did you enjoy the arts festival?' my friend asked me. My friend asked me if/whether I had enjoyed the arts festival.

B Answer the questions a–c below.

a When a direct question has a question word, do we use it in the reported question? _____

b When a direct question doesn't have a question word, which words can we use in the reported question? _____

c Is the word order in the reported questions the same as the word order in the direct questions? _____

C Read the sentences and answer the questions below.

1 The museum employee told us not to touch the exhibits.

2 Our music teacher asked us to join the choir.

a Which sentence is an example of a reported request? ☐

b Which sentence is an example of a reported command? ☐

▶ Grammar Focus p.171 (10.4 to 10.6)

D Change the direct speech into reported speech.

1 'Turn down the volume!' my sister told me.
My sister told me _____.

2 'Where is the concert hall?' the tourist asked.
The tourist asked _____.

3 'Do you like hip-hop music,' Maria asked.
Maria asked me _____.

4 'Don't play your drums all day!' Mum told me.
Mum told me _____.

5 'Do you like the film?' asked Melanie.
Melanie asked us _____.

6 'Please don't be late,' Aunt Judy said to us.
Aunt Judy asked us _____.

7 'Please sit down,' our teacher told us.
Our teacher asked us _____.

8 'Can you get me a ticket for the play, please?' my friend asked me.
My friend asked me _____.

E Change the reported speech into direct speech in your notebooks.

1 Joanna asked Harry if he liked the lyrics.

2 Grant told us that he had been chosen for the school band.

3 She asked her best friend to download some songs for her.

4 Brett asked me what type of music I was listening to.

5 Julia told her friend not to take a photo of her.

Writing: a letter or story

Learning Focus

Ordering ideas

- When you write a letter or story, there are words and phrases that can help you to order your ideas.
- Use *First of all* to introduce the first event or action, e.g. *First of all we went to the theatre.*
- You can use *while* for two things happening at the same time, e.g. *He looked at the posters while she was buying the tickets.*
- Use *then, after that, after* or *before* for things that happen one after another, e.g. *After going into the theatre, they sat down and looked around. Then they …*
- To introduce a final event, use *Finally* or *In the end*, e.g. *Finally, the lights went off and the play started.*

A Write the sentences in the correct order in your notebook.

1 stage / actor / First of all / came / onto / the / the
2 began / he / to say / Then / lines / his
3 started / spoke / He / beautifully / then / and / to sing
4 while / audience / performed / listened / he / The
5 closed / After / had / curtain / finished / the / he
6 cheered / audience / Finally / the / and clapped

B Read the two exam writing questions. What do you need to write for each one?

1 This is part of a letter you receive from your Australian pen-pal.

> *In after-school club we are doing a project on what young people do at the weekend all over the world. What do you usually do? Please tell me so I can write about you!*

2 Your English teacher has asked you to write a story. Your story must begin with this sentence: *Charlie woke up and remembered it was the weekend.*

C Now read the example writing and answer the questions.

a Which question in B did the student answer?
b Did she answer the exam question? Why? / Why not?

Hi Ella,

Thanks for your letter. Yes, I can help you! Your project sounds interesting.

(1) _____, on Saturdays I have a piano class at 10am and (2) _____ we go swimming at 11.30. (3) _____, I go home for lunch and a rest.
I'm always very tired by lunchtime! In the afternoon, I go to my cousin's house (4) _____ my mum is working.

On Sundays, we watch TV (5) _____ breakfast (6) _____ get dressed.
I love Sundays! Do you like Sundays?

Love,

Katie

D Read the example letter again and complete it with the words and phrases below.

> while   before   then   First of all   then
> After that

E Put Katie's paragraph plan in the correct order. Write 1, 2 and 3.

Para ____: Best day! Programmes, food, clothes.

Para ____: thank you, help - yes, good project

Para ____: morning activities, tired! pm to auntie Carol's

F Read the *Exam Close-up*. Then read the *Exam Tasks* and decide which one is the best for you.

G Complete the *Exam Task*. Remember to use the *Useful Expressions* to help you.

Exam Close-up

Choosing the right question

- If you can't choose which question to do in the exam, look at the options and decide which one will be the easiest for you to do.
- Read the options carefully and spend a short time thinking of ideas for each one.
- Choose the one you have the most ideas for.

Useful Expressions

Free-time activities

I play football / tennis / volleyball …

I'm in an orchestra / choir …

We usually …

I do aerobics / judo / karate

I have a … class.

After-school club

… until late

I go swimming / running … with

… is great fun!

I love my … because

Exam Task

Write an answer to one of the questions below. Write your answer in about 100 words.

1   This is part of a letter you receive from a Canadian friend.

In school we are doing a project on what young people do after-school all over the world. What do you usually do? Please tell me so I can write about you!

2   Your English teacher has asked you to write a story. Your story must begin with this sentence:
Finally, school finished and Charlie quickly ran to …

A girl plays a bandurria in a youth orchestra

10 Steel Drums

Trinidad and Tobago, Caribbean

Before you watch

A Look at the photos below and read the captions. How do you think steel drums are made?

While you watch

B Watch the video and circle the words you hear.

1 Steelband music is a famous / popular part of life here.
2 Through the island's streets and markets, you can't escape / avoid the music.
3 At first, people played these African rhythms / sounds by hitting old tin cans.
4 Most players don't use notes / music written on paper.
5 It takes a long time to make / tune the drums.
6 It's part of the local culture, showing the world the music / creativity of the island's people.

After you watch

C Complete the summary of the video below using these words.

backgrounds   belongs   culture   fills   influenced   instruments   invented   lively

Trinidad and Tobago is home to a(n) **(1)** _____ kind of music. The sound of the steelband drum, which is called *pan* by the locals, **(2)** _____ the air of this island nation and brings people of different **(3)** _____ together. The steelband sound comes from Trinidad and Tobago and was **(4)** _____ in the 20th century. How was it created? Trinidad produces oil and during the 1940s, people began using oil drums as musical **(5)** _____. The steelband sound has **(6)** _____ all kinds of music throughout the Caribbean region. Most steelband players do not read music. They play music by ear until they get a song right. For the people of Trinidad, the steelband drum is more than just an instrument. It is part of their **(7)** _____. Steelband music **(8)** _____ to the people of Trinidad and Tobago, but they want to share it with the world.

Steel drum: A steel drum is a musical instrument

Oil drum: An oil drum is a large container that holds oil

Ideas Focus

- Most steelband drummers play music 'by ear'. What does this mean?
- Do you think steelband music is similar or different to other music discussed in this unit Why / Why not?

Vocabulary

A Match.

1	USB	☐	**a**	lab
2	surveillance	☐	**b**	oven
3	science	☐	**c**	control
4	state	☐	**d**	TV
5	battery	☐	**e**	exploration
6	box	☐	**f**	energy
7	closed-circuit	☐	**g**	camera
8	remote	☐	**h**	powered
9	microwave	☐	**i**	stick
10	renewable	☐	**j**	of the art
11	space	☐	**k**	office
12	dressing	☐	**l**	room

B Complete the sentences using these words.

> revolutionised   microchip   gadget   log in   install   lyrics   lines   release

1 The famous rock star will _____ his new album next month.
2 That singer writes all the _____ and the music for his songs.
3 I just have to get this _____. It's a pocket-sized computer!
4 Ricky is a technician, so he can help you _____ software on your PC.
5 The actor didn't learn his _____, so his acting wasn't very convincing.
6 It's amazing that this gadget works on just a tiny _____.
7 The arrival of the Internet completely _____ the way people work and entertain themselves.
8 I can't _____ on Stella's computer because I don't know her password.

C Choose the correct answers.

1 Mum's got a headache! Please turn ___ the music.
   a up   **b** into   **c** down

2 As soon as iPhones came out, they caught ___.
   a up   **b** off   **c** on

3 The producer was concerned ___ the amount of money being spent on the film.
   a for   **b** about   **c** at

4 The computers at work have crashed and this could lead ___ problems in production.
   a to   **b** on   **c** by

5 The composer is looking ___ talented singers to perform his songs.
   a for   **b** to   **c** down

6 I can't log ___ to my computer. I've forgotten my password.
   a in   **b** at   **c** up

7 The director didn't expect the film to turn ___ to be so successful.
   a out   **b** in   **c** down

8 He is an expert ___ computers.
   a with   **b** on   **c** for

9 The alarm next door was set ___ and went on ringing for hours.
   a of   **b** off   **c** on

10 We didn't see the play because all the tickets were sold ___.
   a off   **b** by   **c** out

Grammar

A **Change the sentences from the Active into the Passive or from the Passive into the Active.**

1　The technician has installed a new sound system in the studio.
　_____

2　Discovery Channel is going to broadcast a new documentary on wildlife.
　_____

3　This new film was recommended by all the critics.
　_____

4　Were the actors given their roles by the director last night?
　_____

5　The company may develop a new gadget next year.
　_____

6　The famous film star doesn't enjoy fans and photographers following him.
　_____

7　The director is admired by a great number of actors.
　_____

8　The singer wasn't recording a new album last year.
　_____

9　The company wanted the new device to be manufactured.
　_____

10　The release of the soundtrack had been announced before 9 o'clock.
　_____

B **Complete the sentences in reported speech.**

1　'I'm not going to this concert tonight,' John said.
　John told his friend _____.

2　'I will buy you a laptop!' Mr White said.
　Mr White promised his son that _____.

3　'The head teacher wants to see me tomorrow,' Jess said.
　Jess said _____.

4　'When are we rehearsing the play?' I asked.
　I asked _____.

5　'I have had enough of actors not listening to me,' the director said.
　The director said _____.

6　'Please don't play your music so loudly,' she said.
　She asked me _____.

7　'I'll have the results ready by next month,' said the scientist.
　The scientist promised _____.

8　'Did you get a signed autograph from Rihanna?' we asked Sue.
　We asked Sue _____.

9　'Let's go and buy that new CD by Britney Spears,' John said.
　John suggested _____.

10　'Bob, I think you should replace that old mobile with a new one,' his brother said.
　His brother advised _____.

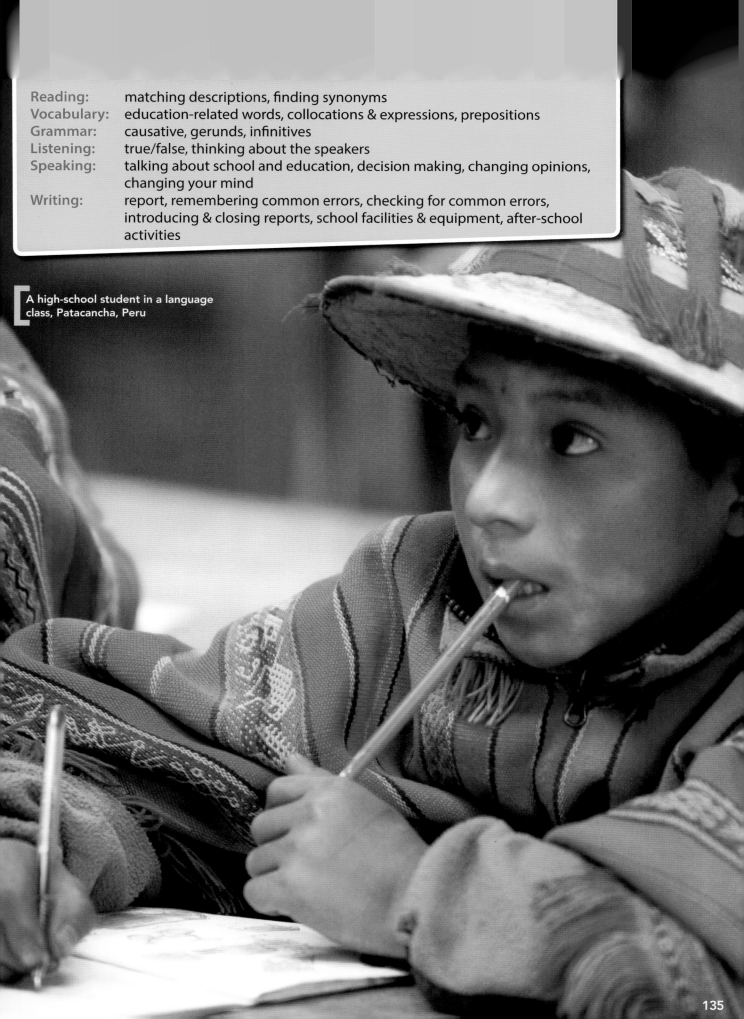

Reading:	matching descriptions, finding synonyms
Vocabulary:	education-related words, collocations & expressions, prepositions
Grammar:	causative, gerunds, infinitives
Listening:	true/false, thinking about the speakers
Speaking:	talking about school and education, decision making, changing opinions, changing your mind
Writing:	report, remembering common errors, checking for common errors, introducing & closing reports, school facilities & equipment, after-school activities

A high-school student in a language class, Patacancha, Peru

Reading

A Which school subjects do you enjoy the most? Why?

B Are any of the subjects below taught at your school? If not, which ones would you like to be taught? Why?

- dance
- drama
- design
- film-making
- computers

C Quickly scan the eight advertisements. Which courses are creative?

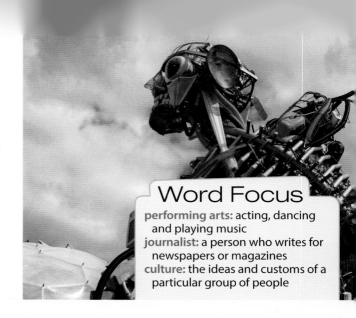

Word Focus

performing arts: acting, dancing and playing music
journalist: a person who writes for newspapers or magazines
culture: the ideas and customs of a particular group of people

THINGS TO DO THIS SUMMER

a | COMPUTERS!

For young fans of computers, a computer course can teach you all kinds of interesting things. How about building your own website or developing your own computer game? It isn't as difficult as it sounds. After just a few weeks, you will be surprised by how much you have learnt.

b | parla italiano!

A beginner's course in Italian takes only six weeks. In that time, you can learn the basic phrases and grammar of the language. It's the perfect course for people who want a good start. After that, you can continue to higher levels.

Love to dance?

Modern dance is a fantastic way to express yourself. There are many different kinds of modern dance and they all make you move! You'll become hot and tired in the classes, but you'll learn a lot, too. Unlike ballet, which has many rules, you can create your own style.

d | BRACELETS, NECKLACES, AND MORE!

Necklaces, earrings, rings and bracelets can say a lot about you and your style. If you can't find exactly what you want in the shops, or if it's too expensive, do a course in jewellery making and create your own unique pieces. It's fun and creative.

DO YOU HAVE WHAT IT TAKES TO SURVIVE?

If you think the summer holidays are dull, then a survival course could add some excitement to your life. The course teaches young explorers how to build a fire and put up a tent, how to climb a tree and how not to get lost in a forest.

Writing courses near you

Do you need to work on your grammar or spelling? Are you creative? Perhaps you want to work for a newspaper one day? These are all very good reasons to do a writing course this summer. It can improve your writing skills for school or work.

LEARN MAGIC!

What could be more fun in the boring summer school holidays than a magic course? You can learn lots of incredible tricks that will amaze and impress your friends. You will be able to make objects vanish, cut someone in half and pull a rabbit out of a hat!

COOK GOOD FOOD

Everyone loves eating, so why not impress your friends and family with great food? Do a cooking course and learn how to make delicious meals like the ones you eat in restaurants. You'll also learn how to cook traditional dishes from around the world.

Finding synonyms

- Remember to underline the key words in the descriptions and to look for synonyms in the texts.
- You will only need to match five of the eight texts, but you must read all of them carefully.
- After you have matched the descriptions and the texts, remember to re-read the three texts you have not used and make sure they don't match any of the descriptions.

D Read the *Exam Close-up*. Then read the *Exam Task* below and underline the key words.

E Now complete the *Exam Task*. Remember to read the descriptions you didn't use again and check they don't match any texts.

Exam Task

The teenagers below are all looking for a summer course to do. Read about the eight summer courses for young people. Decide which course would be the most suitable for the teenagers. For questions 1–5, mark the correct letter a–h.

1 Toby is keen on the performing arts and he's in the drama club at school. He enjoys being creative, and he would like to do a course that will keep him fit. ☐

2 Mei is a sports fan, but she enjoys watching sport more than she likes playing it! Her dream is to be a sports journalist and write about competitions, matches and athletes. ☐

3 Samuel is interested in different cultures. He loves travelling to different countries with his family and enjoying the food and the music there. He wants to remember those experiences again at home. ☐

4 Emma can't afford to spend a lot of money, but she is very good with her hands and makes some of her own clothes. She is very interested in fashion and likes to look trendy. ☐

5 Hans is very interested in cinema and likes classic, black and white European films. One day, he would like to watch his favourite films in their original language and understand them. ☐

F Find words in the course descriptions (in brackets) to complete the sentences below.

1 A(n) _____ is a group of pages on the Internet. (A)

2 Someone who is doing something for the first time is a(n) _____ (B)

3 _____ means not the same as something else. (C)

4 If something is _____, it is special and different. (D)

5 Something that is _____ is very boring. (E)

6 When you _____ something, you try to improve it. (F)

7 _____ is another way of saying 'disappear'. (G)

8 If something is _____, it has continued for a long time without changing. (H)

Ideas Focus

- Are you interested in any of the activities mentioned in the texts? Which ones?
- Would you like to do a summer course? Why? / Why not?
- What kind of courses are the best for people of your age? Why?

Vocabulary

A Circle the odd ones out.

1	education	knowledge	exam
2	diploma	project	certificate
3	fees	grant	application
4	tutor	lecturer	graduate
5	arts	studies	sciences
6	uniform	stapler	folder
7	backpack	timetable	schedule
8	biology	chemistry	physical education (PE)

B Choose the correct answers.

1 My sister has her university _____ paid by my parents.

   a applications   b grants   c fees

2 Professor Oakes is the best _____ in the college; there are queues of students when he gives a talk.

   a tutor   b graduate   c lecturer

3 As far as I'm concerned, nothing is more important in life than a good _____.

   a knowledge   b test   c education

4 Could you put these books in your _____ for me? I'll get them later.

   a schedule   b backpack   c timetable

5 Do students have to wear _____ at your secondary school?

   a uniforms   b folders   c staplers

6 Students must have their _____ graded by no later than 31 January.

   a projects   b diplomas   c certificates

7 Is your brother completing his _____ at the local college?

   a studies   b arts   c sciences

8 I was in my _____ class and I twisted my ankle playing basketball.

   a biology   b chemistry   c physical education

C Complete the sentences using both words.

1 **behave   expel**

The school will _____ this student if he doesn't make more effort to _____.

2 **primary   secondary**

I was in _____ school last year but this year I will be starting _____ school.

3 **fail   pass**

I'm so pleased! I managed to _____ all my exams at school this year. I didn't even _____ maths!

4 **courses   qualifications**

Students can get very good _____ if they manage to complete our computer studies _____.

5 **miss   lose**

Be careful you don't _____ any questions on the test. If you do, you'll _____ some marks.

6 **examiner   candidate**

The _____ taking his oral exam was very nervous before meeting the _____.

7 **lesson   subject**

History is my favourite _____, but today's _____ was unbelievably boring.

8 **accent   pronunciation**

When you learn to speak a foreign language, it doesn't matter if you have a(n) _____, but your _____ should be correct.

D Read the list and tick (✓) the things that are true for you. Then work with a partner and explain why.

- behave well ☐
- miss lessons ☐
- practise pronunciation ☐
- revise for an exam ☐
- fail exams ☐
- pass exams ☐
- have a tidy folder ☐
- enjoy studying ☐
- enjoy PE ☐
- do extra courses after school ☐

Grammar

Causative

A **Read the sentences and then answer the questions.**

    a The student **will have** his essay **checked**.
    b The student **will check** his essay.

    1 In which sentence will the student check his essay himself? ☐
    2 In which sentence will somebody else check his essay? ☐

B **Complete the rule.**
We use the causative to say that we have arranged for somebody to do something for us. We form the causative with _____ + object + past participle. When we want to mention the agent, we use the word *by*.

C **Tick (✓) the sentence which contains the causative.**

    1 She **had** her computer **repaired** before she went to school. ☐
    2 She **had repaired** her computer before she went to school. ☐

> **Be careful**
> 1 Remember that only the verb *have* changes tense.

> ⟳ **Grammar Focus p.171 (11.1)**

D **Put the words in the correct order to make sentences with the causative. Write the sentences in your notebook.**

    1 ? / their sports class / have / the students / had / today / cancelled
    2 will / my project / I / a teacher / by / graded / have
    3 ? / exhibited / going to / are / in the gallery / have / the students / their paintings
    4 taken / at the end / the teachers / of the year / their photos / had
    5 must / their application / by their parents / children under 16 / have / signed
    6 our staff / first aid / had / yet / haven't / we / trained in

E **Complete the sentences using the causative.**

    1 Mr Brown's laptop was stolen at school.
       Mr Brown _____.
    2 New computers have been installed at the college.
       The college _____.
    3 Someone's going to make a new key for me.
       I'm going to _____.
    4 Jane's friend will type her essay for her.
       Jane _____.
    5 Is a swimming pool being built at our school?
       Are we _____?
    6 Mrs Fletcher's children are driven to school every day.
       Mrs Fletcher _____.
    7 The teachers must mark the students' tests by Friday.
       The students must _____.
    8 New desks were delivered to the school.
       The school _____.

Listening

A Match the words and expressions 1-5 with the definitions a-e.

1 an exchange programme ☐
2 a host family ☐
3 embarrassed ☐
4 to miss ☐
5 to adapt ☐

a feel stupid or self-conscious
b accept, get used to
c remember and want someone / something
d a school trip where students live in a different country
e people who offer students a place to live and stay

B Read the *Exam Close-up* and the *Exam Task* below. Then underline the key words in the questions.

C Work with a partner. Compare the words you underlined in the *Exam Task*. What do you think the speakers will say.

D 11.1 ▶️ Now complete the *Exam Task*.

Exam Close-up

Thinking about the speakers

- Remember, it's important to read the instructions carefully to understand what the listening will be about.
- Read the sentences and underline any key words or expressions.
- Think about similar words or expressions the speakers could use.
- Try to imagine what the speakers will say if each answer is true and if each answer is false.

Exam Task

Look at the six sentences. You will hear two friends, a boy, Robin, and a girl, Anna, talking about a school trip abroad. Decide if each sentence is correct or incorrect. Write **T** (True) or **F** (False).

1 Robin's school is planning an exchange trip to France next year. ☐
2 Anna got on very well with her host family and Chantal. ☐
3 At first, Anna felt uncomfortable because of problems with the language. ☐
4 Anna didn't do any fun activities with her host family. ☐
5 Anna loved Paris, but wanted more time to visit it. ☐
6 Anna found the food and eating times a bit strange. ☐

E 11.1 ▶️ Listen again and check your answers.

Speaking

A **Work with a partner and answer these questions.**

- Which is your favourite subject at school? Why?
- Which subject is the most difficult? Why?
- Is there anything else that you would like to learn in the future?
- Can you think of something that you would be able to teach somebody?

B **Look at the photos in D of school facilities. Decide which facility could be described by these statements.**

computer room   canteen   football pitch
gymnasium   library   pool   common room

1   The grass needs a lot of watering.
_____

2   Students can exercise there, but it's also good for parties.
_____

3   Students can surf the Internet and use CD-Roms.
_____

4   It provides students with a quiet place to study.
_____

5   Students can do water sports. _____

6   Students can eat there which is useful if your home is far from the school. _____

7   Students can relax there which is good if the weather is bad. _____

D **Now work with a partner and complete the *Exam Task*.**

Exam Task

Imagine that a school is trying to improve different facilities for students. Talk together about why these facilities are important for students.

pool table   swimming pool   canteen   computer room   gymnasium   library   football pitch

Which facility is best?

Now decide which facility would be best.

C **Read the *Exam Close-up* and look at the *Useful Expressions*. Then work in pairs and try and change each other's minds.**

Student A: Say why it's important to use computers to study at school.

Student B: You disagree. Try to convince your partner to agree with you!

Student B: Say why it's important to have a school library.

Student A: You disagree. Try to convince your partner to agree with you!

Useful Expressions

Changing your mind

Are you sure about that?

Do you really think that …?

I'm sure … is better because …

Actually, I think you're right …

Yes, that's a good point, I hadn't thought of that.

OK then, yes, I agree with you!

Exam Close-up
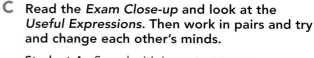

Changing opinions

- Ask your partner for his or her opinion about the options and give your own.
- Remember that it's OK to disagree. If you don't agree with your partner you can try to change his or her opinion. You can also change your opinion and decide that you do agree with your partner.
- Remember to talk about all the different options before you make a final decision.

- Are you happy with the sports facilities at your school? Why? / Why not?
- Do you prefer to study on your own or with friends? Why / Why not?

Ideas Focus

11 Lessons to Learn

Vocabulary
Collocations & Expressions

A Choose the correct answers.

1 When students **make progress**, they _____.
  a get worse at doing something
  b get better at doing something

2 If you **break the rules**, you _____.
  a do what you are supposed to do
  b do something you aren't supposed to do

3 When you **are in your teacher's good books**, he or she is _____.
  a pleased with you
  b unhappy with you

4 When you **get the hang of** something, you _____.
  a learn how to do something new
  b don't learn anything new

5 If you **get a taste for something**, you _____.
  a no longer enjoy doing it
  b start to enjoy doing it

6 If you **make an effort**, you _____.
  a don't try to do something
  b try to do something

B Complete the text with phrases from A.

High-school help!

Secondary school can be very difficult, but if you want to do well and be in your teacher's (1) _____, then we have some advice for you! First of all, to (2) _____ at school, you need to manage your time well. This means that you must (3) _____ to do your homework on time and make sure that you aren't late for school. Students who (4) _____ and are repeatedly late or absent are only going to get into trouble. If getting ready for school is a problem because you're sleepy, establish a morning routine and stick to it. You will soon (5) _____ it and you won't be late any more.
Finally, don't forget that if you study hard, you'll soon see results and, who knows, you may even (6) _____ for learning!

Prepositions

C Complete the sentences with these prepositions. You need to use some of them more than once.

about   at   for   from   in   of   on   with

1 There has been an increase _____ the number of students leaving school _____ eighteen.
2 Please concentrate _____ what your teacher is saying.
3 Some parents are prepared to spend large amounts _____ money _____ their children's education.
4 Jen never speaks up in class. She suffers _____ a lack of confidence.
5 My brother is going to apply _____ a place _____ Oxford University.
6 Try not to worry _____ your exams, Phil. I'm sure you'll do well.
7 Jane is good _____ French. She loves learning languages.
8 Most of Gordon's teachers are satisfied _____ his progress this year.

Ideas Focus

- Do you want to apply for a place at university? Why / Why not? What would you like to study?
- Do you have to pass exams in your country to go to university? Are they difficult?
- Are you satisfied with the progress you've made at school this year? Why? / Why not?

Grammar

Gerunds

A Look at the gerunds in bold in these sentences. How are gerunds formed?

  a John is interested in **studying** biology.
  b The teacher avoids **shouting** at students.
  c It isn't worth **revising** all night for a test.
  d She loves **swimming**.
  e **Surfing** the Net is his favourite pastime.

B Read the sentences in A again and answer the questions below. Which sentence(s) include(s) an example of

  1 a gerund after a verb or phrase? ☐ ☐ ☐
  2 a gerund after a preposition? ☐
  3 a gerund used as the subject of a sentence? ☐
  4 a gerund used as the object of a sentence? ☐

Infinitives

C Read the sentences. What do the words in bold all have in common?

  1 He was too busy **to go out**.
  2 James wants **to become** an engineer.
  3 They went to the exhibition **to see** the latest inventions.
  4 Jenny was very happy **to finish** university this year.

D Match the sentences in C with the uses of the full infinitive below.
We use the full infinitive

  a to express purpose. ☐
  b after adjectives such as *afraid, scared, happy, glad, sad*, etc. ☐
  c after the words *too* and *enough*. ☐
  d after certain verbs and phrases. ☐

E Read these sentences and underline the bare infinitives.

  1 She must do a seminar on language teaching.
  2 He can't decide what to study at university.
  3 I would rather go out than stay in tonight.
  4 We had better be careful when using this machine.

F Complete the rule.
We use bare infinitives after _____ verbs and the phrases _____ and _____ .

Gerund or Infinitive?

G Read the sentences and underline the gerund and full infinitives.

  a Scientists have begun to research new ways of communication.
     Scientists have begun researching new ways of communication.
  b The teacher stopped to write on the board.
     The teacher stopped writing on the board.

H Read the sentences in G again. In which pair of sentences does the meaning of the sentences
  1 stay the same? ☐   2 change? ☐

I Look at the full infinitive and the gerund in bold in these sentences and answer the questions below.

  a Sam remembered **calling** his professor.
  b Sam remembered **to call** his professor.

In which sentence did Sam

  1 first remember something and then an event happened? ☐
  2 remember an event after it happened? ☐

▶ Grammar Focus pp.171 & 172 (11.2 to 11.6)

J Complete the text with the gerund or the correct form of the infinitive of the verbs in brackets.

Nature as a blackboard

Would you like (**1**) _____ (go) to a school that doesn't expect students (**2**) _____ (be) in class all day? What student wouldn't enjoy (**3**) _____ (attend) such a school if it existed?

Well, at Southern Cross School near South Africa's famous Kruger National Park, you can (**4**) _____ (do) just that. Teachers and children spend time in nature (**5**) _____ (look) for things that can be used (**6**) _____ (study) anything from maths and science to language. For example, young students learn how to count by (**7**) _____ (count) how many different animals come to drink water during the night. Students can't help (**8**) _____ (become) involved in their lessons.

This school aims (**9**) _____ (teach) students the importance of (**10**) _____ (care) for the natural environment and the school's motto is 'Southern Cross is a School for the Planet'.

K Circle the correct words.

  1 Some students can't afford *going / to go* to university.
  2 I don't feel like *to study / studying* when the weather is warm.
  3 Jason was glad *to learn / learning* that he had passed his exams.
  4 She'd better *get / to get* some advice on her studies.
  5 It's no use *staying / to stay* up all night studying.
  6 Teachers should be prepared *to answer / answering* students' questions.
  7 The children are too young *attending / to attend* these classes.
  8 Is she interested in *train / training* to become a photographer?

Writing: a report

Remembering common errors
- It's a good idea to keep a list of common errors that you make in English.
- Think about words, collocations and expressions which are different in English to your language and note them down in your list, e.g.

both and *either* to talk about two people or things – positive meaning.
both + plural noun, *I like both my teachers.*
both + two singular nouns *I like Mrs Brown and Mr White.*
both of + plural noun *Both of my teachers are great.*
either + singular noun *We could have either Mrs Brown or Mr White today.*
either of + plural noun *Either of our teachers could come today.*

neither – **negative** meaning
neither + singular noun, *Neither Mrs Brown nor Mr White can teach today.*
neither of + plural noun *Neither of the teachers can teach today.*

neither … nor / either … or to compare two people or things, … etc.

A Circle the correct words.

1 We can spend the break neither / either in the playground or in the common room.
2 Neither / Neither of the teachers were worried about the student's performance.
3 You can do both / both of woodwork and design at our school.
4 It was suggested that either drama nor / or dance should be offered next term.
5 Both students / student have been given a laptop.
6 Neither / Nor the principal nor the teachers feel action should be taken.

B Underline the key words and phrases in the writing task below and then answer the questions in your notebook.

> You recently carried out a student survey on facilities at your school as part of a social studies project. Write a report summarising opinions on two facilities mentioned in the survey and suggest how these facilities could be improved. (100–120 words)

1 What will you write?
2 What are school facilities?
3 How many facilities will you discuss?
4 What two things must your report include?

C Read the model report and complete it with *both*, *either* or *neither*.

Introduction
This report presents the findings of a survey on the facilities at Torringdon High School. It also suggests some improvements to the facilities.

The library
Most students think the library is (1) _____ big enough nor well equipped. As a result, it is not as useful as it should be. A different location for the library could be (2) _____ the old science lab or the common room as (3) _____ of these are much bigger than the library. Students also suggested we have more computers put in so students can do research on the Internet there.

Classrooms
In general, most students believe the classrooms are good. They particularly like the interactive whiteboards as they make lessons more interesting. However, students complained about the temperature during winter. The students felt that the classrooms should have (4) _____ central heating or air conditioning.

Conclusion
To sum up, the main recommendations are to (5) _____ move the library and to improve equipment in it, as well as to provide a better heating system.

D Read the model report again and tick (✓) the things the writer has done.

1 given a short explanation of the survey ☐
2 written about two facilities ☐
3 only included negative points ☐
4 used a heading for each paragraph ☐
5 forgotten to make suggestions ☐
6 used informal language ☐

E Complete the plan for the model report with these sentences.

a Discuss the first facility and make a suggestion for improvement.
b Discuss the second facility and make a suggestion for improvement.
c Bring the report to an end by summing up the suggestions made.
d State the reason for writing the report.

Paragraph 1 ☐
Paragraph 2 ☐
Paragraph 3 ☐
Paragraph 4 ☐

F Look at the *Useful Expressions* and choose the correct answers.

1 Each classroom would benefit from ___ whiteboards.
   a common   b interactive   c after-school
2 The ___ of this report is to present the findings of a survey.
   a recommendation   b writing   c purpose
3 Some school ___, such as the theatre, need to be improved.
   a facilities   b activities   c labs
4 The cookery class could move to the school ___.
   a toilets   b science lab   c canteen
5 The report will ___ recommendations for improvements.
   a make   b do   c put
6 Either the gym or the ___ is the best location for sports teams to practise.
   a canteen   b library   c playground

G Read the *Exam Close-up* and complete the *Exam Task* below.

Exam Close-up

Checking for common errors
- Remember to review your writing to make sure you have answered the exam question fully.
- It's a good idea to also check your writing carefully and make sure you haven't made any simple spelling mistakes or language errors.
- Thinking about your common errors list will help you correct your writing.

Exam Task

You recently carried out a student survey on the after-school activities at your school as part of a social studies project. Write a **report** summarising opinions on two activities mentioned in the survey and suggest how these activities could be improved. (100–120 words)

Useful Expressions

Introducing reports
The aim / purpose of this report is to …
This is a report on …
This report will present the findings of …

Closing reports
To sum up, the main recommendations / suggestions are …
In conclusion, …

School facilities & equipment

canteen	interactive whiteboard
classrooms	library
common room	playground
computer room	science labs
theatre	toilets
gym	

After-school activities
arts and crafts
choir practice
cooking
music and drama
sports teams

Video ▼

11 The Maasai Teacher

Before you watch

A Work with a partner and answer these questions.

- What are schools like in your country? How are they different to schools in other counties?
- What do you think is the most important skill you learn in school? Why?
- Do you, as students, want to learn more about the world? What would you like to learn?

Kenya, Africa

While you watch

B Watch the video and decide if these statements are T (True) or F (False).

1 Joseph Lekuton was born in a small village in Northern Virginia. ☐
2 Lekuton used to look after his family's cattle when he was a young boy. ☐
3 The book *Facing the Lion* is about his life in Kenya. ☐
4 The title of the book *Facing the Lion* refers to an event in his childhood, when he came face to face with a lion. ☐
5 Lekuton believes that not all people face challenges in life. ☐
6 Lekuton encourages children to have hope, determination and courage, to try to conquer their 'lions'. ☐

After you watch

C Complete the summary of the video below using these words.

| ability aim apply consists lectures principles project skills |

Joseph Lekuton is a teacher in Northern Virginia, USA. He gives **(1)** _____ to his students about American history. But his own country, Kenya, is very different. Joseph is a Maasai tribesman. Maasai children lead a very different life from American children. For example, a ten-year-old's day **(2)** _____ of taking care of cattle all day long. Maasai children also learn various **(3)** _____ like how to survive in the wild. Unlike many Maasai children, Lekuton was very lucky and went to school. With his **(4)** _____ to speak English, he was able to study and then teach in America. Lekuton wrote a book about his childhood called *Facing the Lion*. His **(5)** _____ is to help children learn about a culture that's very different from their own. He also wants to teach them **(6)** _____ like strength and hope, which they can **(7)** _____ to their own lives. Joseph hopes that his first **(8)** _____ will help children face their own 'lions'.

Maasai children spend much of their life taking care of cattle and other animals. Ndutu area, Tanzania

Ideas Focus

- Would you rather lead the life of a Maasai child or of an American child? Why?
- What 'lions' do you face in your life?

12 The Body Beautiful

Reading:	multiple-choice questions, choosing the best option
Vocabulary:	body-related words, phrasal verbs
Grammar:	adjectives, adverbs, *so* & *such*, comparison of adjectives and adverbs
Listening:	multiple-choice questions (pictures), keeping calm
Speaking:	talking about your body, general conversations, interacting with your partner, talking about health and fitness
Writing:	dramatic stories, making stories more interesting, leaving enough time, relationships

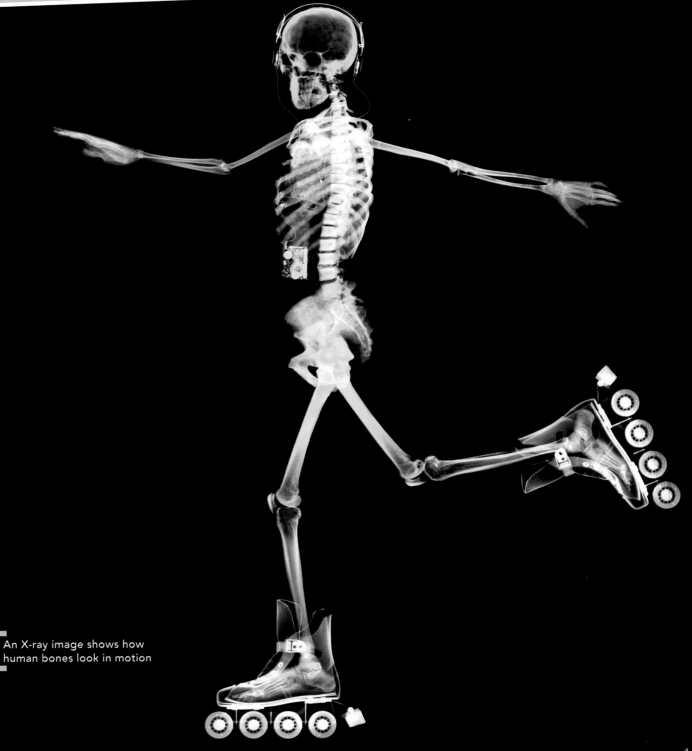

An X-ray image shows how human bones look in motion

Reading

A **How much do you know about the human body? Do the quiz and find out! Your teacher will give you the correct answers.**

1 Which is the largest organ in the human body?
- **a** the heart
- **b** the lungs
- **c** the brain
- **d** the skin

2 How many bones are there in the adult human body?
- **a** 206
- **b** 276
- **c** 106
- **d** 186

3 What is the total length of all the blood vessels in a child's body?
- **a** about 23,000 km
- **b** about 97,000 km
- **c** about 36,000 km
- **d** about 65,000 km

4 How much does the adult human brain weigh on average?
- **a** 1 kg
- **b** 2 kg
- **c** 1.3 kg
- **d** 2.3 kg

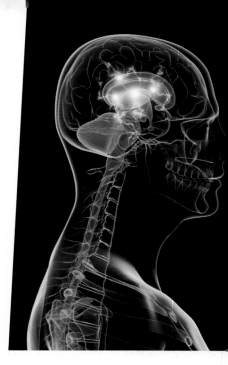

B **Can you read and understand the short text below?**

It deosn't mttaer in what oredr the ltteers in a wrod are, the olny iprmoatnt tihng is taht the frist and lsat ltteer be in the rghit pclae. The rset can be a tatol mses and you can sitll raed it wouthit any porbelms. Tihs is bcuseae the huamn bairn deos not raed ervey lteter by istlef, but the wrod as a wlohe. Amzanig!

Write your own sentence in your notebook with jumbled up letters, following the rule above. Swap with a partner!

C **Quickly read the article about the human brain. What advice is suggested for students who are unable to do their homework?**

Your Amazing Brain

A room at the Virginia Science Museum in Richmond, USA, is designed as an optical illusion – something that is not what it seems

Your brain controls everything you do. It makes it possible for you to think, learn, create and feel emotions; to blink and breathe and for your heart to beat — this fantastic control centre is your brain. It is so amazing that a famous scientist once called it 'the most complex thing we have yet discovered in our universe'.

Trying to make <u>sense</u> of the brain isn't easy. We know it's the organ that makes us human by giving us the ability to create art and language, make decisions and produce rational thought. It's also responsible for our personalities, memories, movements and how we understand the world.

Can this small grey organ, which weighs less than one and a half kilos, really do so much? Amazingly, your brain contains about 100 billion microscopic cells called neurons — it would take you over 3,000 years to count them all. Whenever you dream, laugh, think, see or move, it's because

D Read the *Exam Close-up*. Then read the *Exam Task* below and underline the key words.

Exam Task

Read the text and questions below. For each question, choose the correct letter **a**, **b**, **c** or **d**.

1 Why does the writer mention computers?
   a to compare them to the human brain
   b to show how fast they have become
   c to say that computers have no abilities
   d to say that computers need eyes and ears

2 We know that neurons
   a send messages very slowly.
   b are only found in your skin.
   c deliver messages to your brain.
   d need electricity to work.

3 When you have a new thought,
   a your heart beats faster.
   b the structure of your brain changes.
   c you learn something new.
   d you remember something.

4 What does the writer tell us about exercise?
   a It can make you less intelligent.
   b It needs a special chemical.
   c Its effects are not well known.
   d It can make you feel better.

5 What is the article generally about?
   a All the steps that are involved when your brain learns things.
   b What an incredible organ the human brain is.
   c How the brain makes people smarter than computers.
   d The things you can do to speed up your brain.

Exam Close-up

Choosing the best option

- Remember, if you see the same word in an answer option and in the text, it may not be the correct answer.
- Read the section in the text with the same word carefully and check it is the best option.
- Remember to read all the answer options before you choose the best one.

E Find these words in the text and use them to complete the definitions below.

structure   mood   organs   sense   signals

1 Electrical messages in the body are known as _____.
2 Your _____ is the way you are feeling at a certain time.
3 The way something is built is known as its _____.
4 If the meaning of something is not clear, it doesn't make _____.
5 The eyes, ears, nose, mouth and skin are all _____.

F Work with a partner to solve the brain teaser below. You have two minutes!

A man went for a walk. After about an hour, he came to a deep, wide river. There was no bridge. He didn't have a boat or raft, or any materials to make one. He couldn't swim. How did he get across the river?

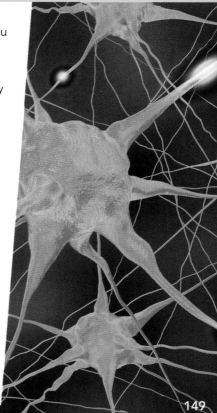

signals are racing between these neurons. Believe it or not, the activity in your brain never stops. Your neurons create and send more messages than all the phones in the world. And although one neuron creates only a very small amount of electricity, all your neurons together can produce enough electricity to power a light bulb.

So exactly how fast does your brain work? Well, imagine this: a bee lands on your foot. Neurons in your skin send this information to your brain at a speed of more than 240 kilometres per hour. Your brain then uses other neurons to send the message back to your foot to shake the bee off quickly. These neurons can send this information at more than 320 kilometres per hour. No computer has your brain's incredible ability to cope with the amount of information coming from your eyes, ears and other sensory organs.

But how does your brain allow you to learn things that you will use in the future? The structure of your brain changes every time you have a new thought, remember

or learn something. For example, riding a bike seems impossible at first, but soon you are able to do it. How? As you practise, your brain sends 'bike riding' messages again and again. Soon, the actions are learnt and you are able to ride a bike easily from then on.

How quickly we learn things varies from person to person, but there are some things which can help us to learn faster and, surprisingly, exercise is one of them. We know that any exercise that makes your heart beat faster is great for your body and can even help improve your mood, but we know less about the effects of exercise on learning. However, scientists have recently discovered that for a period of time after you've exercised, your body produces a chemical that makes it easier for your brain to learn. So, if you're stuck on a homework problem that is too difficult to solve, go out and play a game of football, then try the problem again. You just might discover that you're able to solve it.

Vocabulary

A Match the parts of the body a–j with the words below.

1 ankle ☐
2 calf ☐
3 chest ☐
4 elbow ☐
5 forehead ☐
6 hip ☐
7 shoulder ☐
8 stomach ☐
9 thigh ☐
10 thumb ☐

B Read these amazing facts about the human body and choose the correct answers.

1 A man's ___ contains between 7,000 and 15,000 hairs.
   a chest   b beard   c eyelid

2 On average, a person ___ 15,000 times a day.
   a blinks   b laughs   c cries

3 The human ___ is used for pronunciation as well as tasting food.
   a neck   b cheek   c tongue

4 It's impossible to ___ and keep your eyes open.
   a sneeze   b cough   c yawn

5 When you're angry, your ___ pressure rises.
   a blood   b water   c sweat

6 50% more males than females are ___.
   a left   b left-handed   c handed

7 The ___ in the heart work involuntarily. This means you don't have to think about using them.
   a muscles   b bones   c cells

8 On average, a person ___ 23,000 times a day.
   a sighs   b breathes   c bites

C Complete the text with these words.

| confident ears eyebrows features personality shy successful thin |

What's in a face?

It is said that the eyes are the window of the soul, but did you know that according to the ancient Chinese art of face reading, all your facial (1) _____ reveal secrets about your (2) _____?

In this ancient art, all parts of the face give an experienced 'reader' information. Large eyes indicate that you are generous, while long, thick (3) _____ above the eyes indicate that you are very wise. Large, flat (4) _____ show that you are a good listener, and the type of mouth you have says a lot about your ability to communicate. A large mouth shows that you are probably loud and (5) _____ when you speak, whereas a small mouth shows that you may be quiet and (6) _____. If your lips are large and thick, this indicates that you are honest and loyal. However, if your lips are small and (7) _____, don't despair! This means that you will be (8) _____ later in life.

Ideas Focus

- Do you believe what is being suggested in C? Why? / Why not?
- 'If you can dream it, you can do it.' Walt Disney. Do you agree with this statement? Why? / Why not?

Grammar

Adjectives

A Read and underline the adjectives in the sentences.

My mum has a beautiful red Italian car.
What a horrible huge straw hat!
Jenny gave me a gorgeous white woollen scarf.

B Read the sentences in A again and answer the questions.

1 Which adjectives describe opinion?
_____, _____ and
_____

2 Which adjectives describe colour?
_____ and _____

3 Which adjective describes origin?
_____

4 Which adjective describes size?
_____

5 Which adjectives describe material?
_____ and _____

6 Do adjectives of opinion come before or after other kinds of adjectives? _____

C Read the sentences and complete the rule below by choosing the correct endings.

a Basketball is a very **tiring** sport.
b They're **tired** because they've been playing basketball.

Adjectives that end in –ing / –ed describe the effect something can have on someone. Adjectives that end in –ing / –ed describe how someone feels.

Adverbs

D Adverbs give us information about how, where, when, how often and to what degree something happens. Look at these sentences and the adverbs in bold and answer the questions below.

The little boy wrote his name **carefully**.
Our PE teacher left **yesterday**.
My grandad is **quite** fit.
I **often** go to the gym **opposite** my house.

Which adverb is used to answer the question

1 how?   _____
2 where?   _____
3 when?   _____
4 how often?   _____
5 to what degree? _____

So & Such

E We use *so* and *such* for emphasis. Look at these sentences and answer the questions below.

Looking after your health is **so** important.
Oranges are **such** a good source of vitamin C.

1 What part of speech follows *so*?
_____

2 What parts of speech follow *such*?
_____

▶ Grammar Focus pp.172 & 173 (12.1 to 12.6)

F Complete the sentences with the adjectives in brackets.

1 Julie has _____ hair. (blonde / lovely / short)
2 Lisa bought some _____ boots. (Italian / leather / new)
3 I saw a(n) _____ statue. (amazing / huge / marble)
4 What a(n) _____ ring! (diamond / expensive / pink)
5 We sat around the _____ table. (large / round / wooden)

G Complete the sentences with the pairs of words given.

amazed/amazing   bored/boring   excited/exciting
interested/interesting

1 Medicine is a(n) _____ subject to study.
   Mandy is _____ in becoming a doctor.
2 Riding a rollercoaster is _____.
   The children are _____ because they are going to the funfair today.
3 I think watching tennis is _____. I'd much rather play it.
   I'm _____! What can I do?
4 The human body is _____. It can do so many things.
   Janet was _____ when her brother learnt to ride a bike in half an hour.

H Circle the correct words.

1 I always brush / brush always my hair before I go to school.
2 My little sister is too / enough short to go on the rollercoaster.
3 This book is almost / very never read.
4 The doctor told my father not to work such / so hard.
5 Peggy goes on Saturdays to the gym / to the gym on Saturdays.
6 People usually are / are usually at home at the weekend.
7 We should all exercise and eat healthily / healthily eat.
8 The seminar was such a / so success that it will be held again next year.

151

Listening

A Where on the body are each of these things found? Write **L** (leg), **A** (arm) or **H** (head).

ankle	☐	knee	☐
calf	☐	shoulder	☐
chin	☐	thumb	☐
ear	☐	tongue	☐
elbow	☐		

B 🔊 12.1 **Listen to four speakers and circle the body part they are describing.**

1 **a** ankle **b** neck **c** elbow
2 **a** calf **b** hip **c** neck
3 **a** toes **b** fingers **c** hands
4 **a** ears **b** eyes **c** legs

C 🔊 12.2 **Read the *Exam Close-up* and then complete the *Exam Task*.** Remember to focus on each question and write notes while you listen.

Exam Task

There are six questions in this part. For each question, there are three pictures and a short recording. Circle the correct answer **a**, **b**, or **c**.

1 What activity do the friends decide to do?

 a   b   c

2 When will the man leave hospital?

a **MARCH**
1	2	3	4	5	6	7
8	9	10	11	12	13	14
15	16	17	18	19	20	21
22	23	24	25	26	27	28
29	30	31				

b **MARCH**
1	2	3	4	5	6	7
8	9	10	11	12	13	14
15	16	17	18	19	20	21
22	23	24	25	26	27	28
29	30	31				

c **MARCH**
1	2	3	4	5	6	7
8	9	10	11	12	13	14
15	16	17	18	19	20	21
22	23	24	25	26	27	28
29	30	31				

3 How does the girl think she hurt her shoulder?

 a   b   c

4 Which picture shows the boy's uncle?

 a   b   c

5 Which part of her body did the woman hurt?

 a   b   c

6 What does the man decide to buy?

 a   b    c

D 🔊 12.2 **Listen again and check your answers.**

Electrodes are used to measure the brain activity of a meditating Buddhist monk, Dru-gu Choegyal Rinpoche – according to scientist Richard Davidson, one monk they studied was proven to be 'the happiest man in the world'.

Speaking

A Work with a partner and answer these questions.

- Do you ever feel tired or lack energy? Why do you think that is?
- Do you enjoy physical activity or would you rather watch TV or use a tablet or computer?

B Look at the list of ideas related to caring for your body. Put a tick (✓) next to the ones which are good for you and a cross (✗) next to the ones which are bad. Compare with a partner.

1 watching a lot of TV ☐
2 eating lots of fruits and vegetables ☐
3 exercising three or more times a week ☐
4 brushing your teeth three times a day ☐

5 drinking lots of water ☐
6 sleeping for five hours a night ☐
7 eating fast food ☐
8 riding your bike to school or work ☐

C Work with a partner. Student A, describes photo 1 and Student B, describes photo 2. Remember to listen to each other's descriptions.

Exam Close-up

Interacting with your partner

- Remember to listen carefully to the instructions before you start.
- When you are asked to talk about a topic with your partner, make sure you interact with him or her.
- Ask his or her opinion on the topic and react to the answers.
- Say if you agree or not and give your reasons.
- It's a good idea to ask your partner questions to get more information and to keep the conversation going.

Useful Expressions

Talking about health and fitness

So, what do you do to stay healthy?
Do you do anything special to stay fit and healthy?
How often do you do exercise / go to the gym?
Do you go swimming / play any sports?
Do you think it's important to … ? Why?
Do you have enough time to … ? Why not?

D 12.3 ▶❚❚ Read the *Exam Close-up*. Then listen to the instructions for the *Exam Task*. What do you have to do?

E Work with a partner and complete the last part of the *Exam Task*. Use the *Useful Expressions* to help you.

- Why is it important for us to look after our bodies?
- Do you think people in your country have a healthy diet? Why? / Why not?

Ideas Focus

Vocabulary

Phrasal verbs

A In the following exercise, two of the options given are used with each verb in bold to make a phrasal verb. For each question, cross out the option that cannot be used with the verb in bold.

1 **back:** away / over / out of
2 **hand:** over / against / out
3 **head:** together / for / off

4 **run:** out of / over / of
5 **think:** over / around / up
6 **stand:** out / in / across

B Complete sentences 1–12 with words from A.

1 If you **run** _____ breath, stop exercising until you feel better.
2 They started to **back** _____ as soon as the smell hit them.
3 I'm going to **head** _____ now. I've got a dentist's appointment soon.
4 I knew Jenny would **back** _____ coming jogging with me. She hates it!
5 I need a new haircut that will make me **stand** _____.
6 You aren't allowed mobile phones in class. **Hand** it _____.
7 Paul got **run** _____ by a car last week! He's got a broken arm and a bruised hip.
8 If you **head** _____ the DVD shop, I'll catch you up in five minutes.
9 They had to get another biology teacher to **stand** _____ for ours when she was off sick.
10 I'm trying to **think** _____ an easy way to lose weight.
11 Could you do me a favour and **hand** _____ these leaflets about my hair salon?
12 Please **think** _____ my proposals for the beauty salon. I think they'll improve business.

C Complete the sets of sentences with the correct form of the phrasal verbs from A.

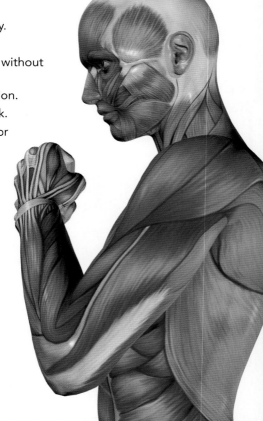

1 a If you come across an angry dog, _____ from it slowly.
  b You can't _____ our deal; we shook hands on it!
2 a Can you help me _____ some ways to plan the party without Mum knowing about it?
  b Let's _____ her offer to help before we make a decision.
3 a Where is John going? It looks like he's _____ the park.
  b Well, I think we'd better _____ now or we'll be late for the meeting.
4 a The race was nearly over and many of the runners had _____ breath.
  b Don't ride your bike in the road! You'll get _____ by a car.
5 a She had gorgeous long blonde hair which really made her _____ in a crowd.
  b Our biology teacher was off sick, so the PE teacher had to _____ for her.
6 a Stop right there, thief! _____ the stolen money or we'll shoot!
  b There's a man on the corner _____ leaflets for the new museum.

Ideas Focus

• Do you like to stand out in crowd? Why? / Why not?
• Do you think you are good at thinking up new ideas? Why? / Why not?

154

Grammar

Comparison of Adjectives & Adverbs

A **Look at these sentences and answer the questions below.**

  a Grandad's moustache is the longest I have ever seen.

  b Paul's feet are bigger than his father's feet.

  c My classmate James complains the most in our class.

  d Steven wakes up earlier than the rest of his family.

  1 Which sentences contain the comparative form?
    ☐ and ☐

  2 Which sentences contain the superlative form?
    ☐ and ☐

B **Look at these sentences and answer the questions below.**

  a My brother is**n't as tall as** Dad.

  b Lucy can run **as fast as** Beth.

  1 In sentence a, who is the tallest? _____

  2 In sentence b, can Beth run faster than Lucy?

    _____

C **Complete the rules.**

We use _____ + adjective/adverb + _____ to show that two people or things are similar in some way. When they are not similar, we can use _____ as/so + adjective/adverb + as.

> ⤹ **Grammar Focus p.173 (12.7 & 12.8)**

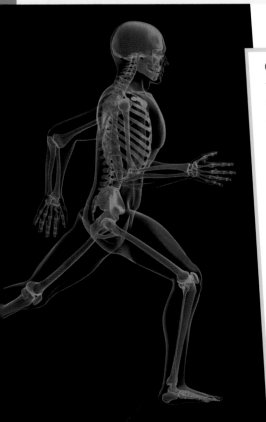

D **Complete the second sentences so that they have a similar meaning to the first sentences. Use the words in bold.**

  1 Mum and Dad go to bed at midnight. I go to bed at ten o'clock. **late**

    I don't go to bed _____
    Mum and Dad.

  2 Cathy's hair reaches her waist. My hair is shoulder-length. **than**

    My hair _____ Cathy's.

  3 I try hard to do well at school. My best friend doesn't try hard enough. **harder**

    I _____ my best friend to do well at school.

  4 Both Melinda and I run for two kilometres every morning. **far**

    Melinda runs _____ I do every morning.

  5 I haven't seen a better documentary than the one about the human body. **the**

    The documentary about the human body was _____ I have ever seen.

  6 Kelly takes less time to solve maths problems than the rest of the class. **quickly**

    Kelly solves maths problems _____
    _____ the rest of the class.

  7 I can see better than my grandma. **well**

    My grandma can't see _____ as I can.

  8 Mum says that nobody sings as beautifully as I do. **most**

    Mum says that I sing _____ of all.

E **Complete the text with these words.**

| longest | many | more | most | smaller | smallest |

Our skeleton

The human skeleton is amazing. Some of its many functions include enabling us to move, supporting and protecting our internal organs and producing blood cells.

Not surprisingly, the bones of children and young teenagers are **(1)** _____ than those of adults. However, babies have **(2)** _____ bones than adults. A baby is born with about 300 bones. As it grows, some bones join together. An adult skeleton has 206 bones and half of them are in the hands and feet. However, the foot doesn't have as **(3)** _____ bones as the hand; it has one less.

Bones have different shapes and functions. Some bones are flat, others are long or short and others are irregular in shape. The thighbone is the **(4)** _____ and strongest bone of the human skeleton, whereas the **(5)** _____ bone in our body is found in the ear. It is only 2.8 mm long.

Even though bones are strong and tough, they can break. Did you know that the collar bone breaks the **(6)** _____ easily? Luckily for us, bones are made of living cells. When a bone breaks, lots of new cells are produced to rebuild it.

Writing : a dramatic story

Learning Focus

Making stories more interesting

There are several ways to make your stories interesting.

- Interesting stories start with a dramatic opening sentence, which will make the reader want to read on.
- Descriptive adjectives and adverbs help the reader to imagine the characters and the action.
- You can also use some idiomatic expressions to make your writing more colourful.
- Direct speech and short dramatic sentences in places add variety and drama.
- Introducing a twist in the story in which something unexpected happens can add suspense.
- Finally, an interesting ending to the story is also important.

A Match the ways of making your story more interesting 1–8 with the examples a–h.

1 descriptive **adjectives** ☐
2 dramatic **opening sentence** ☐
3 descriptive **adverbs** ☐
4 direct **speech** ☐
5 idiomatic **expressions** ☐
6 short, **dramatic sentence** ☐
7 a **twist in the story** ☐
8 an **interesting ending** ☐

a Unfortunately, the two cousins have never seen eye to eye.
b 'Please don't leave me! I promise I won't hurt you again,' she said.
c Today was the day when Hannah was going to meet her sister for the first time.
d He jumped quickly out of bed, rushed downstairs and opened the door nervously.
e Like most teenagers, Hannah was independent and not very communicative.
f He left the building with tears in his eyes. That part of his life was over.
g They had always been a loving family, but one day something happened to change that forever.
h He stopped and stared.

B Read the writing task below and then answer the questions about it in your notebook.

> Your teacher has asked you to write a story. Your story must begin with this sentence.
> *Sally was extremely nervous.*
> (100 words)

1 How will your story start?
2 How does Sally feel?
3 Do you have to explain why she feels this way in the story?

C Read the example story and underline techniques from A that make the story more interesting.

Sally was extremely nervous. It was their turn to dance. Sally breathed deeply while Maddy was completely relaxed. 'Come on!' said Maddy. 'We've got to win!'

Maddy and Sally met at dance class a year ago. They quickly discovered they had a lot in common. When their teacher entered them in a competition, they were very excited.

This was their big chance. However, when the music started Sally froze. Maddy was angry but carried on. When the music stopped, Maddy headed for the door. Sally knew she had let Maddy down. Worst of all, she had lost a friend.

D Read the example story again and answer the questions.

1 Why does Sally feel nervous?
2 Where did Maddy and Sally meet?
3 How did the girls react when their teacher told them about the competition?
4 Which girl does something disappointing?
5 How does the other girl react?

E Match to complete the plan for the example story.

a Give background details about the characters' relationship.
b Set the scene and introduce the main characters.
c Introduce a twist in the story and bring the story to an end.

Paragraph 1 ☐
Paragraph 2 ☐
Paragraph 3 ☐

F Look at the *Useful Expressions* and choose the correct answers.

1 She was relieved to see that everyone looked very _____ .
   a suspicious   b embarrassing   c friendly
2 Can I give you _____ with your suitcases?
   a a hand   b an eye   c an arm
3 I don't find it easy to _____ on with new people.
   a see eye to eye   b respect   c get
4 We don't have a lot in _____ .
   a trust   b friendship   c common
5 The two brothers grew _____ when they left home.
   a apart   b out   c up for

G Read the *Exam Close-up*. Then read the *Exam Task* below and make a paragraph plan.

Dancing competition at the Highland games in Ballater, Scotland

Exam Close-up

Leaving enough time
- In the exam, remember to leave yourself enough time to write the story.
- Try to decide quickly which question to do and then make a plan thinking of ideas and useful expressions for each paragraph.
- Leave a few minutes to check your writing at the end.

H Complete the *Exam Task*. Remember to include techniques to make your story more interesting and to leave time at the end to check your writing.

Exam Task

Your teacher has asked you to write a **dramatic story**. Your story must begin with this sentence.
Alex was the best friend anyone could have.
(100 words)

Useful Expressions

Relationships
friendship
stranger
trust
(not) have a lot in common
make friends with
get on
give someone a hand
grow apart
help someone out
let someone down
see eye to eye
embarrassing
friendly
suspicious
rely on
respect

Before you watch

A How much do you know about the human brain? Look at the statements below and write T (True) or F (False).

1 The brain is the most complex organ in the body. ☐

2 Our brain sleeps when we sleep. ☐

3 The right side of the brain controls the left side of the body and vice versa. ☐

Italy

While you watch

B Watch the video and circle the words you hear.

1 The young Italian man calls it 'the art / ability of memory'.

2 It's a kind of memory that is connects / connected to what I see.

3 Gianni has a very special kind of gene / memory.

4 Researchers are now studying how memory and learning / knowledge change the brain.

5 He practises continuously to increase / improve the power of his memory.

6 If there is a memory gene, Gianni Golfera probably / definitely has it.

After you watch

C Complete the summary of the video below using these words.

correctly   genes   information   memorised   memory   numbers   result   wonder

Gianni Golfera is a man with a wonderful (1) _____. He can remember a lot of (2) _____. In one experiment, people choose 60 numbers and someone reads the (3) _____ to Golfera, who is blindfolded. Then, after hearing them only once, Golfera says the numbers (4) _____ from memory. After that, he says the numbers again, backwards this time. And again, he does it perfectly. Golfera has (5) _____ over 250 books and he can remember every detail of every day of his life. Doctors (6) _____ why he has such a great memory. Is it because he received good memory (7) _____ from his family? Or is it the (8) _____ of a lot of practice? Whatever the reason, Golfera is making good use of it. He teaches classes that help people 'remember to remember'.

610 542 584 5697

Ideas Focus

• Do you think it's important to study how the brain 'works'? Why / Why not

• Do you have a good memory? Why? / Why not?

Vocabulary

A Circle the correct words.

1   I hope to graduate / pass from university this year.
2   Did you know that an adult's body consists of 212 bones / eyelids?
3   Jamie has been trying harder at school and has done / made progress.
4   The students found the lecture boring and started to sneeze / yawn.
5   The candidate / examiner was very pleased with how easy her oral examination had been.
6   Private schools usually charge very high grants / fees.
7   She was unhappy and we could hear her breathe / sigh quite often.
8   We are taught many different lessons / subjects at school.
9   The principal had to expel / behave a student who was rude to a teacher.
10 I know you have a busy timetable / schedule, but could we meet on Tuesday?

B Complete the sentences with both phrasal verbs.

1   back away   back out

  a   You promised to help me with my project! You can't _____ now!
  b   The policeman asked people to _____ from the injured man.

2   head for   head off

  a   Dan will _____ the library after class to study in peace.
  b   I think I will _____ now. I'm late for my biology class.

3   think over   think up

  a   James wanted to _____ the matter of choosing a college very carefully.
  b   She had put on a lot of weight and had to _____ a diet plan to slim down.

4   run out of   run over

  a   I was so upset when my cat was _____. Fortunately, it survived.
  b   The teacher has _____ patience with the badly-behaved student.

5   stand in   stand out

  a   The actress always wears clothes that make her _____ in a crowd.
  b   Our tutor broke his leg and so his assistant had to _____ for him.

6   hand out   hand over

  a   The secretary will _____ the application forms for the course.
  b   'OK, John! I think you should _____ the purse you stole,' the detective said.

C Complete the sentences with the correct preposition.

about   at   for   from   in   on   out   with

1   My mother is very satisfied _____ my marks at school this year.
2   My best friend is going to apply _____ a course at the same university as me.
3   I should have concentrated _____ what the teacher was saying rather than daydreaming.
4   Vicky suffers _____ a lack of confidence because of how often her father criticised her.
5   My brother is so good _____ English, people think he is English.
6   Don't worry _____ your dad. He probably got delayed in heavy traffic.
7   There has been a big increase _____ the number of unemployed people this year.
8   Becky helped hand _____ food at the shelter for homeless people.

Review 6 Units 11 & 12

Grammar

A Complete the sentences using the correct form of the causative.

1 The patient _____ (his brain / scan) four times since last month.
2 Sammy _____ (her hair / cut) since I saw her last.
3 I can't talk to you because I am at the dentist's. I _____ (my teeth / clean) at the moment.
4 The owners _____ (their gym / renovate) next summer.
5 _____ the college _____ (its classrooms / paint) every year?
6 Jane _____ (her eyes / test) by 10 o'clock yesterday.
7 _____ you _____ (the photo / frame) after you took it?
8 The university graduate _____ (his qualifications / recognise) by the government last month.

B Complete the sentences with the gerund or the correct form of the infinitive of the verbs in brackets.

1 My friend is having difficulty _____ (cope) with his studies.
2 Try _____ (look) up unknown words in a dictionary. It's good practice.
3 The young boy refused _____ (go) to school this morning.
4 I suggest _____ (enrol) on an art course this summer.
5 Helen must _____ (revise) for her exams if she wants to pass.
6 He went on _____ (talk) for an hour. It was so boring!
7 I'd rather _____ (call) for information on each course than send an email.
8 David denied _____ (be) rude to his English teacher.

C Write the words in the correct order to make sentences.

1 never / allowed / to choose / have / I / my own clothes / been
   _____

2 find / so / children / it / I / that / learn / quickly / things / wonderful
   _____

3 human brain / know / scientists / enough / about / the / don't
   _____

4 touches / big / my dog's / that / the ground / it / is / stomach / so
   _____

5 a prize / interesting / the book / to win / wasn't / enough
   _____

6 speak / his uncle / several / fluently / can / languages
   _____

7 left / the scientist / the lab / after lunch / quickly
   _____

8 ? / blue / horrible / bag / whose / old / this / is / leather
   _____

D Complete the sentences with the correct form of the word in brackets.

1 I wish I could sing _____ (good) my brothers.
2 Our teacher is always _____ (early) of all the teachers to arrive at school.
3 That is _____ (bad) painting I have seen in my life!
4 I don't think Jenny is _____ (pretty) her sisters.
5 That scientist is one of _____ (intelligent) people I know.

160

Unit 1

1.1 Present Simple

Affirmative
I/we/you/they play he/she/it play**s**

Negative
I/we/you/they **don't** play he/she/it **doesn't** play

Questions
Do I/we/you/they play? **Does** he/she/it play?

Short Answers	
Yes, I/we/you/they **do**. **Yes**, he/she/it **does**.	**No**, I/we/you/they **don't**. **No**, he/she/it **doesn't**.

We use the Present Simple for
- facts or general truths.
  *My grandmother **speaks** five languages.*
- routines or habits (often with adverbs of frequency).
  *My sister always **plays** volleyball at the weekend.*
- permanent states.
  *We **live** in Sevenoaks.*
- timetabled events in the future.
  *The film **starts** at 8 o'clock in the evening.*

Note: Some common time expressions that are often used with the Present Simple are *every day/week/month/ summer, every other day, once a week, twice a month, at the weekend, in January, in the morning/afternoon/ evening, at night, on Tuesdays, on Friday mornings,* etc.
*Jane visits her mother **twice a week**.*

1.2 Adverbs of frequency

We use adverbs of frequency to say how often something happens. They come before the main verb, but after the verb *be*.
*Jeremy **is often** tired in the morning.*
*Susan **rarely argues** with her brother.*
*Mum **always makes** our birthday cakes.*
Some common adverbs of frequency are:

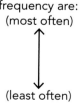

always	(most often)
usually	
often	
sometimes	
rarely/hardly ever/seldom	
never	(least often)

1.3 Present Continuous

Affirmative
I **am ('m)** play**ing** he/she/it **is ('s)** play**ing** we/you/they **are ('re)** play**ing**

Negative
I **am ('m) not** play**ing** he/she/it **is not (isn't)** play**ing** we/you/they **are not (aren't)** play**ing**

Questions
Am I play**ing**? **Is** he/she/it play**ing**? **Are** we/you/they play**ing**?

Short Answers	
Yes, I **am**. **Yes**, he/she/it **is**. **Yes**, we/you/they **are**.	**No**, I'm **not**. **No**, he/she/it **isn't**. **No**, we/you/they **aren't**.

Spelling: make → mak**ing**, swim → swi**mming**, study → study**ing**
We use the Present Continuous for
- actions that are in progress at or around the time of speaking.
  *We**'re watching** a DVD about elephants.*
- actions that are temporary.
  *My cousin **is staying** with us this weekend.*
- situations that are changing or developing in the present.
  *Family members **are living** further and further away from each other.*
- an annoying habit (often with *always, continually, constantly* and *forever*).
  *My brother **is forever complaining** about his homework.*
- plans and arrangements for the future.
  *We**'re visiting** my aunt this Saturday.*

Note: Some common time expressions that are often used with the Present Continuous are *at the moment, now, for the time being, this morning/afternoon/evening/week/ month/year, today,* etc.
*Jenny is getting married **in December**.*

1.4 Stative Verbs

Some verbs are not usually used in continuous tenses. They are called *stative* because they describe states and not actions. To talk about the present, we use these verbs in the Present Simple tense. The most common of these are:
- verbs of emotion: *hate, like, love, need, prefer, want.*
  *Jane **loves** her new house.*
- verbs of senses: *feel, hear, see, smell, sound, taste.*
  *This soup **tastes** delicious.*
- verbs which express a state of mind: *believe, doubt, forget, imagine, know, remember, seem, suppose, think, understand.*
  *I **think** that's a great idea!*
- verbs of possession: *belong to, have, own, possess.*
  *This flat **belongs to** my aunt.*
- other verbs: *be, consist, contain, cost, include, mean.*
  *Those curtains **cost** a fortune.*

Some verbs can be both stative verbs and action verbs, but with a different meaning. The most common of these verbs are:
- be
  *John **is** very honest.* (usual behaviour)
  *Ken **is being** very rude.* (at the moment; not his normal behaviour)

- expect
  I **expect** you enjoyed your holiday. (expect = think or believe)
  I'm **expecting** a letter from my grandma. (expect = wait for)
- have
  Lucy **has** a lovely house. (have = own/possess)
  Susan's **having** a great time at her cousin's house! (have = experience)
  Gerty's **having** lunch with her parents today. (have = eating)
- look
  She **looks like** her mother. (look like = resemble)
  Are you **looking** for your keys? (look = search)
- taste
  This soup **tastes** horrible! (taste = have a particular flavour)
  Why **are you tasting** the sauce? (taste = test the flavour)
- think
  I **think** you're mad! (think = have an opinion)
  Jenny's **thinking** of going to France. (think = consider)
- see
  'My uncle Paul is my mum's brother.' 'Oh, I **see**.' (see = understand)
  'I'm **seeing** Wendy tomorrow evening.' (see = meet)
- smell
  These flowers **smell** wonderful. (smell = have a particular smell)
  Why **are you smelling** the milk? (smell = action of smelling)
- weigh
  Jill **weighs** 48 kg. (weigh = have a particular weight)
  I'm **weighing** my suitcase to see how heavy it is. (weigh = measure the weight)

1.5 Countable Nouns

Most nouns are countable and have singular and plural forms.

sister → sisters	leaf → leaves
family → families	child → children
toy → toys	woman → women
tomato → tomatoes	foot → feet

We usually use a or an with singular countable nouns.
a wedding
an opinion

We can use some, any or a number (eg three) with plural countable nouns.
There are **some** birds in the park.
Are there **any** biscuits?
We're moving house **in three** weeks.

We use singular or plural verb forms with countable nouns depending on whether we are talking about one or more items.
A family get-together **is** just what we need.
My sisters **live** in Hull.

Note: Some countable nouns don't end in –s. Remember to use a plural verb form with them.
Children **are** sometimes unkind.
His feet **are** very big!

1.6 Uncountable Nouns

Some nouns are uncountable. They do not have plural forms.

advice	history	progress
cheese	homework	research
chocolate	information	rubbish
equipment	knowledge	salt
food	luggage	time
fruit	milk	traffic
fun	money	water
furniture	music	weather

We don't use a or an with uncountable nouns. We can use some and any.
I'd like **some** cheese in my sandwich.
Have you got **any** homework tonight?

We always use singular verb forms with uncountable nouns.
This fruit **is** so delicious.
Milk **is** good for you.

Note: Some uncountable nouns end in –s. Remember to use a singular verb form with them
The **news isn't** good.
Maths is my favourite subject.

We can use phrases describing quantity with uncountable nouns to say how much we have. The most common of these phrases are:

- a bag of
- a bottle of
- a bowl of
- a can of
- a carton of
- a cup of
- a glass of
- a jar of
- a kilo of
- a loaf of
- a number of
- a packet of
- a piece of
- a tin of

A bowl of soup
A glass of water

1.7 Quantifiers

We use some with both uncountable and plural countable nouns in affirmative sentences and in requests or offers.
Here are **some books** for your research.
Can you give me **some advice**?
Would you like **some chocolate**?

We use any with both uncountable and plural countable nouns in negative sentences and in questions.
Did Julia buy **any fruit** at the market?
Sarah hasn't got **any brothers**.

We use a lot/lots of with both uncountable and plural countable nouns.
There's **a lot/lots of traffic** today.
There are **a lot/lots of people** in town.

We use a little with uncountable nouns and a few with plural countable nouns in affirmative sentences.
I like **a little milk** in my tea.
James always eats **a few biscuits** for breakfast.

We use much with uncountable nouns and many with plural countable nouns in negative sentences and in questions.
There wasn't **much snow** last night.
Have **many of your friends** seen that film?

Unit 2

2.1 Past Simple

Affirmative
I/he/she/it/we/you/they cook**ed**

Negative
I/he/she/it/we/you/they **didn't** cook

Questions
Did I/he/she/it/we/you/they cook?

Short Answers	
Yes, I/he/she/it **did**. **Yes**, we/you/they **did**.	**No**, I/he/she/it **didn't**. **No**, we/you/they **didn't**.

Spelling: dance → danc**ed**, travel → travel**led**, ti**dy** → ti**died**, play → pl**ayed**

Note: Some verbs are irregular and do not follow these spelling rules. See a list of irregular verbs on pages 174 & 175.

We use the Past Simple for
- something that started and finished in the past.
  *John **made** some coffee a few minutes ago.*
- past routines and habits (often with adverbs of frequency).
  *Sue never **ate** fast food at school.*
- actions that happened one after the other in the past, for example when telling a story.
  *We **went** to the park and **had** a picnic.*

Note: Some common time expressions that are often used with the Past Simple are *yesterday, last night/week/ month/summer, a week/month/year ago, twice a week, once a month, at the weekend, in March, in the morning/ afternoon/evening, at night, on Thursdays, on Monday mornings*, etc.
*The farmer harvested the olives **last week**.*

2.2 Past Continuous

Affirmative
I/he/she/it **was** cook**ing** we/you/they **were** cook**ing**

Negative
I/he/she/it **was not (wasn't)** cook**ing** we/you/they **were not (weren't)** cook**ing**

Questions
Was I/he/she/it cook**ing**? **Were** we/you/they cook**ing**?

Short Answers	
Yes, I/he/she/it **was**. **Yes**, we/you/they **were**.	**No**, I/he/she/it **wasn't**. **No**, we/you/they **weren't**.

Spelling: write → writ**ing**, travel → travel**ling**, tidy → tid**ying**

We use the Past Continuous for
- actions that were in progress at a specific time in the past.

*Mum **was making** hamburgers for us at 7 o'clock last night.*
- two or more actions that were in progress at the same time in the past.
  *I **was cooking** while my brother **was watching** TV.*
- giving background information in a story.
  *The sun **was shining** and the children **were playing** outside when suddenly **there was** a loud bang.*
- an action that was in progress in the past that was interrupted by another.
  *We **were getting** ready to have dinner when the doorbell **rang**.*

Note: Some common time expressions that are often used with the Past Continuous are *while, as, all day/week/ month/year, at ten o'clock last night, last Sunday/week/ year, this morning*, etc.
*Mario was working all night **yesterday**.*

2.3 Used To & Would

We use *used to* + bare infinitive for
- actions that we did regularly in the past, but that we don't do now.
  *Our family **used to produce** olive oil when I was young.*
- states that existed in the past, but that don't exist now.
  *I **used to love** eating out but now I prefer cooking at home.*

We use *would* + bare infinitive for actions that we did regularly in the past, but that we don't do now. We don't use it for past states.
*Their mother **would cook** something special at the weekends.*

2.4 Be Used To & Get Used To

We use *be used to* + gerund/noun to talk about something that is usual or familiar.
*Her daughter **is used to eating** late at night.*

We use *get used to* + gerund/noun to talk about the process of something becoming familiar.
*I **am getting used to salty food**. I don't mind it.*

Note: *Be* and *get* change depending on the tense that is needed in the context.
*He**'s used to waking** up early.*
*Julie **has never got used to eating** a lot of olive oil.*

Unit 3

3.1 Present Perfect Simple

Affirmative
I/we/you/they **have ('ve) seen** he/she/it **has ('s) seen**

Negative
I/we/you/they **have not (haven't) seen** he/she/it **has not (hasn't) seen**

Questions
Have I/we/you/they **seen**? **Has** he/she/it **seen**?

Short Answers	
Yes, I/we/you/they **have**. **Yes**, he/she/it **has**.	**No**, I/we/you/they **haven't**. **No**, he/she/it **hasn't**.

Spelling: walk → walk**ed**, dance → danc**ed**, travel → trave**lled**, ti**dy** → ti**died**, play → pl**ayed**

Note: Some verbs are irregular and do not follow these spelling rules. See a list of irregular verbs on pages 174 & 175.

We use the Present Perfect Simple for
- something that started in the past and has continued until now.
  *That scientist **has studied** global warming since 2001.*
- something that happened in the past, but we don't know or we don't say exactly when.
  *Biologists **have found** new marine species.*
- something that happened in the past and has a result that affects the present.
  *Pollution **has endangered** the survival of many animals.*
- actions that have just finished.
  *The museum **has just closed** for the day.*
- experiences and achievements.
  *Lynda **has travelled** to many countries.*

Note: Some common time expressions that are often used with the Present Perfect Simple are *already, ever, for, for a long time/ages, just, never, once, recently, since 2007/June, so far, twice, three times, until now, yet,* etc.
*Mary has lived in this house **since 2003**.*

3.2 Have Been & Have Gone

Notice the difference between *have been* and *have gone.*
have been = someone has gone somewhere and has now returned
*I **have been** to that natural history museum. It's great.*
have gone = someone has gone somewhere and is still there
*Mum is not here. She**'s gone** to work.*

3.3 Ago, For & Since

We often use *ago* with the Past Simple, and *for* and *since* with the Present Perfect Simple.

We use *ago* at the end of a sentence with the Past Simple.
*He went to a conference a month **ago**.*

We use *for* with an expression that shows a period of time at the end of a sentence with the Present Perfect Simple.
*The Tasmanian Wolf has been extinct **for** about 50 years.*

We use *since* with a point of time in the past at the end of a sentence with the Present Perfect Simple.
*The Dodo bird has been extinct **since** 1681.*

3.4 Present Perfect Simple & Past Simple

We use the Present Perfect Simple when we talk about something that happened in the past and has a result that affects the present. We also use the Present Perfect Simple when we don't know or we don't say when something happened in the past. We use the Past Simple when we say when something happened.
*The use of fossil fuels **has caused** air pollution.*
*He **has explored** many places in the Amazon.*
*We **met** the famous scientist at a conference last year.*

3.5 Present Perfect Continuous

Affirmative		
I/we/you/they **have ('ve) been** seeing he/she/it **has ('s) been** seeing		
Negative		
I/we/you/they **have not (haven't) been** seeing he/she/it **has not (hasn't) been** seeing		
Questions		
Have I/we/you/they **been** seeing? **Has** he/she/it **been** seeing?		
Short Answers		
Yes, I/we/you/they **have**. **Yes**, he/she/it **has**.	**No**, I/we/you/they **haven't**. **No**, he/she/it **hasn't**.	

Spelling: make → mak**ing**, swim → swi**mming**, stud**y** → stud**ying**

We use the Present Perfect Continuous
- for actions that started in the past and are still in progress now or have happened repeatedly until now.
  *The team of biologists **has been searching** for new species in the Amazon.*
- for actions that happened repeatedly in the past and have finished recently, but that have results that affect the present.
  *My eyes hurt because I **have been working** on the computer for hours.*
- to emphasise how long actions have been in progress for.
  *Her brother **has been researching** global warming for a decade.*

Note: Some common time expressions that are often used with the Present Perfect Continuous are *all day/night/week, for years/a long time/ages, lately, recently, since.* We can use *How long ...?* with the Present Perfect Continuous in questions and *for (very) long* in questions and negative sentences.
*We have been going on holiday to a tropical island **for ages**.*
***How long** has Bob been working in this lab?*
*I haven't been researching coral reefs **for very long**. It's only been two months.*

3.6 Present Perfect Simple & Present Perfect Continuous

We use the Present Perfect Simple to talk about something we have done or achieved, or an action that is complete. It is also used to say how many times something happened.
*We **have watched** that documentary five times in the last month.*

We use the Present Perfect Continuous to talk about how long something has been happening. It is not important whether or not it has finished.
*The tropical storm **has been going** on for days.*

3.7 The Indefinite Article: A/An

We use a before a consonant sound.
a fisherman
a uniform

We use an before a vowel sound.
an octopus
an hour

We use *a/an*
- with singular countable nouns.
  *He always has **a** laptop with him.*
- to mean *per/each* in expressions of frequency.
  *Our teachers meet once **a** week.*
- to mention something for the first time. (When we continue talking about it we use *the*.)
  ***An** elephant was born at the zoo.*
  ***The** baby elephant is very popular with visitors.*
- to show job, status, etc.
  *He is **an** archaeologist.*

3.8 The Definite Article: The

We use *the* with singular and plural countable nouns and uncountable nouns, to talk about something specific when the noun is mentioned for a second time.
*Look! There's a fisherman on **a** boat. **The** boat looks very old.*

We also use *the* before
- unique nouns.
  ***The** sun is yellow and **the** sky is blue.*
- names of cinemas, theatres, ships, hotels, etc.
  *When did **the** Titanic sink?*
  *We're staying at **the** Intercontinental in Athens.*
- names of rivers, deserts, mountain ranges, and names or nouns with *of*.
  *Where is **the** Sahara Desert?*
  ***The** Andes are covered in snow.*
- countries or groups of countries whose names are plural.
  *Have you visited **the** United States?*
  *She comes from **the** Philippines.*
- musical instruments.
  *Brian plays **the** violin and **the** piano.*
- nationalities.
  ***The** British are well-known for drinking tea.*
  ***The** Chinese invented the modern abacus.*
- adjectives used as nouns.
  ***The** poor should get help from the government.*
- superlatives.
  *He is **the** best student in the class.*
- the following words *beach, countryside, station, jungle,* etc.
  *We love going to **the** beach in summer.*
- *morning, afternoon, evening.*
  *Most people watch TV in **the** evening.*

We do not use *the* before
- proper nouns.
  *Is **Anna** at work today?*
- names of sports, games, colours, days, months, drinks, holidays, meals and languages (not followed by the word *language*).
  ***Blue** is my favourite colour.*
- subjects of study.
  *We have to study **physics** at school.*
- names of countries, cities, streets (BUT: *the High Street*), squares, bridges (BUT: *the Golden Gate Bridge*), parks, stations, individual mountains, islands, lakes, continents.

London is a very popular tourist destination.
- *bed, church, school, hospital, prison, university, college, court* when we talk about something related to the main purpose of the place. (*Work* never takes *the*.)
  *Fran is in **hospital**. (She's had an accident and is a patient there.)*
  *Angela has gone to **the hospital** to visit Fran. (She's not a patient; she's gone to visit someone.)*
- means of transportation in expressions like *by car*, etc. (*in the car*).
  *A huge number of people go to work **by train**.*

Unit 4

4.1 Relative Clauses: defining & non-defining

Relative clauses give more information about the subject or the object of a sentence. They are introduced by the following words (relative pronouns):
- *who* for people.
  *The book is about a boy **who** is homeless.*
- *which* for things.
  *The programme **which** was about guide dogs was very interesting.*
- *whose* to show possession.
  *The woman **whose** dog got lost was very upset.*
- *when* for time.
  *A birthday is a time **when** you feel a bit emotional.*
- *where* for places.
  *This is the house **where** we grew up.*

4.2 Defining Relative Clauses

This type of relative clause gives us information that we need to be able to understand who or what the speaker is talking about. We do not use commas to separate it from the rest of the sentence. We can use *that* instead of *who* and *which* in defining relative clauses.
*These are the rescue workers **who/that** rescued hundreds of people in the flood.*

4.3 Non-defining Relative Clauses

This type of relative clause gives us extra information which isn't necessary to understand the meaning of the main clause. We use commas to separate it from the rest of the sentence.
*His father, **who** is a trainer, has a great love for dogs.*

4.4 Temporals

When we use temporals such as *when, before, after, until, once, by the time,* etc to talk about the future, we follow them with a present or a present perfect tense. We do not use them with a future tense.
***After** I **finish** my homework, I'll help you with yours.*
***By the time** Janet **arrives**, the film will have finished.*

We use a present perfect tense to emphasise that the first action is finished before the other one starts. We cannot use a present tense if one action has finished.
*You can watch TV **when** you**'ve cleared** the table. (You'll clear the table first and then you'll watch TV.)*
***Once** everyone **has eaten**, we'll begin. (Everyone will eat first and then we'll start.)*

Unit 5

5.1 Will

Affirmative
I/he/she/it/we/you/they **will** build

Negative
I/he/she/it/we/you/they **will not (won't)** build

Questions
Will I/he/she/it/we/you/they build?

Short Answers	
Yes, I/he/she/it **will**. **Yes**, we/you/they **will**.	**No**, I/he/she/it **won't**. **No**, we/you/they **won't**.

We use *will*
- for decisions made at the time of speaking.
  I'll ring my friend to borrow her car.
- for predictions without having evidence.
  My son will be famous one day.
- for promises.
  He won't be late again. He promised.
- for threats.
  Don't tell anyone my secret or I'll never speak to you again!
- to talk about future facts.
  John will be seventeen years old tomorrow.
- after verbs like *think, believe, be sure, expect*, etc and words like *probably, maybe*, etc.
  I think I will move house next year.
- to offer to do something for someone.
  Dad will help you clean the house.
- to ask someone to do something.
  Will you please cook dinner tonight?

5.2 Be Going To

Affirmative
I **am ('m) going to** build he/she/it **is ('s) going to** build we/you/they **are ('re) going to** build

Negative
I **am ('m) not going to** build he/she/it **is not (isn't) going to** build we/you/they **are not (aren't) going to** build

Questions
Am I **going to** build? **Is** he/she/it **going to** build? **Are** we/you/they **going to** build?

Short Answers	
Yes, I **am**. **Yes**, we/you/they **are**. **Yes**, he/she/it **is**.	**No**, I'm **not**. **No**, we/you/they **aren't**. **No**, he/she/it **isn't**.

We use *be going to* for
- future plans.
  They're going to paint the living room green at the weekend.
- predictions for the near future based on present situations or evidence.
  Oh no! The window is open and the rain is going to come in.

Note: Some common time expressions that are often used with *will* and *be going to* are *this week/month/summer, tonight, this evening, tomorrow, tomorrow morning/afternoon/night, next week/month/year, at the weekend, in January, in a few minutes/hours/days, on Thursday, on Wednesday morning*, etc.
He is going to leave the house in a few minutes.

5.3 Future plans & events

Affirmative		
I/he/she/it/we/you/they **will be** build**ing**		

Negative		
I/he/she/it/we/you/they **will not (won't) be** build**ing**		

Questions		
Will I/he/she/it/we/you/they **be** build**ing**?		

Short Answers			
Yes, I/he/she/it **will**. **Yes**, we/you/they **will**.		**No**, I/he/she/it **won't**. **No**, we/you/they **won't**.	

Spelling: make → mak**ing**, swim → swi**mming**, study → stud**ying**

We use the Future Continuous for
- actions that will be in progress at a specific time in the future.
  She will be decorating the baby's room all afternoon.
- plans and arrangements for the future.
  They will be moving into their new flat tomorrow.

Note: Some common time expressions that are often used with the Future Continuous are *this time next week/month/summer, this time tomorrow morning/afternoon/night*, etc.
This time next week we will be living in New York.

5.4 Future predictions

Affirmative	
I/he/she/it/we/you/they **will have built**	

Negative
I/he/she/it/we/you/they **will not (won't) have built**

Questions
Will I/he/she/it/we/you/they **have built**?

Short Answers	
Yes, I/he/she/it **will**. **Yes**, we/you/they **will**.	**No**, I/he/she/it **won't**. **No**, we/you/they **won't**.

Spelling: walk → walk**ed**, dance → danc**ed**, travel → trave**lled**, tidy → ti**died**, play → play**ed**

Note: Some verbs are irregular and do not follow these spelling rules. See a list of irregular verbs on pages 174–175.

We use the Future Perfect Simple to talk about
- something that will be finished by or before a specific time in the future.
  The architect will have finished the design for the skyscraper by next month.

- the length of time that an action will have lasted for at a point of time in the future.
  *Next year we **will have worked** on this project for two years.*

Note: Some common time expressions that are often used with the Future Perfect Simple are *by the end of this week/month/year, by this time tomorrow, by tomorrow morning/10 o'clock/2012,* etc.
*The electrician **will have fixed** the problem by tomorrow.*

Note: Other tenses that describe the future are the Present Simple for timetabled events, and the Present Continuous for plans and arrangements. See Grammar Reference 1.1 and 1.3.

Unit 6

6.1 Zero Conditional: zero & first, second conditional, if

If clause	Main clause
present simple	present simple

We use the zero conditional to talk about the results of an action or situation that are always true. We can use *when* instead of *if*.
If a football player is shown a red card, he leaves the pitch.
When a football player is shown a red card, he leaves the pitch.

6.2 First Conditional

If clause	Main clause
present tense	*will* + bare infinitive

We use the first conditional to talk about the results of an action or situation that will probably happen now or in the future.
*If my team **wins** the match, I'll be thrilled!*
*If it's still **raining** later, we'll play indoors.*

We can use *can, could, may* or *might* in the main clause instead of *will*. We can also use an imperative.
*If John scores a goal, we **might** win the game.*
*If you aren't doing anything tonight, **watch** the match at my house.*

6.3 Second Conditional

If clause	Main clause
past tense	*would* + bare infinitive

We use the second conditional to talk about the results of an action or situation
- that probably won't happen now or in the future.
  *You **would be** healthier if you **took** some exercise.*
- that we know will not happen now or in the future.
  *If I **won** an Olympic gold medal, I'd be famous!*

We can also use the second conditional to give advice.
*If I **were** you, I'd **take up** a sport.*

We can use *could* or *might* in the main clause instead of *would*.
*Jack **could** win the tournament if he trained harder.*
*If you left now, you **might** be on time for the match.*

Note: We usually use *were* for all persons in second conditional sentences.
*If Luke **were** better at football, he'd be on the team.*

6.4 Unless

We can use *unless* in first and second conditional sentences. It means the same as *if not*.
*Lucy won't be happy **unless** she gets chosen for the netball team.*
*Mr Martins couldn't go to the match **unless** he had a ticket.*

Unit 7

7.1 Past Perfect Simple

Affirmative		
I/he/she/it/we/you/they **had ('d)** climb**ed**		
Negative		
I/he/she/it/we/you/they **had not (hadn't)** climb**ed**		
Questions		
Had I/he/she/it/we/you/they climb**ed**?		
Short Answers		
Yes, I/he/she/it **had.** **Yes,** we/you/they **had.**		**No,** I/he/she/it **hadn't.** **No,** we/you/they **hadn't.**

Spelling: walk → walk**ed**, dance → danc**ed**, travel → travel**led**, tidy → tid**ied**, play → play**ed**

Note: Some verbs are irregular and do not follow these spelling rules. See a list of irregular verbs on pages 174–175.

We use the Past Perfect Simple for an action or situation that finished before another action, situation or time in the past.
*The lost climber **had been** on the mountain for days before he was rescued.*

Note: Some common time expressions that are often used with the Past Perfect Simple are *already, for, for a long time/ages, just, never, once, since 2007/June, so far, yet,* etc.
*A light rain had **already** begun when we set out for a run.*

7.2 Past Simple & Past Perfect Simple

In some sentences, it is clear which action happens first. In this case, we can use the Past Simple for both actions. However, when the order of events is not clear, or when we want to emphasise which action happened first, we can use the Past Perfect Simple for the first action.
*We **went** to a talk and **met** a famous explorer.*
*He **realised** later that he **had done** a very dangerous thing.*

Remember that we must use the Past Simple for both actions when one past action happens quickly after another or one is the immediate result of the other.
*When the little boy **heard** the thunder, he **hid** under the bed.*

7.3 Past Perfect Continuous

Affirmative
I/he/she/it/we/you/they **had ('d) been** climb**ing**

Negative
I/he/she/it/we/you/they **had not (hadn't)** been climb**ing**

Questions
Had I/he/she/it/we/you/they **been** climb**ing**?

Short Answers	
Yes, I/he/she/it **had**. **Yes**, we/you/they **had**.	**No**, I/he/she/it **hadn't**. **No**, we/you/they **hadn't**.

Spelling: make → mak**ing**, swim → swi**mming**, study → stud**ying**

We use the Past Perfect Continuous

*   for actions that started in the past and were still in progress when another action started or when something happened.
    *He **had been free falling** for several seconds before he opened his parachute.*
*   for actions that were in progress in the past and had an effect on a later action.
    *The hiker **had been walking** for days and collapsed just before reaching his destination.*

Note: Some common time expressions that are often used with the Past Perfect Continuous are *all day/night/week, for years/a long time/ages, since*. We can use *How long ...?* with the Past Perfect Continuous in questions and *for (very) long* in questions and negative sentences.
*Ben had been climbing mountains **for years**.*
***How long** had you been competing in races?*

7.4 Question Tags

Question tags are short questions at the end of a positive or negative sentence. They are formed with a modal or an auxiliary verb + a personal pronoun.
We usually use an affirmative question tag after a negative sentence, and a negative question tag after an affirmative sentence.
*You haven't competed in a marathon, **have you**?*
*The athletes are training hard, **aren't they**?*
When an affirmative sentence contains a verb in the Present Simple or the Past Simple we use *do/does, don't/doesn't* and *did/didn't* in the question tag.
*You go swimming every day, **don't you**?*
*You went swimming yesterday, **didn't you**?*
We use question tags when we want

*   someone to agree with what we are saying.
    *It's a beautiful day, **isn't it**?*
*   to make sure that what we are saying is right.
    *The tennis match starts at 3 o'clock, **doesn't it**?*

Note: Some question tags are irregular. Notice the way these tags are formed.
*I am lucky to be alive, **aren't I**?*
*Everyone is looking forward to the trip, **aren't they**?*
*Let's hike in the mountains, **shall we**?*
*Don't forget to let me know you've arrived safely, **will you**?*

*Be careful, **won't you**?*
*This/That is so dangerous, **isn't it**?*
*These/Those are brave men, **aren't they**?*

7.5 Subject & Object Questions

When *who, what,* or *which* asks about the subject of a question, the word order stays the same as in an affirmative sentence.
***Who survived** yesterday's climbing accident?*
*(**Everyone** survived.)*

When *who, what,* or *which* are the object of a question, the word order changes in the question form.
***Who did** the rescue **team** save?*
*(They saved **the captain**.)*

7.6 Negative Questions

We use negative questions

*   to express surprise.
    *'**Didn't** Jamie **finish** the race?' 'No, he collapsed before the finish line.'*
*   in exclamations.
    ***Isn't** bungee jumping one of the most thrilling extreme sports?*
*   when we expect the listener to agree with us.
    ***Wasn't** that such an interesting documentary?*

To answer negative questions we just use a *Yes* or *No* answer depending on what we think. A *Yes* answer confirms a positive opinion, whereas a *No* answer confirms a negative opinion.
Isn't it a lovely day today?
Yes. / Yes, it is. (=agreement)
No. / No, it isn't. (= disagreement)

Unit 8

Modals & Semi-modals
8.1 Can & Could

We use *can* + bare infinitive

*   to talk about general ability in the present and the future.
    *He **can** make beautiful things out of stone.*
*   for requests.
    ***Can** we go to the concert tonight?*
*   for permission.
    *People **can** enter this cave and explore if they like.*

    We use *can't* + bare infinitive to show that we are sure that something isn't true.
    *That **can't** be Jane! Isn't she away on a trip?*

    We use *could* + bare infinitive

*   to talk about general ability in the past. (past form of *can*)
    *I **could** ski when I was only seven years old.*
*   to talk about possibility.
    *We **could** go sailing if the wind went down by tomorrow.*
*   for polite requests.
    ***Could** you please give me that magazine?*
*   to make suggestions.
    *We **could** go to the cinema.*

8.2 May & Might

We use *may* + bare infinitive
- to talk about possibility in the future.
  *I **may** take up painting as a hobby next month.*
- for polite requests. (with *I* and *we*)
  ***May** we borrow your camera?*
- for polite permission.
  *You **may** ask me any question you like.*

We use *might* + bare infinitive
- to talk about possibility in the future.
  *Sue **might** decide to join a gym soon.*
- as the past tense of *may*.

8.3 Must

We use *must* + bare infinitive to
- say that something is necessary.
  *I **must** be home at 7 o'clock at the latest.*
- talk about obligations.
  *You **must** wear a helmet when riding a motorbike in this country.*
- show that we are sure that something is true.
  *My sister **must** be nervous about the dance competition.*
- recommend something.
  *You really **must** go and see that play! It was great!*

We use *mustn't* + bare infinitive to talk about something that is not allowed.
*People **mustn't** speak on their mobiles while driving.*

8.4 Should

We use *should* + bare infinitive to
- give advice.
  *People of all ages **should** take some exercise every week.*
- ask for advice.
  *What **should** I do about losing weight?*

Note: *Ought to* can also be used to give advice, but it is not usually used in the question form.

8.5 Would

We use *would* + bare infinitive for
- actions that we did regularly in the past, but that we don't do now.
  *I **would** always go for a run in the morning before I started work.*
- polite requests.
  ***Would** you please buy some batteries for my camera?*

8.6 Needn't

We use *needn't* + bare infinitive to say that something is not necessary. We don't use it in affirmative sentences.
*You **needn't take** photos at the party because my brother is videotaping it.*

Note: We can also use *need* as an ordinary verb. It has affirmative, negative and question forms and it is usually used in the Present Simple and the Past Simple. It is followed by a full infinitive.
*Mary **needs to find** a new hobby.*
*The twins **didn't need to walk** to the cinema because their mum took them in the car.*
***Did** he **need to** pay to join the chess club?*

8.7 Be Able To

We use *be able to* to talk about
- ability.
  *I **will be able to** play the guitar tonight.*
- a specific ability in the past. (*Could* cannot be used here.)
  *She **wasn't able to** practise the new dance at the weekend.*

8.8 Have To

We use *have to* to
- say that something is necessary.
  *You **have to** rehearse your part in the play every day.*
- talk about obligation.
  *We **have to** have some training before we can go parachuting.*

8.9 Mustn't & Don't Have To

There is an important difference between *mustn't* and *don't have to*. We use *mustn't* to say that something is not allowed, whereas we use *don't have to* to show that there is no obligation or necessity.
*In basketball, players **mustn't kick** the ball.*
*You **don't have to play** basketball with us this afternoon if you don't want to.*

Unit 9

9.1 The Passive Voice: Tenses

We use the passive voice when
- the action is more important than who or what is responsible for it (the agent).
  *Two people **were injured** during the robbery.*
- we don't know the agent, or it is not important.
  *You can use the computer now. It **was repaired** yesterday.*

The passive is formed with the verb *be* and a past participle. Notice how the active verb forms change to passive verb forms.

Tense	Active	Passive
Present Simple	take/takes	am/are/is taken
Present Continuous	am/are/is taking	am/are/is being taken
Past Simple	took	was/were taken
Past Continuous	was/were taking	was/were being taken
Present Perfect Simple	have/has taken	have/has been taken
Past Perfect Simple	had taken	had been taken
Future Simple	will take	will be taken

Note: There is no passive form for Future Continuous, Present Perfect Continuous and Past Perfect Continuous.

We change an active sentence into a passive sentence in the following way:

The object of the verb in the active sentence becomes the subject of the verb in the passive sentence. The verb *be* is used in the same tense of the main verb in the active sentence, together with the past participle of the main verb in the active sentence.

*They **are watching** us! We **are being watched**!*
In this example, we do not know who is watching us and it is not very important, so we do not include the word *they* in the passive sentence.

Note: When we want to change a sentence with two objects into the passive voice, one becomes the subject of the passive sentence and the other one remains an object. Which object we choose depends on what we want to emphasise. If the personal object remains an object in the passive sentence, then we have to use a suitable preposition (*to, for*, etc).
He gave me a video camera.
***I was given** a video camera.*
*A video camera **was given to me**.*

9.2 By & With

Sometimes it is important to mention the agent (who or what is responsible for the action) in a passive sentence. We use the word *by* before the agent to do this.
*Alexander Graham Bell **invented** the telephone.*
*The telephone **was invented by** Alexander Graham Bell.*

Sometimes we want to mention a tool or material in the passive sentence. We use the word *with* to do this.
*The window **was broken with** a rock.*
*The room **was painted with** a new kind of paint.*

9.3 The Passive Voice: Gerunds, Infinitives & Modals

Tense	Active	Passive
Modal	can take	can be taken
Gerund	taking	being taken
Bare Infinitive	take	be taken
Full Infinitive	to take	to be taken

*Surveillance cameras **should be installed** here to prevent crimes.*
*He avoided **being recognised** by wearing dark glasses.*
*The project had better **be finished** by tomorrow.*
*The battery needs **to be recharged**.*

Unit 10

10.1 Reported Speech: Statements

When we report direct speech, the tenses used by the speaker usually change as follows:

Present Simple	Past Simple
'He **likes** hip-hop,' she said.	She said (that) he **liked** hip hop.
Present Continuous	**Past Continuous**
'He **is listening** to his new CD,' she said.	She said (that) he **was listening** to his new CD.
Present Perfect Simple	**Past Perfect Simple**
'They **have bought** a new CD,' she said.	She said (that) they **had bought** a new CD.

Present Perfect Continuous	Past Perfect Continuous
'They **have been recording** all day,' she said.	She said (that) they **had been recording** all day.
Past Simple	**Past Perfect Simple**
'He **watched** a film on TV,' she said.	She said (that) he **had watched** a film on TV.
Past Continuous	**Past Perfect Continuous**
'He **was reading** about Imiz,' she said.	She said (that) he **had been reading** about Imiz.

Other changes in verb forms are as follows:

can	could
'Jane **can** play the piano,' she said.	She said (that) Jane **could** play the piano.
may	**might**
'He **may** come to the concert,' she said.	She said (that) he **might** come to the concert.
must	**had to**
'He **must** collect the tickets later,' she said.	She said (that) he **had to** collect the tickets later.
will	**would**
'They **will** never like opera,' she said.	She said (that) they **would** never like opera.

Note:
1 Remember to change pronouns and possessive adjectives where necessary.
*'**We** are going to form a band,' he said.* → *He said (that) **they** were going to form a band.*
*'Those are **my** music magazines,' she said.* → *She said (that) those were **her** music magazines.*
2 We can leave out *that*.
*They **said that** they had seen the film before.* → *They **said they** had seen the film before.*
3 The following tenses and words don't change in Reported Speech: Past Perfect Simple, Past Perfect Continuous, *would, could, might, should, ought to, used to, had better, mustn't* and *must* when they refer to deduction.

10.2 Say & Tell

We often use the verbs *say* and *tell* in reported speech. We follow *tell* with an object.
Julia said they would love her new single.
*Julia told **her friends** they would love her new single.*

10.3 Reported Speech: Change in time & place

When we report direct speech, there are often changes in words that show time and place too.

now	then
'I'm playing the guitar **now**,' she said.	She said she was playing the guitar **then**.
today	**that day**
'We're going to the theatre **today**,' he said.	He said they were going to the theatre **that day**.

tonight	**that night**
'They can go to the cinema **tonight**,' she said.	She said they could go to the cinema **that night**.
yesterday	**the previous day/the day before**
'I saw them in concert **yesterday**,' she said.	She said she had seen them in concert **the previous day/the day before**.
last week/month	**the previous week/month / the week/month before**
'He released the CD **last month**,' she said.	She said he had released the CD **the previous month/the month before**.
tomorrow	**the next day/the following day**
'I'll buy the tickets **tomorrow**,' she said.	She said she would buy the tickets **the next day/the following day**.
next week/month	**the following week/month**
'We're going to the show **next week**,' she said.	She said they were going to the show **the following week**.
this/these	**that/those**
'**This** is my music magazine,' she said.	She said **that** was her music magazine.
ago	**before**
'I bought that CD two weeks **ago**,' she said.	She said she had bought that CD two weeks **before**.
at the moment	**at that moment**
'He's singing in a band **at the moment**,' she said.	She said he was singing in a band **at that moment**.
here	**there**
'Your CDs are **here** on the table,' she said.	She said my CDs were **there** on the table.

10.4 Reported Speech: Questions

When we report questions, changes in tenses, pronouns, possessive adjectives, time and place are the same as in reported statements. In reported questions, the verb follows the subject as in ordinary statements and we do not use question marks.

When a direct question has a question word, we use this word in the reported question.
'**When** did you start making records?' he asked.
He asked **when** I had started making records.

When a direct question does not have a question word, we use *if* or *whether* in the reported question.
'Do you like classical music?' he asked.
He asked **if/whether** I liked classical music.

10.5 Reported Speech: Commands

When we report commands, we usually use *tell* + object + full infinitive.
'Turn the volume down!' he shouted at me.
He **told me to turn** the volume down.
'Don't take my MP3 player!' he said to his sister.
He **told his sister not to take** his MP3 player.

10.6 Reported Speech: Requests

When we report a request, we usually use *ask* + object + full infinitive.
'Can you lend me your headphones, please?' she asked.
She **asked me to lend** her my headphones.
(Also: She asked if I could lend her my headphones.)
'Please don't tell anyone,' he said.
He **asked us not to tell** anyone.

Unit 11

11.1 Causative

We use the causative
- to say that someone has arranged for somebody to do something for them.
  John **is having his new computer delivered** in the morning.
- to say that something unpleasant happened to someone.
  Mrs Temp **has had her car broken into**.

We form the causative with *have* + object + past participle. It can be used in a variety of tenses.
I **was having my kitchen painted** last weekend.
Aunt Maureen **has been having her clothes made** for her for years.
The school **has its rubbish collected** every day.

Note: We can also use *get* + object + past participle. This structure is less formal.
Joseph **got his mobile phone taken away** in English yesterday!

11.2 Gerunds

We form gerunds with verbs and the –ing ending. We can use gerunds
- as nouns.
  Swimming is my favourite hobby.
  Ben likes **cycling**.
- after prepositions.
  Jenny's only five but she's very good **at reading**.
- after the verb *go* when we talk about activities.
  My class **are going canoeing** at the weekend.

We also use gerunds after certain verbs and phrases.

admit	finish	love
avoid	forgive	miss
be used to	hate	practise
can't help	have difficulty	prefer
can't stand	imagine	prevent
deny	involve	regret
dislike	it's no good	risk
(don't) mind	it's no use	spend time
enjoy	it's (not) worth	suggest
fancy	keep	
feel like	like	

Some students **are having difficulty doing** their maths exercises.
It's no good only studying for tests. You won't get good grades.

11.3 Infinitives

	Active	Passive
Present	(to) send	(to) be sent
Perfect	(to) have sent	(to) have been sent

*The teacher threatened **to expel** the badly behaved student.*
*Photos can **be edited** on a computer.*
*You should **have tried** harder to pass your exams.*
*He should **have been awarded** a prize.*

11.4 Full Infinitives

We form full infinitives with *to* and the verb. We use full infinitives
- to explain purpose.
  *They went to the library **to look up** information for their project.*
- after adjectives such as *afraid, scared, happy, glad, sad,* etc.
  *Jenny was so **happy to pass** her exams.*
- after the words *too* and *enough*.
  *It was **too** late **to change** his mind about his studies.*
  *His grades weren't good **enough** for him **to go** to university.*

We also use full infinitives after certain verbs and phrases.

afford	fail	prepare
agree	forget	pretend
allow	hope	promise
appear	invite	refuse
arrange	learn	seem
ask	manage	start
begin	need	want
choose	offer	would like
decide	persuade	
expect	plan	

*The teacher **offered to give** the weak student some extra help with maths.*

11.5 Bare Infinitives

We use bare infinitives after
- modal verbs.
  *You **should ask** your teacher for advice on your studies.*
- *had better* to give advice.
  *You**'d better be** careful when you go mountain climbing.*
- *would rather* to talk about preference. We often use the word *than*.
  *I**'d rather stay** at home than go out tonight.*

11.6 Gerund or Infinitive?

Some verbs can be followed by a gerund or a full infinitive with no change in meaning. Some common verbs are *begin, bother, continue, hate, like, love* and *start*.
*The students started **writing/to write** the test at 9 o'clock.*
*John failed the test because he didn't bother **revising/to revise**.*
*Mr Cairn continued **teaching/to teach** until he was 70 years old.*

*Young children love **learning/to learn** new things.*
*Don't start **running/to run** until you hear the whistle.*

There are other verbs that can be followed by a gerund or a full infinitive, but the meaning changes. Some common ones are *regret, forget, go on, remember, stop* and *try*.
*I **regret studying** French at university. (I studied French, but now I wish I hadn't.)*
*I **regret to tell** you that I've lost my maths book. (I'm sorry that I have to give you this news.)*
*Paul **forgot meeting** Belinda and walked straight passed her this morning! (He didn't remember that he had met Belinda, and he didn't recognise her when he saw her this morning.)*
*Paul **forgot to revise** for his test, and he failed. (Paul didn't remember he had a test and so he didn't revise for it.)*
*Mr Jones **went on talking** about photography for hours! (He continued to talk about the same thing.)*
*Mr Jones **went on to talk** about photography. (He had been talking about a different subject, and then started talking about a new subject – photography.)*
*My dad **remembers learning** Latin at school. (He learnt Latin at school and now he remembers learning it.)*
*My dad **remembered to pick** me **up** from school. (He remembered first and then came to pick me up from school.)*
*I **stopped going** to karate classes. (I don't go to karate classes any more.)*
*I **stopped to do** my homework. (I stopped doing something else so I could start my homework.)*
*If you can't remember things very easily, **try making** notes while you read. (You can make notes, but it might not help you.)*
*If you're doing a test, **try to answer** all the questions. (You might not be able to answer them all.)*

Unit 12

12.1 Ordering Adjectives

Sometimes more than one adjective is used in front of a noun:
*She was a **nice, old** woman.*
*He has a **large, black, leather** sofa.*

Opinion adjectives

Some adjectives give a general opinion, which describe almost any noun:
*He's a **nice** boy.*
*She's a **good** student.*
*They're **wonderful** parents.*

However, some adjectives give a specific opinion to describe particular kinds of nouns:
***tasty** meal, **comfortable** bed, **intelligent** child*

Usually a general opinion adjective is placed **before** a specific noun:
a nice, tasty meal
a beautiful, comfortable bed
a lovely, intelligent child

When we use two or more adjectives to describe something or someone, we usually put them in a certain order. Notice the correct order.

N O U N	general opinion	nice	beautiful	strong
	size	small	large	big
	age	old	new	ancient
	shape	round	oval	long
	colour	pink	beige	white
	nationality	French	Italian	Japanese
	material	cotton	wooden	silk

She has **beautiful long brown** hair.
He usually wears an **awful green woollen** jumper at the weekend.
They live in a **huge old English** cottage.

12.2 Adjectives ending in –ed & –ing

Adjectives that end in -ed describe how someone feels whereas adjectives that end in -ing describe a person, place or thing.
He's **interested** in the human body and he wants to be a doctor.
This book on the human body is very **interesting**.

12.3 Types of Adverbs

There are adverbs of frequency, manner, time, place and degree.
- Adverbs of frequency answer the question *How often?*.
  They see each other **regularly**.
- Adverbs of manner answer the question *How?*.
  She sings so **beautifully**.
- Adverbs of time answer the question *When?*.
  Tom broke his leg **yesterday**.
- Adverbs of place answer the question *Where?*.
  There is a great supermarket **near** my house.
- Adverbs of degree answer the question *To what extent?*.
  It's **rather** difficult to think when there is a lot of noise around you.

12.4 Order of Adverbs (manner, place & time)

When we use two or more adverbs in a sentence, the usual order is **manner + place + time**.
He put the envelope **carefully into his pocket after the meeting**.

After verbs like *come, leave, go*, etc, the usual order is **place + manner + time**.
She went to **the dentist quickly after work**.

Time adverbs can also come at the beginning of a sentence.
After the meeting he put the envelope carefully into his pocket.
After work she went to the dentist quickly.

12.5 Order of Adverbs (degree & frequency)

Adverbs of degree such as *quite, rather, too* and *very* usually come before an adjective.
He is **quite** good at maths.
The film was **rather** scary.
She is **too** young to see that film.
His mother is a **very** talented musician.

Enough is also an adverb of degree, but it comes after an adjective or a verb.
The film wasn't good **enough** to win an oscar.
She earns **enough** to afford a new car every two years.
Adverbs of frequency such as *always, never, seldom*, etc usually come after the verb *be* but before the main verb. (See also 1.2 on page 161.)
She **always** brushes her teeth in the morning and at night.
He **seldom** eats sweets.

12.6 So & Such

We use *so* and *such* for emphasis. They are stronger than *very*.
- We use *so* + adjective/adverb.
  This course is **so interesting**! I am really enjoying it!
- We use *such* + (adjective) + noun.
  Her brother is **such a clever boy**!

We can also use *so* and *such* to emphasise characteristics that lead to a certain result or action.
It was **such an interesting book that** I read it twice.
The film was **so bad that** I left the cinema half way through.

12.7 Comparison of Adjectives & Adverbs

We use the comparative to compare two people or things. We usually form the comparative by adding –er to an adjective or adverb. If the adjective or adverb has two or more syllables, we use the word *more*. We often use the word *than* after the comparative.
Judy has got **longer** hair than me.
This black dress is **more expensive** than the white one.

We use the superlative to compare one person or thing with other people or things of the same type. We usually form the superlative by adding –est to the adjective or adverb. If the adjective or adverb has two or more syllables, we usually use the word *most*. We use the word *the* before the superlative.
You are **the best** friend I've ever had.
He is **the most intelligent** person I have ever met.
Spelling: big → big**ger**/big**gest**, nice → nic**er**/nic**est**, brave → brav**er**/brav**est**, tidy → tid**ier**/tid**iest**
Some adjectives and adverbs are irregular and form their comparative and superlative in different ways.

Adjective/Adverb	Comparative	Superlative
good/well	better	the best
bad/badly	worse	the worst
many	more	the most
much	more	the most
little	less	the least
far	farther/further	the farthest/ furthest

12.8 Other comparative structures

We use *as* + adjective/adverb + *as* to show that two people or things are similar in some way.
My computer is **as fast as** your laptop.

We use *not as/so ... as* to show that one person or thing has less of a quality than another.
I am **not as successful as** my brother is.

Infinitive	Past Simple	Past Participle
be	was/were	been
beat	beat	beaten
become	became	become
begin	began	begun
bite	bit	bitten
blow	blew	blown
break	broke	broken
bring	brought	brought
broadcast	broadcast	broadcast
build	built	built
burn	burnt	burnt
buy	bought	bought
can	could	–
catch	caught	caught
choose	chose	chosen
come	came	come
cost	cost	cost
cut	cut	cut
deal	dealt	dealt
do	did	done
draw	drew	drawn
dream	dreamt	dreamt
drink	drank	drunk
drive	drove	driven
eat	ate	eaten
fall	fell	fallen
feed	fed	fed
feel	felt	felt
fight	fought	fought
find	found	found
fly	flew	flown
forecast	forecast	forecast
forget	forgot	forgotten
get	got	got
give	gave	given
go	went	gone
grow	grew	grown
have	had	had
hear	heard	heard
hide	hid	hidden
hit	hit	hit
hold	held	held
hurt	hurt	hurt
keep	kept	kept
know	knew	known
lead	led	led
learn	learnt	learnt
leave	left	left
lend	lent	lent
let	let	let

Infinitive	Past Simple	Past Participle
lie	lay	lain
light	lit	lit
lose	lost	lost
mean	meant	meant
make	made	made
meet	met	met
pay	paid	paid
prove	proved	proven
put	put	put
read	read [red]	read [red]
ride	rode	ridden
ring	rang	rung
rise	rose	risen
run	ran	run
say	said	said
see	saw	seen
sell	sold	sold
send	sent	sent
set	set	set
shake	shook	shaken
shine	shone	shone
show	showed	shown
shoot	shot	shot
shut	shut	shut
sing	sang	sung
sink	sank	sunk
sit	sat	sat
sleep	slept	slept
slide	slid	slid
smell	smelt	smelt
speak	spoke	spoken
speed	sped	sped
spend	spent	spent
stand	stood	stood
steal	stole	stolen
stick	stuck	stuck
stink	stank	stunk
sweep	swept	swept
swim	swam	swum
take	took	taken
teach	taught	taught
tell	told	told
think	thought	thought
throw	threw	thrown
understand	understood	understood
wake	woke	woken
wear	wore	worn
win	won	won
write	wrote	written

Writing Reference

Email

When writing an email,

- make it clear why you are writing.
- be friendly and use informal language.
- don't use *texting* language (for example, *ur* for *you're* and *lol* for *laugh out loud*).

Plan

Greeting
Hi...! / Hello...! / Dear ...,

Paragraph 1
Begin with polite phrases. Thank the reader for his/her email or ask about him/her and say why you are writing.
How are you? / I hope you're well.
Thank you for your email. / It was great to get your email.
That's why I'm writing. / As you know, ... / I'm writing to ...

Paragraph 2
Give more details about why you are writing.
We're planning ... / I'm thinking of ... / We've decided to ...

Paragraph 3
Give more information.
In addition, ... / Also, ... / As for ...

Signing off
See you soon! / Keep in touch. / That's all for now. / Write back soon! / Talk to you later!
Keep in touch! Love, ...

Email checklist

- Have you followed the plan? ☐
- Have you used grammatically correct forms? ☐
- Have you checked for spelling and punctuation mistakes? ☐
- Did you use informal language, such as short forms of verbs? ☐
- Is your writing style suitable for the situation and the reader? ☐
- Did you use linking words? ☐

Informal letter and email

When writing an informal letter or email,

- use informal language.
- make it clear why you are writing.
- make sure you focus on the subject you're writing about.

Plan

Greeting
Dear ..., / Hi ...,

Paragraph 1
Ask about the person you're writing to and explain why you're writing.
How are you? / Guess what? / Thanks for ...

Paragraphs 2 & 3
*Give more details regarding what you are writing about and what you want to find out or do.
There is/are ... / If you're interested, ... / Let me know ... / When are you available? / Let's
go together!*

Paragraph 4
Ask the person you're writing to further questions and suggest what needs to be done next.
*Could you do me a favour? / Maybe / Perhaps you could ... for me? / Do we need to ... ? /
I was wondering if ...*

Signing off
*See you soon! / Keep in touch. / That's all for now. / Write back soon! / Talk to you later! /
Keep in touch! / Love, ...*

Informal letter checklist

- Have you followed the plan? ☐
- Have you used grammatically correct forms? ☐
- Have you checked for spelling and punctuation mistakes? ☐
- Have you used informal language? ☐
- Have you used linking words correctly? ☐

Postcard

When writing a postcard:

- open and close your postcard in a friendly way.
- use informal language
- use linking words and phrases to join your ideas.
- explain the good points about your holiday.

Plan

Opening
Use an informal greeting
Dear Eric, Hi, Eric

Paragraph 1
Write about the holiday and explain what you have done so far:
We're having a lovely/terrible time. The food is delicious/horrible/spicy. We've had special pizza and fresh fish.

Paragraph 2
Write what your future plans are:
We're going to visit a Roman villa tomorrow.

Paragraph 3
Ask a question:
When are you going on holiday? How is your holiday going?

Closing:
Use an informal phrase for closing the postcard:
Bye. See you soon.
Jenny

Postcard checklist:

- Have you followed the plan? ☐
- Have you used informal language that is grammatically correct? ☐
- Have you checked for spelling and punctuation mistakes? ☐
- Have you asked a question? ☐
- Have you included all the information you were given? ☐

Story

When writing a story,

- spend a few minutes thinking about how you want your story to develop and make notes.
- set the scene in the first paragraph and create a strong atmosphere.
- use narrative tenses (past tenses) to describe events better.
- use linking words to make your sentences flow.
- make sure you give your story an interesting ending.
- remember to talk about how the people felt in the end.

Plan

Paragraph 1
Set the scene and introduce the main characters. Make the introduction sound interesting or dramatic. Use the sentence you are given in the task if necessary.
It was a cold, dark evening. / John was very scared.

Paragraph 2
Give background information about the characters and what is going on.
Maddy and Sally met at their dance class a year ago.

Paragraph 3
Describe the main events in order.
At first, ... / Then, ... / The moment that ... / Meanwhile, ...

Paragraph 4
Introduce a twist in the story (if appropriate).
That was when ... / Soon after that ... / Suddenly, ... / Just then, ... / As soon as ...

Paragraph 5
Bring the story to an end.
Eventually, ... / We never went to the castle again. / Sally knew it would never happen again.

Story checklist

- Have you followed the plan? ☐
- Have you used grammatically correct forms? ☐
- Have you checked for spelling and punctuation mistakes? ☐
- Have you made your story interesting to the reader? ☐
- Is the storyline clear and coherent? ☐
- Have you used a range of tenses, direct speech and dramatic sentences? ☐
- Have you used appropriate adjectives, adverbs and expressions to give life to your story? ☐
- Have you used linking words and time expressions? ☐

Review

When writing a review,

- think of a suitable title for your review.
- try to catch the reader's attention in the first paragraph.
- remember to give your negative or positive opinion.

Plan

Paragraph 1
Introduce what you are reviewing.
Try ... / Why not try ...? / If you like ... / ... is worth a try ...

Paragraph 2
Describe what you are reviewing. Give the reader an idea of what you are writing about.
... set in ... / ... combines ... with ... / ... is ideal for ...
For example, ... / For instance, ...
Give further details about what you are reviewing.
By the way, ... / That doesn't mean that, ... / On the other hand, ...
One example of this, ... / In this case, ...

Recomendation
End the review give your opinion.
I highly recommend ... / I wouldn't recommend ... / ... should not be missed

---

Review checklist

- Have you followed the plan? ☐
- Have you checked for grammar, punctuation and spelling mistakes? ☐
- Have you clearly stated what your opinion is? ☐
- Have you used appropriate adjectives for your descriptions? ☐
- Does the review summarise the important points? ☐

Report

When writing a report,

- think of a suitable title for your report.
- use formal language and long forms.
- remember to use headings to organise your report and make your ideas clearer.
- allow yourself time to plan what you will be including in your report.
- consider the advantages and disadvantages of each option.
- each part of your report should be separated from the next with clear paragraphs.

Plan

Paragraph 1
Say why you are writing the report.
The aim/purpose of this report is to present/recommend/review/examine ... / This is a report on ... / This report will present the findings of ... / It will also make suggestions/ recommendations for ... / It will also suggest/recommend/discuss/analyse ...

Paragraph 2
Discuss the first point or option and evaluate it and/or make suggestions.
The first option is/would be ... / This may be a good choice ... because ... / On the other hand, there may be some disadvantages.

Paragraph 3
Discuss the second point or option and evaluate it and/or make suggestions.
An alternative possibility would be to ... / Alternatively, ... / However, ... / In general, ... / This option has several disadvantages ... / However, there may be some reservations about/problems with ...

Paragraph 4
Bring the report to an end by summing up the suggestions made. Recommend one of the options or refer to future action.
In conclusion, ... / To sum up, the main recommendations/suggestions are ... / As can be seen from this report, ... / For these reasons, I feel that the best option is ...

Report checklist

- Have you followed the plan? ☐
- Have you used grammatically correct forms? ☐
- Have you checked for spelling and punctuation mistakes? ☐
- Have you used formal language and the full forms of verbs? ☐
- Have you used linking words correctly? ☐
- Have you made suggestions and/or recommendations? ☐

Speaking References

Describing photos
… lying on the floor.
I can see a … in the foreground /
background.
There's a white …
There are four …
She's got long …
He's behind / in front of / next to / on
the right
He's wearing …
She's … tall, slim good-looking
He / She's got… long, dark hair
They look … relaxed / happy / easy-
going

Inviting
You're invited to …
Can you come?
I want to invite you to …
Asking for a reply
Let me know if you can come.
Tell me if you can come or not.

Writing about special events
celebration
guests
invitation
special occasion
surprise party
celebrate
invite
organise
plan
have a party

Using adjectives
It looks / seems to be + adjective
I think they / he / she are + adjective
That is / isn't good for you because it's +
adjective
I often eat / don't usually eat
that because it's + adjective
I like / don't like that because it's
+ adjective

Recommending
I highly recommend …
I wouldn't / don't recommend …
It's the perfect place / cafe / restaurant
for …
It's the worst …

Adjectives for food
bitter
undercooked
overcooked
colourful
delicious
healthy
unhealthy
bland
processed
tasty
tasteless

Adjectives for restaurants
scruffy
dirty
trendy
bright
old-fashioned
expensive
slow
unfriendly
rude

Opening discussions
Shall we start with this …?
Let's begin / start by looking at …
First of all, …
To begin with, …
Let's move on to …
Shall we talk about … now?

Friendly openings
Hi!
Hello
How are you?
How are things?
How is it going?
It's good to hear from you!

Useful phrases
I really miss you!
I love reading your emails.
Good luck!
Sorry for not answering your last email.

Friendly endings
Write back soon and tell me all about it.
Bye!
Bye for now.
See you soon.
Speak to you later.
That's all for now.
Write soon!

Giving advice
If I were him, I'd …
I think it would be better to … because
…
Perhaps he should … then he …
He should also …
I really think it's best to … because
To be honest, I'd …

Describing people
tall /short
slim / overweight
kind / unkind
friendly / unfriendly
clever / stupid
young / old
easy-going / nervous
scared / happy

Describing place/time
morning / lunchtime / afternoon / evening
dark / bright
clean / dirty
cold / hot
early / late

Talking about a topic
My favourite room is … because
… and / but …

If I could change something about my
house / flat, it would be / I'd …
because …
Do you like the … in your house / flat?
How much time do you spend in … ?
Would you change the same things as
me in … ?
What about your … ?

Making suggestions
If I were you, I'd / I wouldn't …
Why don't you …?
How / What about …?

Accepting / Rejecting invitations
I'd love to come …
I'll definitely be there.
I'm sorry, I can't make it.
Unfortunately, I won't be able to come.

Responding to news
What exciting / sad / great … news!
I'm really pleased for / proud of you.
It'll be fun / great … !

Giving your opinion
I think … is a good idea because …
Well, I don't think he / she should …
But if he / she … , he / she'll … !

Asking if someone agrees
Do you agree (with me)?
Would you agree that …?
Do you think so, too?

Agreeing
I agree.
Yes, I totally / quite agree
with you.
I think you're (quite / absolutely) right.

Disagreeing
Actually, I don't really agree.
I'm afraid I don't agree.
I don't think that's a very good idea
because …

Paraphrasing
It's a sort of …
It's a kind of …
It's a an activity that … / a place where
… / a person who …
I think it's a …
It could be / might be a ….
It's similar to …
It's dangerous because …
You need … to do it.
You shouldn't do it on your own because
…
You have to be careful of …
Some equipment, such as … is necessary
to …

Creating suspense

At that point …
During the minutes / hours / days that followed …
All of a sudden …
As quick as lightning, / As fast as he could, …
He'd never been in such an extreme situation.
Without thinking, …
There was no sign of …
He thought of a plan.
To make things worse, …
They were just about to give up when …

Talking about possibility

Do you think … might be good?
I don't think … would be a good idea because …
… could be good? What do you think?
Yes, I think … would be good because …
No, I don't think that would work because …

Writing a postcard

We're having a lovely time.
The weather is …
The hotel / campsite / apartment is …
The beach is …
The food is …
We've had …
We've been to …
We've seen …
We've done some sightseeing.
See you soon!
Miss you!

Deciding

OK, so let's decide …
Right, let's make a decision …
Do we think the best one is … ?
So, do we agree that … is the best one?
So, to sum up …
In the end we think … because …

Describing people

She's got …
He's wearing …
They're smiling …
He's sitting …
Describing places
There are lots of …
It looks like a …
I can see a … behind / in front of
There's a … in the foreground / background

Describing things

It's a kind of …
I think it's a …
It looks old / new / expensive …
It could be …

Free-time activities

I play football / tennis / volleyball …
I'm in an orchestra / choir …
We usually …
I do aerobics / judo / karate
I have a … class.
After-school club
… until late
I go swimming / running … with
… is great fun!
I love my … because

Changing your mind

Are you sure about that?
Do you really think that …?
I'm sure … is better because …
Actually, I think you're right …
Yes, that's a good point, I hadn't thought of that.
OK then, yes, I agree with you!

Introducing reports

The aim / purpose of this report is to …
This is a report on …
This report will present the findings of …

Closing reports

To sum up, the main recommendations / suggestions are …
In conclusion, …

School facilities & equipment

canteen
classrooms
common room
computer room
theatre
gym
interactive whiteboard
library
playground
science labs
toilets

After-school activities

arts and crafts
choir practice
cooking
music and drama
sports teams

Talking about health and fitness

So, what do you do to stay healthy?
Do you do anything special to stay fit and healthy?
How often do you do exercise / go to the gym?
Do you go swimming / play any sports?
Do you think it's important to … ? Why?
Do you have enough time to … ? Why not?

Relationships

friendship
stranger
trust
(not) have a lot in common
make friends with
get on
give someone a hand
grow apart
help someone out
let someone down
see eye to eye
embarrassing
friendly
suspicious
rely on
respect

Collocations & Expressions

as quick as lightning	(U7)	keep calm	(U7)
be in one's good books	(U11)	make a journey	(U7)
be on a safari	(U9)	make a mess	(U5)
break the ice	(U4)	make an effort	(U11)
break the rules	(U11)	make progress	(U11)
can't stand somebody	(U8)	make one's bed	(U5)
climate change	(U3)	man's best friend	(U4)
do one's best	(U7)	move house	(U5)
do judo	(U9)	move with the times	(U5)
do the dishes	(U5)	natural habitat	(U3)
do the housework	(U5)	pay a compliment	(U1)
endangered species	(U9)	pay a visit	(U1)
fall in love with somebody	(U1)	power station	(U3)
fall to pieces	(U1)	renewable energy	(U3, U9)
fossil fuels	(U3)	save someone's life	(U7)
get a taste for something	(U11)	scared to death	(U7)
get divorced	(U1)	solar power	(U3)
get lost	(U7)	take a bath	(U5)
get married	(U1)	take a break	(U5)
get the hang of something	(U11)	tasty food	(U9)
go missing	(U7)	without thinking	(U7)
have a family	(U1)		
have sympathy	(U1)		
keep a diary	(U1)		
keep a secret	(U1)		

above sea level	(U7)	increase **in**	(U11)
about the same size	(U7)	**in** love **with**	(U4)
after years **of** + ing	(U3)	instead **of**	(U9)
agree **with**	(U4)	interact **with**	(U4)
angry **with**	(U4)	interested **in**	(U4, U5)
appear **in**	(U3)	**in** the water	(U7)
apply **for** ... **at** ...	(U11)	invite **to**	(U1)
argue **with**	(U4)	jealous **of**	(U1, U4)
ashamed **of**	(U4)	keen **on**	(U4, U6)
at the end **of**	(U1)	lead **to** something	(U9)
at the moment	(U3)	listen **to**	(U4)
at the weekend	(U1, U5)	look **for** something	(U9)
before something happens	(U3)	**on** the planet	(U7)
belong **to**	(U4)	**over** the years	(U7)
below freezing	(U7)	**over** 32 degrees Celsius	(U7)
beneficial **to**	(U4)	pick **up**	(U4)
close **to**	(U5)	protect **from**	(U3)
come **under** threat	(U9)	proud **of**	(U4)
communicate **with**	(U9)	relate **to**	(U4)
concentrate **on**	(U4, U11)	rely **on**	(U4, U5, U9)
concerned **about**	(U9)	responsible **for**	(U4)
cope **with**	(U9)	runs **across**	(U7)
disappear **from**	(U4)	satisfied **with**	(U11)
dress **in**	(U1)	similar **to**	(U4)
expert **on** something	(U9)	spend money **on** something	(U11)
find information **about**	(U1)	successful **in**	(U9)
for over (20) years	(U3)	suffer **from**	(U11)
get **from** this to this	(U3)	take action **on**	(U3)
get **onto** something	(U3)	talk **about**	(U4)
go **from** here to there	(U3)	turn **into** something	(U3)
good **at**	(U11)	the top **of** the/a mountain	(U7)
go **on** safari	(U9)	wait **for**	(U6)
in a desert	(U7)	worry **about**	(U11)
in common	(U4)		

act out	perform	(U10)
ask someone out	invite on a date	(U4)
back away	move slowly backwards	(U12)
back out of	decide not to do something you had previously agreed to do	(U12)
break up	separate	(U4, U9)
call for	require	(U8)
call out	announce	(U8)
carry on	continue	(U4, U7)
catch on	become popular	(U10)
clear up	make a place tidy	(U4)
cut out for	suited to	(U8)
deal with	do what is necessary	(U7)
eat out	go to a restaurant	(U2)
fall down	move quickly down onto the ground	(U5)
fall off	drop to the ground	(U5, U6)
fall over	fall to the ground	(U6)
find out	discover	(U1, U8)
get down	write down	(U10)
get on	be friends	(U4, U7)
give out	distribute	(U10)
give up	stop trying	(U7)
go along	continue to happen	(U7)
go away	travel away from a person or place	(U7)
grown out of	become too old for	(U10)
hand out	give each person in a group something	(U12)
hand over	give	(U12)
hang out	spend time relaxing	(U4)
head for	start moving/travelling towards a place	(U12)
head off	leave	(U12)
let someone down	disappoint someone	(U4)
log in	start using a computer	(U9)
look after	take care of someone or something	(U1_
look at	read or examine something	(U1)
look for	search for something	(U1, U5)
look up to	admire/have respect for someone	(U4)
look up something	attempt to find	(U9)
make up	forgive each other	(U4)
pass down	give	(U1)
pick up	collect	(U10)
pull from	save or rescue from danger	(U9)
put in	install	(U9)
put someone down	make someone feel stupid	(U4)
put up	build, erect	(U5)
put up	display	(U9)
run out of	have no more of something left	(U12)
run over	drive over something	(U12)
sell out	run out of tickets for an event	(U10)
set off	cause an alarm to make a sound	(U9)
show off	behave in a boastful way	(U8)
stand in	take someone's place	(U12)
stand out	look different	(U12)
take after	to look or behave like an older relative	(U1)
take to	start to like	(U8)
take up	begin	(U8)
think over	consider carefully	(U12)
think up	use one's imagination or intelligence to come up with an idea	(U12)
try out	test something first	(U9)
try out for	audition	(U8)
turn away	refuse admission	(U10)
turn down	decrease the volume	(U10)
turn into	be transformed into	(U3)
turn off	stop something working	(U4, U10)
turn on	switch on	(U10)
turn out	end in a particular way	(U10)
turn up	increase the volume	(U10)
warm up	prepare one's body for exercise	(U6)

NATIONAL GEOGRAPHIC

L E A R N I N G

Close-up B1 Student's Book, Second Edition

Angela Healan
Katrina Gormley
with Karen Ludlow

Publisher: Sharon Jervis

Editors: Bruce Nicholson and Jain Cook

Content Project Manager: Jon Ricketts

Text/Cover Designer: Ken Vail Graphic Design

Acknowledgements

The Publisher has made every effort to trace and contact copyright holders before publication. If any have been inadvertently overlooked, the publisher will be pleased to rectify any errors or omissions at the earliest opportunity.

For product information and technology assistance, contact us at
Cengage Learning Customer & Sales Support, cengage.com/contact

For permission to use material from this text or product, submit all requests online at **cengage.com/permissions**
Further permissions questions can be emailed to
permissionrequest@cengage.com

ISBN: 978-1-4080-9554-6

National Geographic Learning
Cheriton House, North Way, Andover, Hampshire, SP10 5BE
United Kingdom

National Geographic Learning, a Cengage Learning Company, has a mission to bring the world to the classroom and the classroom to life. With our English language programs, students learn about their world by experiencing it. Through our partnerships with National Geographic and TED Talks, they develop the language and skills they need to be successful global citizens and leaders.

Locate your local office at **international.cengage.com/region**

Visit National Geographic Learning online at **NGL.Cengage.com/ELT**
Visit our corporate website at **www.cengage.com**

Printed in China by RR Donnelley
Print Number: 08   Print Year: 2018

Text Credits

6–7 Adapted from 'Family Ties', by Patricia McKissack: NGE, Jan-Feb 2010, **18–19** Adapted from 'Olive Oil – Elixir of the Gods', by Erla Zwingle: NGM, Sep 1999, **32–33** Adapted from 'Coral Reef Color', by Les Kaufmann: NGM, May 2005, and 'Coral in Peril', by Douglas Chadwick: NGM, Jan 1999, **44–45** Adapted from 'Wolf to Woof', by Karen Lange: NGM, Jan 2002, **70–71** Adapted from 'Paddleboard Racing: The Hardest Adventure Sport You've Never Heard of', by Tetsuhiko Endo, NGA blog, Aug 2009, **84–85** Adapted from 'Alive: Then and Now', by James Vlahos: NGA, April 2006, **96–97** Adapted from 'Caves; Deep Into Darkness', by Beth Geiger, NGE, May 2010, **110–111** Adapted from 'Watching You', by David Shank: NGM, May 2005, **148–149** Adapted from 'Your Amazing Brain', by Douglas A. Richards, NGK website

Photo Credits
Cover images: (front cover) © Charles Krebs/Corbis, (back cover) nikkytok/Shutterstock

Shutterstock:

5 Renata Sedmakova; **6** Psv; **7** Kudryashka; **7** Kaarsten; **8** Four Oaks; **8** Kaarsten; **9** Monkey Business Images; **10** Igorlale; **10** Gaja1; **10** Shutterstock; **10** Nikkytok; **10** Tena Rebernjak; **10** Shutterstock; **11** Nikkytok; **11** Monkey Business Images; **11** Perry Correll; **11** Kostudio; **12** Kostudio; **14** Wavebreakmedia; **15** Melis; **16** Kaarsten; **18** Maxuser; **18** Javier Martin; **18** Mickyso; **19** Nikkytok; **19** Flower_Power; **19** Kostudio; **20** Sbego; **21** Steve Lovegrove; **22** Nikkytok; **23** Nikkytok; **23** Kostudio; **24** Ruth Black; **24** Kaarsten; **25** Monkey Business Images; **26** Michael Kemp; **27** Hxdyl; **28** Gandolfo Cannatella; **28** Kostudio; **33** Nikkytok; **33** Jc Photo; **33** Kaarsten; **34** Peter Wollinga; **34** Elnavegante; **34** Sigapo; **34** Yurok; **34** Ramunas Bruzas; **34** Vanderwolf Images; **34** Sybanto; **34** Eky Studio; **34** Kostudio; **36** Nikkytok; **37** Spwidoff; **37** Nikkytok; **37** Kostudio; **38** Baloncici; **38** Nikkytok; **38** Kaarsten; **40** Shaiith; **41** Nikkytok; **41** Jan Martin Will; **42** Kostudio; **44** Waldemar Dabrowski; **44** Boris Djuranovic; **44** K. Miri Photography; **44** Margouillat Photo; **45** Nikkytok; **45** Jim Parkin; **45** Kaarsten; **46** Kostudio; **48** Wavebreakmedia; **48** Photographee. Eu; **48** Nikkytok; **49** Nikkytok; **49** Nicoelnino; **49** Accord; **49** Kostudio; **50** Kostudio; **50** Sergiyn; **51** S-F; **52** Shevs; **52** Zaretska Olga; **53** Nikkytok; **54** Eric Isselee; **54** Erik Lam; **54** Eric Isselee; **54** Geoffrey Kuchera; **54** Kaarsten; **55** Odua Images; **56** Edyta Pawlowska; **57** Apurva Madia; **58** Andreas G. Karelias; **58** Iakov Filimonov; **58** Iakov Filimonov; **59** Nikkytok; **59** Kaarsten; **60** David Acosta Allely; **60** Seleznev Oleg; **60** David Burrows; **60** Sam100; **60** Markabond; **60** Gergo Orban; **60** Adam Fraise; **60** Yanik Chauvin; **60** Royalty Free Stock Photos; **60** Kostudio; **62** Nigel Paul Monckton; **62** Zcw; **62** Sima; **62** Zeljko Radojko; **62** Stillfx; **62** Sura Nualpradid; **62** Nikkytok; **63** Photobank.Ch; **63** Nikkytok; **65** 3000Ad; **67** Nikkytok; **68** Alexey Arkhipov; **68** Kostudio; **70** Tyler Olson; **71** Nikkytok; **71** Kostudio; **72** Ipatov; **72** Maxim Petrichuk; **72** Kaarsten; **73** Nejron Photo; **74** Tumar; **74** Nikkytok; **74** Opel; **74** Vertes Edmond Mihai; **74** Mitrofanov Alexander; **74** Luca_Luppi; **74** Luca_Luppi; **74** Luca_Luppi; **74** Toonstyle; **74** Toonstyle; **74** Toonstyle; **74** Ankomando; **74** Ankomando; **74** Ankomando; **74** Virinaflora; **74** Virinaflora; **74** Virinaflora; **74** 3Drenderings; **74** Tele52; **74** Kaarsten; **75** Nikkytok; **75** Kostudio; **76** Kaarsten; **77** Vetrovamaria; **79** Nikkytok; **80** Brandon Stein; **80** Kostudio; **82** Edyta Pawlowska; **83** Vitalii Nesterchuk; **84** Im_Photo; **85** Nikkytok; **85** Kostudio; **86** Kaarsten; **87** Shutterstock; **88** Nikkytok; **89** Nikkytok; **89** Greg Epperson; **89** Armin Rose; **89** Kostudio; **90** Kostudio; **91** Thomas Barrat; **92** Berserg; **93** Nikkytok; **93** Bule Sky Studio; **94** Kaarsten; **96** Salajean; **97** Nikkytok; **97** Kaarsten; **98** Alexsutula; **98** Arina P Habich; **98** Kzenon; **98** Oksmit; **98** Ruslan Guzov; **98** Noam Armonn; **98** Kostudio; **99** Mikadun; **100** Ekler; **100** Sovisdesign; **100** Kokandr; **100** Phoelix; **100** Pavel L Photo And Video; **100** Robert Adrian Hillman; **100** Nikkytok; **100** Adrian Niederhaeuser; **101** Nikkytok; **101** Oleksiy Mark; **101** Hong Vo; **101** Vipavlenkoff; **101** Filip Fuxa; **101** Armin Staudt; **101** Oleksiy Mark; **101** Kaarsten; **104** Epicstockmedia; **105** Nikkytok; **106** Kostudio; **107** Odua Images; **108** Edyta Pawlowska; **110** 24Novembers; **110** Linda Bucklin; **110** Terrym; **111** Nikkytok; **111** Kaarsten; **112** Scyther5; **112** Vartanov Anatoly; **112** Fotografos; **112** Tkemot; **112** Ivan Montero Martinez; **112** Aquila; **112** You Can More; **112** Tatiana Popova; **112** Kostudio; **114** Nikkytok; **115** Nikkytok; **115** Nebuto; **115** Xtrekx; **115** Neelsky; **115** Thaiview; **115** Kaarsten; **116** Ewan Chesser; **116** Kostudio; **119** Nikkytok; **120** Kostudio; **121** Shutterstock; **122** User Friendly; **122** Daseaford; **122** Slavoljub Pantelic; **122** VladislavGajic; **123** Nikkytok; **123** Olga Borisenko; **123** Kostudio; **124** Pakhnyushchy; **124** Kaarsten; **127** Photobank Gallery; **127** Nikkytok; **127** Allison Achauer; **127** Monkey Business Images; **127** Kostudio; **128** Kaarsten; **129** Paul Atkinson; **131** Nikkytok; **132** 1125089601; **132** Kostudio; **133** Odua Images; **134** Edyta Pawlowska; **136** Stokkete; **136** Davidtb; **136** Olesya Kuznetsova; **136** Falcon Eyes; **137** Nikkytok; **137** Everett Collection; **137** Anjelikagr; **137** Kostudio; **138** National Geographic; **139** MatejKastelic; **140** Nikkytok; **140** Gorillaimages; **141** Nikkytok; **141** Andrey_Kuzmin; **141** Monkey Business Images; **141** Volodymyr Kyrylyuk; **141** Picsfive; **141** Wlg; **141** Ferenc Szelepcsenyi; **141** Kaarsten; **142** Monkey Business Images; **142** Kostudio; **144** Kristin Smith; **145** Nikkytok; **145** Shutterstock; **146** Kaarsten; **148** Sebastian Kaulitzki; **148** Lightspring; **149** Nikkytok; **149** Lightspring; **150** Rudall30; **150** Shutterstock; **150** Kaarsten; **152** Nikkytok; **152** Jiri Kaderabek; **152** Theblackrhino; **152** Iarada; **152** Milo827; **152** Malinovskaya Yulia; **152** Pichayasri; **152** Neyro; **152** Neyro; **152** Neyro; **153** Nikkytok; **153** Racorn; **153** Oliveromg; **153** Kostudio; **154** Yorkberlin; **154** Kaarsten; **155** Sebastian Kaulitzki; **156** Shutterstock; **157** Nikkytok; **158** Ktsdesign; **158** Kostudio; **159** Odua Images; **160** Edyta Pawlowska.

6 Photoalto Sas/Alamy; **12** Chris A Crumley/Alamy; **13** James L. Stanfield/National Geographic; **16** John StanmeyerLlc/National Geographic; **20** Xpacifica/National Geographic; **23** Eric Nathan/Alamy; **23** Viktor Pravdica/Alamy; **31** Jonathan Blair/National Geographic; **32** Norbert Wu/ Minden Pictures/National Geographic; **32** Chris Newbert/ Minden Pictures/National Geographic; **36** Mauricio Handler/National Geographic; **39** Jane Sweeney/Jai/Corbis; **40** By Ian Miles-Flashpoint Pictures/Alamy; **42** Brian J. Skerry/National Geographic; **43** Blickwinkel/Alamy; **44** Richard Olsenius/National Geographic; **45** Richard Olsenius/National Geographic; **45** Richard Olsenius/National Geographic; **46** J Marshall - Tribaleye Images/Alamy; **49** Jim West/Alamy; **53** Trigger Image/Alamy; **58** Steve Hix/ Somos Images/Corbis; **58** Zero Creatives/Image Source/Corbis; **61** Markus Lange/Robert Harding; **63** Construction Photography/Alamy; **64** Urs Schweitzer/ Robert Harding; **66** William Arthur/Alamy; **67** Jeff Greenberg 4 Of 6/Alamy; **69** National Geographic; **76** Stephen Frink Collection/Alamy; **78** Ray Roberts/Alamy; **79** Rebecca Wright/Alamy; **84** Larry Minden/ Minden Pictures/National Geographic; **88** Christophe Dupont Elise/Icon Smi/Corbis; **90** National Geographic; **94** Kent Kobersteen/National Geographic; **95** Keith Morris/Alamy; **96** Ryan Mcginnis/Alamy; **97** Stephen Alvarez/National Geographic; **97** Stephen Alvarez/National Geographic; **98** Jeff Greenberg 4 Of 6/Alamy; **98** Universal Images Group Limited/Alamy; **101** Oleksiy Maksymenko/Alamy; **101** Mediablitzimages/Alamy; **102** Bob Daemmrich/Alamy; **103** Tom Corban/Alamy; **105** Blickwinkel/Alamy; **106** Stephen Alvarez/National Geographic; **109** Tim Laman/National Geographic; **110** George Steinmetz/National Geographic; **113** Robert Clark/National Geographic; **114** National Geographic; **117** National Geographic; **118** National Geographic; **119** National Geographic; **122** Oliver Gutfleisch/Robert Harding; **123** Oliver Gutfleisch/Robert Harding; **124** Fotomaton/Alamy; **124** Justin KaseZsixz/Alamy; **124** Zuma Press, Inc/Alamy; **124** Cultura Creative/Alamy; **125** Moodboard/Corbis; **128** Jack Hollingsworth/Corbis; **130** B. Anthony Stewart/National Geographic; **131** Ted Spiegel/National Geographic; **132** Todd Gipstein/National Geographic; **135** Michael S. Lewis/National Geographic; **136** Tony French/Alamy; **139** Bob Daemmrich/ Alamy; **141** Jason Smalley Photography/Alamy; **146** Randy Olson/National Geographic; **148** Richard Nowitz/National Geographic; **152** Cary Wolinsky/National Geographic; **157** Imagebroker/Robert Harding.